Archaeologies of Materiality

Edited by Lynn Meskell

© 2005 by Blackwell Publishing Ltd

BLACKWELL PUBLISHING
350 Main Street, Malden, MA 02148-5020, USA
9600 Garsington Road, Oxford OX4 2DQ, UK
550 Swanston Street, Carlton, Victoria 3053, Australia

The right of Lynn Meskell to be identified as the Author of the Editorial Material in this Work has been asserted in accordance with the UK Copyright, Designs, and Patents Act 1988.

All rights reserved. No part of this publication may be reproduced, stored in a retrieval system, or transmitted, in any form or by any means, electronic, mechanical, photocopying, recording or otherwise, except as permitted by the UK Copyright, Designs, and Patents Act 1988, without the prior permission of the publisher.

First published 2005 by Blackwell Publishing Ltd

1 2005

Library of Congress Cataloging-in-Publication Data

Archaeologies of materiality / edited by Lynn Meskell.
p. cm.
Includes bibliographical references and index.
ISBN-13: 978-1-4051-3617-4 (hard cover : alk. paper)
ISBN-10: 1-4051-3617-0 (hard cover : alk. paper)
ISBN-13: 978-1-4051-3616-7 (pbk. : alk. paper)
ISBN-10: 1-4051-3616-2 (pbk. : alk. paper)
1. Social archaeology. 2. Material culture. I. Meskell, Lynn.
CC72.4.A7325 2006
930.1 — dc22
2005008557

A catalogue record for this title is available from the British Library.

The publisher's policy is to use permanent paper from mills that operate a sustainable forestry policy, and which has been manufactured from pulp processed using acid-free and elementary chlorine-free practices. Furthermore, the publisher ensures that the text paper and cover board used have met acceptable environmental accreditation standards.

For further information on
Blackwell Publishing, visit our website:
www.blackwellpublishing.com

Contents

List of Figures		vii
Acknowledgments		ix
1	Introduction: Object Orientations *Lynn Meskell*	1
2	Mastering Matters: Magical Sense and Apotropaic Figurine Worlds of Neo-Assyria *Carolyn Nakamura*	18
3	The Social Life of Rock Art: Materiality, Consumption, and Power in South African Heritage *Lindsay Moira Weiss*	46
4	With a Hint of Paris in the Mouth: Fetishized Toothbrushes or the Sensuous Experience of Modernity in Late 19th Century Bogotá *Felipe Gaitán Ammann*	71
5	Faith in Objects: American Indian Object Lessons at the World in Boston *Erin Hasinoff*	96
6	The Texture of Things: Objects, People, and Landscape in Northwest Argentina (First Millennium A.D.) *Marisa Lazzari*	126

Contents

7 Building an Architecture of Power: Electricity in
 Annapolis, Maryland in the 19th and 20th Centuries 162
 Matthew M. Palus

8 The Voices of Stones: Unthinkable Materiality in the
 Volcanic Context of Western Panamá 190
 Karen Holmberg

9 Afterword 212
 Daniel Miller

Index 220

Figures

1.1	Photo of Zulu baskets at the Rosebank Markets, Johannesburg, July 2004 (photo by the author)	10
2.1	Apotropaic figurine deposit found in Room S57 of Fort Shalmaneser at Nimrud. Adapted from Curtis and Reade (1995:112)	20
2.2	Apotropaic figures with associated features. Drawing after Richards in Black and Green (1992:65)	35
4.1	The fetishized toothbrush (courtesy of the Casa Museo Quinta de Bolivar – Bogotá, Colombia)	74
4.2	Bogotanos at Choachí. From Holton (1857) New Granada: Twenty Months in the Andes. New York: Harper & Brothers	86
5.1	Floorplan of the World in Boston. Handbook and Guide to the World in Boston, 1911	100
5.2	Pomo burden basket (AMNH #50/773), California. Collected by Carl Purdy. Photo courtesy of the Division of Anthropology, American Museum of Natural History	112
6.1	Map of northwest Argentina, with dispersion area of obsidian from the Ona source	139
6.2	Fragment of Formative period ceramics from Antigal de Tesoro (western slope of the Aconquija Mountains)	146
7.1	View of the Annapolis Gas and Electric Light Company Plant, ca. 1895 (Maryland State Archives SC182–02–0809)	173

Figures

7.2 The neatly diagrammed system: multiple-series circuits for municipal lighting, from George D. Shepardson's Electrical Catechism (1901) — 181

8.1 The western face of the Caldera petroglyph boulder and (inset) the split boulder that forms a "passageway" — 192

8.2 The larger setting of the Caldera petroglyph boulder — 193

Acknowledgments

This book would not have been possible without several very important supporters of the project. First, we would like to acknowledge the support of Richard Leventhal, then Director of the School of American Research in Santa Fe, who hosted us for this special symposium dedicated to the topic of materiality in archaeology. The staff of the school made our stay an unforgettable one and we are collectively very grateful. Second, we extend our warmest thanks to Jane Huber who has shepherded the project from the outset and went above and beyond the call of duty for us. Louise Spencely has also been a joy to work with, as usual, along with Emily Martin. We thank them for taking the project through to fruition. Danny Miller has also played a key role, as an inspiration for many of our projects and also as a generous commentator on the chapters. Lastly, I would like to thank the participants for all their hard work and professionalism. They have been incredibly smart and stimulating companions not only throughout this project, but also during my time at Columbia University. It is for these reasons, and others that the book is dedicated my students.

LMM
Stanford, California

1

Introduction: Object Orientations

Lynn Meskell

> The invention or practice of the art of pottery, all things considered, is probably the most effective and conclusive test that can be selected to fix a boundary line, necessarily arbitrary, between savagery and barbarism.
>
> Lewis Henry Morgan, *Ancient Society*, 1877

It was said, not so very long ago that the "deeply integrated place of the artifact in constituting culture and human relations has made discussion of it one of the most difficult of all areas to include in abstract academic discourse" (Miller 1987:130). Yet within the last decade materiality has become a topic of increasing interest in the disciplines of anthropology, sociology, architecture, and archaeology, as well as residing at the core of the new material culture studies (Attfield 2000; Buchli 2002; Meskell 2004; Miller 1998; 2005; Renfrew, et al. 2005). Yet as Daniel Miller has argued, we have been notably remiss in producing substantive accounts of materiality for archaeological contexts: this volume is one such attempt to remedy the situation. As archaeologists, we might profitably explore the underpinning philosophies of materiality for specific cultural moments across time and space. This is one of the major aims of this volume, to provide an array of object orientations in particular and varied contexts, indeed the first to showcase substantive archaeological case studies devoted to the exploration of materiality.

Archaeologists have been relatively slow to embrace theories of materiality: with the constitution of the material world in past contexts, and the concomitant construction of selves and culture (but see Hodder 2006; Meskell 2004). As Miller has indirectly indicated, this project falls squarely within the disciplinary realm of archaeology since the "medium of objectification matters" (Miller 1987:129). Yet our theorization of materiality is a rather different project to that traditional within archaeology, namely contextual studies of objects and assemblages. We hope to demonstrate here that our understanding of the potentials of materiality diverges significantly from the conventional study of material culture in archaeology. Studies of material culture can be traditionally understood as oscillating between empirical studies and more theoretical and cultural expressions. The empirical trend is firmly devoted to object analyses – form, materials, and manufacture – and does not automatically engage with social relations. Curiously, as Miller would say, the same object can inhabit both domains, and thus we might do the work of both and interweave between technologies, meanings, practices, and histories. The theoretical perspective we advocate in this volume focuses more directly on the broader interpretive connotations around and beyond the object, on the unstable terrain of interrelationships between sociality, temporality, spatiality, and materiality (Meskell 2004:2). We hope to move beyond simplistic readings of things as either purely functional or deeply symbolic, as archaeologists have tended to taxonomize things previously. In a way this is similar to Geertz's critique, and more recently the insightful work of Keane (2003a; 2003b): both warn of the false dichotomy between symbolic and materialist readings of the world. This is akin the discursive taxonomies we instantiate, of ideas and things, where things are too often read as expressions or communications of ideas: things have been treated as basically epiphenomenal. As Miller and Tilley cautioned almost a decade ago (1996), artifacts have particular properties and, in an age of rapidly burgeoning material culture, ought to be investigated in their own right. This has been the raison d'être for the subfield of material culture studies, yet speaks equally to the refashioning of archaeology to embrace more nuanced studies of our object worlds. We might profitably explore the contours of our material lifeworld and its recursive shaping of human experience. In Miller's case he saw these rich potentials through the lens of Bourdieu's *habitus* (1977; 1980; 1998) whereby the physicality of the artifact is enmeshed in the work of praxis: cultural construction is achieved through action rather than simply conceptualization.

Introduction: Object Orientations

It is worth exploring the notion of a *material habitus*, a formulation that owes significant intellectual debts to Bourdieu and Miller, but perhaps with a genealogy that extends further back to Tylor. The idea of a material lifeworld that is conceived and constructed by us, yet equally shaping of human experience in daily praxis is a provocative one. Where the argument for *habitus* in the purely social realm can be seen as both constraining and generally restrictive toward societal change (Meskell 1999), it may have significant purchase in the grounded materiality of the object world since the duration of physical things have different and oftentimes longer individual histories . . . their residual force of matter has the ability to shape and influence the living. Tylor argued that any particular culture's arts, customs, and ideas were shaped by the combined actions of many individuals, and their inventions, opinions, and ceremonies were the product of various histories of suggestion, modification, and encouragement or opposition. People act in accordance with their own motives, yet collective social action is embedded within a larger frame of society, and of those many individual actions and choices (Tylor 1977:14). However, where *habitus* is usually applied to a single cultural unit, he applied his construction cross-culturally on the basis of similarities in material culture. Cultural survival was the designation given by Tylor to these "processes, customs, opinions, and so forth, which have been carried on by force of habit" (1977:16) to constantly refashion society, and from these older habits newer understandings were constituted. This material *habitus* or lifeworld is a compelling notion: an enmeshing that combines persons, objects, deities, and all manner of immaterial things together in ways that cannot easily be disentangled or separated taxonomically. One can see why the notion of the fetish has been such an evocative device for anthropological studies of material culture (Ellen 1988; Pels 1998), since fetishism arises from an organic unity between people and things, as opposed to the strongly contoured divide between persons and the things they produce to exchange in capitalist societies (Taussig 1980:37). Yet with this new move to a grounded understanding of things we must simultaneously consider immateriality, the need to objectify, to abstract, and our embodied practices in the spheres of magic and making. Fabrication is all about making the world while making ourselves, our quintessential subject making. All our endeavors in the world are about copying, whether in the domains of language or material culture, both are processes of replication, an objectification of the thought world.

Lynn Meskell

The Thing Is

Archaeologists have to move beyond the representational economy. Historically, it is important that we have advanced toward "meaning" after too long focusing upon environmental or economic motivations, yet we must also now consider the embodied realities of being in the world. Studies of materiality cannot simply focus upon the characteristics of objects but must engage in the dialectic of people and things. We might see this as a co-presence or co-mingling. Keane refers to it as *bundling* (2003b:414), the binding qualities that materiality allows, and in this way the concept harks back to Hegel, but also to anthropologists like Mauss, Munn, and Latour, and similarly connects to the project of object biography (Gosden and Marshall 1999). At a very simple level, the cultural constitution and understanding of objects remains a neglected area. Compelling research has been conducted by Latour on this hybrid terrain (1991; 1996; 2000). Archaeologists have not generally succeeded in embedding things, in creating accounts of embodied things or those that effectively blend with subjects, deities, entities, places, technologies and so on. Given that subjects and objects are collapsible in particular contexts, as Nakamura demonstrates in Chapter 2, so too our natural and cultural categories require rethinking, as Holmberg (ch. 8) and Lazzari (ch. 6) suggest. Recently, Latour (2004) has revisited Heidegger's notion of the distinct world of objects and things. In his attempt to tease from the world of materiality the notion of objects and things, Heidegger reconstituted things as a *gathering* (perhaps like Keane's *bundling*), what Latour describes as matters of fact and concern. This Heideggerian bifurcation sees objects as a lesser category and Latour's example, a coke bottle, is devoid of true meaning and simply the physical result of modern science and technology. Like many of us, Latour finds this binary unhelpful and the dichotomy between *Gegenstand* and *Thing* "justified by nothing except the crassest of prejudices" (2004:234). He asks: what if ordinary objects had the rich and complicated qualities of things? This brings us back again to the fundamental issue of taxonomy.

Bruno Latour has been an outspoken critic of what we might call rational taxonomies. He wants to blur the categorical distinctions between objects and societies, cosmologies and sociologies. Past societies recognized this convergence, but the onslaught of terrifying revolutions has to some degree severed the link, that mixture of rational constraints and the needs of their societies. We continue to identify with Enlightenment thinking, the separability of the human and nonhuman when in fact we need to reconfigure modernity in new ways, perhaps even a little like that of the distant past. Latour's own neologism, *factishes*, reminds us that the dichotomy of facts and social constructions is near useless (2000:113). "And if religion, arts or styles are necessary to 'reflect,' 'reify,' 'materialize,' 'embody' society – to use some of the social theorists' favorite verbs – then are objects not, in the end, its co-producers? Is society not built literally – not metaphorically – of gods, machines, sciences, arts and styles?" (Latour 1991:54). Going further, he asserts that as academics we too are guilty of this categorical blurring since we can embrace the seemingly contradictory modalities of antifetishism, positivism, and realism, because we apply them to different topics or strands of our being. We explain the objects we disapprove of as fetishes and concentrate only upon things we deem our passions and worthwhile matters of concern (Latour 2004:241). Using the words of Allan Turing, celebrated father of modern computers, he shows how Turing could not describe his "thinking machine" without recourse to god's power to create souls and that we are simply instruments of his will, providing mansions for those souls. Gods and machines, intertwined from the outset and not so very different to the oracles and predictive technologies we see in ancient cultures (Meskell 2004:ch. 3). Both ancients and moderns have failed to master the things they have fabricated (see also Palus ch. 7).

When we objectify a god or the contours of a deity we usually need to materialize the immaterial, to give it form and visual presence. That can take a natural or manufactured form, or sometimes even both, as in the case of Egypt. Physical presence is the symbolic and experiential bridge that renders abstract thought and belief both tangible and efficacious. That material presence commands our attention. If we take the evocative case of statue-gods in Egypt, the god embodied in its material form (Meskell 2004:ch. 4; see also Nakamura ch. 2) they behave miraculously, they are agentic beings, fetishes that blur the taxonomies of subject and object. Ancient Egyptian oracles were just such statue-beings, fabricated by human hands while that authorship was stripped from the fetish: it became the embodiment of a deified pharaoh in some cases. Oracles could act independently, make proclamations, pass juridical verdicts and determine the fate of mere mortals. Egyptian gods in statue form or manifest in natural places are a salient examples of what Latour describes as the work of *translation*, the creation and instantiation of new types of beings, hybrids blending nature, culture, things, deities, monsters, and so on. What we envisage as our distinctive nature as moderns is our ability to separate domains, in Latour's terms an act of *purification*, that creates two discrete ontological zones (1991:10). As he provocatively goes on to demonstrate, however, this is a false dichotomy that privileges moderns in the sphere of rationality, whereas we too are guilty of similar ontological crossings and hybridities. Taking the example of an anthropologist, to bring this home, he shows how easily one can write a single book that defines the forces at play, incorporating the distribution of powers between gods, humans and non-humans, ancestors, cosmologies, natural taxonomies, property rights, and so on: separate books are unnecessary. It is the common locus that is crucial here, the constitution of a legible world and lifeworld. Matter is defined differently between these broad swathes of society and as interpreters we are constantly called upon to define matter in those particular settings.

Since materiality is not reducible to a set of given conditions or practices common to all cultures and all times, it is surely necessary to undertake study of specific cultural moments to understand particular contextual notions of the material world and its propensity to forge, shape, interpolate, and possibly even challenge and undermine social relations and experiences. What we aim for within the chapters is an understanding of the underlying philosophy of the material, as present in each of the cultural settings examined. Materiality is thus a set of cultural relationships (Pels 2002), as the individual chapters in the volume demonstrate. Imbued matter and embodied objects exist in relationship to the specificities of temporality, spatiality, and sociality, and we must be mindful of the flipping back and forward between ancient and contemporary situated understandings. Like all ethnographic writing (and I believe we are entering this sort of terrain), this impels us to reconsider our own understandings of materiality, its qualities and limitations, but also to eschew the easy promise of essentialism and naturalism.

The aim of the book is to uncover and examine the past and present lives of things, sometimes as objects, other times as active entities or didactic things, often as circulating cultural capital today, things that we have become accustomed to viewing unproblematically or residing in intransigent taxonomies. It is crucial for archaeologists to interrogate the specific moments of crafting, forging, exchanging, installing, using, and discarding objects, their histories in a variety of contexts, whether the historic implementation of power that Palus (ch. 7) underscores, or the exchange relationships focused upon bodily regimes in Republican Colombia that Gaitán (ch. 4) uncovers. This is what the chapters individually examine and move on to consider their fundamental embedding in places, landscapes, fields of power and discourse, local and international arenas. In some contexts outlined here, we need to interrogate the tensions between material and immaterial political forces as Palus, Weiss (ch. 3), and Hasinoff (ch. 5) outline, shifting between traditional and contemporary understandings of those perhaps unnatural categories. Places and landscapes can be similarly modified into a blurring of encultured nature as Holmberg and Lazzari attempt to trace. How do we enculturate the world and make it our own, intrude into the natural "world" and mark that intrusion physically, materially?

As the chapters will outline, an archaeology of materiality can be achieved by looking at the object world in archaeological and ethnohistoric contexts, by tracing the subsequent biographies of things, or examining the deployment of object worlds in historic and contemporary practice. The following section is a short consideration of the contemporary role of traditional, some might even claim ancient, forms of material culture and making in South Africa today, a nation itself going through one of the most visible and palpable periods of refashioning and remaking of itself in material, social, and spiritual arenas (Meskell 2005).

South African Detour

In this short case study I want to pursue a more ethnographic treatment of material culture in contemporary South Africa and the historic underpinnings of those constructions and sedimentations of identity (see also Weiss ch. 3). More generally, I am increasingly interested in the resonant notion of making culture "pay" in South Africa and the material substrate upon which this ethos rests. In post-Apartheid society indigenous groups, often territorialized in the ways colonialism and apartheid subdivided the nation (Mamdani 1996; Mbembe 2000; 2001), are being encouraged through government initiatives and development schemes to present themselves as culturally distinctive through the making and selling of their ethnically respective cultural objects. Such artisan economies are typically supported by neoliberal policies (Colloredo-Mansfeld 2002:113), often operating under the rubric of development. Craft making, with all the associations of "primitive" otherness and essential difference, coupled with tourist-oriented "tribal" performances are presented as a means of celebrating identity and simultaneously promoting a self-sustaining local economy. Craft is also inherently depicted as a worthy pursuit, albeit locked in tradition, a busy-work for people who are conceived as unskilled and also untainted by the mechanistic world of modernity (see Hasinoff ch. 5). To date there are over 150 groups in South Africa that have received governmental support. As the Department of Arts and Culture minister outlined recently:

> poor communities are in many instances, owners of assets – natural and material resources, human resources, cultural assets, indigenous knowledge, traditions and customs that can be the key agents for social and economic development. South Africa is blessed with a rich cultural tradition with artistic individuals and communities living in all corners of the country. Any poverty alleviation programme which aims at creating work opportunities must begin with these assets. We need to invest in people and their ability to make objects and artefacts, production and music. (Sack 2003:4)

Governmental interventions and NGO development strategies are thus seen as inherently positive moves that sediment and protect tribal culture and its material correlates, and it is the fabric of this constructed identity that lies at the center of these negotiations. It is this materiality that hardens identity in a premodern era, that stands as an unchanging hallmark of "black" and "colored" peoples, situated within the very tribal constituencies that the apartheid government sought to maintain for much of the 20th century. Ironically, there seems to have been little internal critique, apart from the challenge to neoliberal notions of development undertaken by a coterie of anthropologists. Archaeologists have yet to seriously engage with these debates. Anthropologist James Ferguson (1994:255) for one has shown effectively that development is not a machine for eliminating poverty that is imbricated with the state bureaucracy. Such interventions may have no effect whatsoever on poverty but do in fact have other concrete effects. Development work around

Introduction: Object Orientations

ethnic craft industries has the potential of formalizing identity categories and boundaries, marking them and relegating people to the material worlds created and instantiated in history. These contemporary "primitivisms" reflect the earlier, and much critiqued, reifications and fetishizations of a notionally simple way of life. More seriously, their distinctive character derives from the politics of identity in the present (Douglas 1997:63) and serves to reinforce the tribalisms of the colonial and then apartheid eras. While historical deconstruction may deprive ethnicity of its mythic sense of timelessness, to claim that ethnicity is artificially constructed does not enable us to dismiss it as inauthentic. This begs the question of what constitutes *genuineness* (Wilmsen et al. 1994:348)? And when is legitimate identity formation initiated and terminated? While archaeologists are increasingly interested in identity and ethnicity and its fluid formations, we are decreasingly able to confront the modalities of this same shifting terrain in the present.

Describing his oppressed hero Michael K, Nobel Prize-winning South African author J. M. Coetzee says "he ought to be in a protected environment weaving baskets or stringing beads, not in a rehabilitation camp" (Coetzee 1983:131). Such craftwork is seen as an exercise of charity, an "object lesson" (see Hasinoff ch. 5) for the impoverished who are both materially and spiritually in need. Despite this deficit, the indigenous South Africans are "rich" in tradition, and simply require channeling into proper physical works. Following this development ideology, the nostalgia and longing woven through such fabrications is the price we pay as outsiders for these objects, while the makers sublate their heritage and ancient identities for our collective wellbeing. Both sides need something from the exchange: one is the purchase of the embodied object of past tradition and ancestral culture; the other requires the commodity price to operate within the sphere of contemporary culture. One is a spiritual need, the other is material.

On National Heritage Day, September 24, 2004, Thabo Mbeki (2004) proclaimed that "the weavers of iHulzo and Isilulu, the baskets from Hlabisa woven with care by Reuben Ndwandwe and Beauty Ngxongo, the makers of Ntwana dolls, the Litema of the Basotho women, the iNcwala, the reed dance – these are only some of the traditions that have survived the passage of time." One is reminded of E. B. Tylor's (1977) famous (and now reductive) categories of objects as reflective of the hierarchical ordering of people, material cultures stand as signifiers for discrete ethnicized identities: the Zulu make telephone wire baskets, the

Khoi-San make ostrich egg shell jewelry and skin bags, and so on. Many of these material culture assemblages hark back to an archaeological or historic past, other, like the Zulu baskets (or *izimbenge*), speak to a very contemporary setting: they are literally the "arts of resistance" (see Scott 1990). The once-stolen telephone wire of the white administration's apartheid infrastructure is turned into a saleable local product that objectifies inequality and persecution – modern and technological. Originating in the 1970s, artists took traditional basketry skills and applied them to the most modern of materials. They are highly aesthetic, desirable, internationally circulated objects which have been re-signified in the West as re-cycled or green art forms. Zulu wire basketry has been more recently identified with specific South African collectivities: runaway children, battered women, and so on, giving an emotional yet ultimately false sense of individual connection and patronage. In a recent exhibition at the Fowler Museum at UCLA Zulu baskets became material indexes of the AIDS epidemic – KwaZulu Natal is the province with the

Figure 1.1 Photo of Zulu baskets at the Rosebank Markets, Johannesburg, July 2004 (photo by the author)

Introduction: Object Orientations

fastest growing number of HIV/AIDS victims – their motifs reflect a tragic materiality and a foreboding memorialization of the dying.

Why are these particular communities deemed to be trapped in the past, shot through with their particular materialities? Indeed why fossilize culture in such ways? As many interviewees have asked me directly: Why is it that Afrikaner culture is not historicized in this way, why is it not the subject of theme parks and craft stalls? White Afrikaners too claim to be African of course, some even desire to be considered "indigenous" (see Kuper 2003:389). Perhaps this inequity resides in the judgment that "Boer" culture is not deemed exotic, much less aesthetically appealing and lacks the necessary historical substrate of real tradition. And why this is of concern for anthropologists especially is the Durkheimian intonation that ethnicity and aesthetic style correlate, which itself grows out of the assumption that such "primitive" objects stem from the collective mind, rather than any individual artist (Steiner 1994:92).

What is it to know a people by their things? Why such unease on my part? As a social evolutionist, Tylor famously argued that a rough scale of civilization could be instigated on the basis of industrial arts, metalworking, manufacture of vessels and implements, scientific knowledge, social and political organization, and so on, leading to a definite basis of compared facts. The races could be arranged from the Australians, to the Tahitians, Aztec, Chinese, and Italian (Tylor 1977:27). He specifically pointed to South Africa as one context in which colonial forces have brought previously primitive people in line with European civilization (1977:53). In fact he went as far as imputing that the role of the ethnographer was to expose "crude old cultures . . . and to mark these out for destruction" which was "urgently needful for the good of humanity" (see Tambiah 1999:44). Tylor had his own hierarchy of substances (see Lazzari, ch. 6, Gaitán ch. 4), where certain practices and techniques were directly correlated to a primitive age. Stone, Bronze, and Iron are still the pertinent taxonomies. The technologies of contemporary peoples are also hierarchically ordered along the same schema, and correlated back into prehistoric time. This is worrisome since it is an idea that continues to hold sway in the modern mind, that technology equals progress and that material sophistication is an index of social complexity and, ultimately, worth. Impoverished material culture equals impoverished culture in general. A paucity of goods is a material shortfall, another index of the evolution of culture and society: we are fixated by material lack – especially in "under-developed" contexts such as the

African continent. The narrative of "under-development" only emerged after the Second World War when the world was being restructured and re-classified according largely to newly emergent American international interests. Discourses of development also fasten firmly onto this view of material impoverishment and technical backwardness, in a self-fulfilling and destructive cycle where anthropologists, governments, and international organizations affix social and cultural value to modern technologies, whereas other traditional industries are de-privileged (Escobar 1995; Ferguson 1994; 1996; Hobart 1993). It would be a national shame for a post-apartheid black government to encourage the same rigid constructions of ethnicity and culture enforced by their now vilified predecessors.

One can also easily deconstruct the assumptions underlying the manufacture of static and historic Bushman crafts, using traditional processes and materials including skins, shells, beads, and so on. Skin bags decorated with worked ostrich shell, fragile and delicately made, are produced to be decorative rather than functional. While such bags may have served their hunter-gatherer owners well in the past, containing small and portable artifacts, they seem unlikely goods for the world of modern mass consumption. Their simplicity speaks to an earlier time, a time when people were less acquisitive and materialistic, and speaks of a culture considered by most to be extinct. The desire for an authentic, unmarked, and untainted, non-Bantu Southern African native, replete with click language and eco-conscious hunting and gathering subsistence has always been of paramount importance within Africa and perhaps more palpably, abroad (Blundell 2004; Gordon 1992; Skotnes 1996). Decades ago Fanon imputed that "the native artist who wishes at whatever cost to create a national work of art shuts himself up in a stereotyped reproduction of details," and further that "the artist who has decided to illustrate the truths of the nation turns paradoxically towards the past and away from actual events. What he ultimately intends to embrace are in fact the castoffs of thought, its shells and corpses, a knowledge which has been stabilized once and for all" (Fanon 1963:224–5). Much could further be teased from the naturalist fabric of colonial desire for true and celebrated primitivism and the willing complicity entrenched within new forms of South African modernity, but I believe that to be a more obvious set of critiques.

Recently, there have been some efforts to take traditional African techniques and apply modern materials (Zulu wire baskets is an obvious example), tinwork, wire sculpture, beading, woodworking, and so on.

Introduction: Object Orientations

Several of these technologies have been raised to the status of "art," or at least "high craft" and are available at expensive boutiques and art galleries in the metropoles of Cape Town and Johannesburg. Going global, it is nothing today to see a "South African pottery bowl or a Zulu milk pail... in a loft in New York or a home in New England:" ancient practices are thus transformed into "designer wares and one-of-a-kind craft objects" (Sellschop, et al. 2002:11). Certain objects are invoked as having a universal attraction that crosses cultural and geographic borders and "transcends time." In *Craft South Africa* (2002) this "timeless/seamless" connection is reinforced by archaeologist Tom Huffman who goes on to provide the archaeological corollaries, and validate those cultural survivals (see again Tylor 1977).

So it is timely that we examine the products of their labor and ours; however, I do not wish to frame judgments about the rights and wrongs of encouraging local indigenous communities to conduct traditional craft production or to support themselves within the nation's fragile economy. An alternative perspective, one perhaps that runs counter to the one outlined here, is that a significant degree of regional national pride is embedded within these objects, whether Ndebele dress designs worn at Cannes Film festival, township-styled fashion epitomized by the expensive *Stoned Cherry* label, or Venda ceramics adorning five star resorts and featured in global travel magazines, and so on. Of course there is a spectrum of designations from high art, to design, craft, and mere objects amongst the myriad things produced. Here we enter an immensely subjective world that requires a detailed ethnography of its own, conducted across broad social strata. However, we can say that such things are consumed in ways that are both celebratory and empowering for various constituencies in South Africa and that set of possibilities resides very much at the heart of the African Renaissance ethos and specifically the self-development policies of the ANC government (Bongmba 2004) – to make culture pay. In this postcolonial liberal state, the hallmark of which must surely be the instigation of the Truth and Reconciliation Commission (Nuttall and Coetzee 1998), identity is constantly being recast in creative and healing ways, albeit with various degrees of success. It was Nelson Mandela who said that "culture should be the language that should heal and transform the nation." In talking about the artistic traditions of South African people and their therapeutic role in the community today, the Chief Director of the Investing in Culture program reminds us that:

> Their influence is evident in the design of the clothes we wear, the buildings in which we work, and many of the objects we use every day. They transmit values and ideas from generation to generation. In a country like South Africa, where much of the fabric of community life was ripped apart this can form the threads that hold communities together and can be used to forge greater bonds. (Sack 2003:5)

Like many postcolonial states there is a long and not so distant history of unjust interaction that serves to complicate the kind of cultural pluralism we might ideally envisage. What academics may see as endemically flawed ethnic constructs and their concomitant materializations, may alternatively be the workable means for social and economic advancement irrespective of the negative potentials of those identity politics. As Ivison rightly states "since we are never in a position to choose social and political norms, practices or institutions *de novo*, but instead work with the imperfect and unjust arrangements we have, sometimes the very institutions we assume to be pluralism-friendly have been experienced by others in a radically different way" (Ivison 2002:3). Through this enmeshing of peoples, identities, and things, he underscores the dangers inherent in the politics of recognition: "If conceived of too literally, they can promote the telescoping and hardening of cultural and political identities that are, in fact, always internally differentiated and inherently dynamic" (Ivison 2002:10). Artisanship has become central "in the new landscapes of group identity" (Colloredo-Mansfeld 2002:124). Part of that constitution is the reformulation of identity in postcolonial, post-apartheid and postmodern terms, as individuals are called upon to refashion themselves to meet new socio-economic landscapes and imperatives. These reconstituted and permeable ethnoscapes and finanscapes (Appadurai 1996) denote that individual and community livelihoods shape and are shaped by "constellations of relationships, resources, and materialized expressive means" (Colloredo-Mansfeld 2002:125).

Anthropologists tread on treacherous terrain when they adjudicate as to what constitutes authenticity in the sphere of identity politics since identities are "constituted as much by our response to others and to the context we find ourselves in, as they are the product of processes of self-identification and determination" (Ivison 2002:10). Put simply, what concerns me here are matters of agency: indigenous peoples whether San, Venda, or Zulu etc. require clear social and economic choices in their crafting and performing of identity and should not be impelled to perform de facto as unchanging minorities, especially in the new South Africa where black empowerment and mobility are high on the agenda. The material expression of those solidarities and the creative new directions being forged should be of great interest to archaeologists and anthropologists alike and has the potential for great import in the lives of many. Here I conclude with a poignant example of this notion of material culture as uplift and national pride, again from Mbeki's (2004) speech on heritage day:

> We are fortunate that there are still some ordinary men and women of our country who are daily weaving a memory, beading a legacy, cutting a spoor, telling a story and loading into these bowls of history, a future for all our people . . .

Acknowledgments

I would like to thank Richard Leventhal and Jane Huber for making this possible. My own research was supported by a Mellon New Directions Fellowship and funding from the Institute for Social and Economic Research and Policy at Columbia University. I am grateful to Ben Smith, Geoff Blundell, Thembi Russell, and all the staff at the Rock Art Research Institute at the University of the Witwatersrand, South Africa. Thanks as well to Martin Hall, Ian Hodder, Daniel Miller, and Lindsay Weiss for conversations and materials that have been influential in the chapter.

References

Appadurai, A. 1996 Modernity at Large: Cultural Dimensions of Globalization. Minneapolis: University of Minnesota Press.
Attfield, J. 2000 Wild Things: Material Culture of Everyday Life. New York: Berg.
Blundell, Geoff 2004 Nquabayo's Nomansland. Uppsala: Uppsala University.
Bongmba, E. K. 2004 Reflections of Thabo Mbeki's African Renaissance. Journal of Southern African Studies 30(2):291–316.
Bourdieu, P. 1977 Outline of a Theory of Practice. R. Nice, trans. Cambridge: Cambridge University Press.
—— 1980 The Logic of Practice. Stanford: Stanford University Press.
—— 1998 Practical Reason: On the Theory of Action. Cambridge: Polity.
Buchli, V., ed. 2002 The Material Culture Reader. Oxford: Berg.
Coetzee, J. M. 1983 Life and Times of Michael K. London: Penguin.
Colloredo-Mansfeld, R. 2002 An Ethnography of Neoliberalism: Understanding Competition in Artisan Economies. Current Anthropology 43(1):113–137.

Douglas, S. 1997 Reflections on State Intervention and the Schmidtsdrift Bushmen. Journal of Contemporary African Studies 15(1):45-66.
Ellen, R. F. 1988 Fetishism. Man 23:213-235.
Escobar, A. 1995 Encountering Development: The Making and Unmaking of the Third World. Princeton: Princeton University Press.
Fanon, F. 1963 The Wretched of the Earth. New York: Grove Press, Inc.
Ferguson, J. 1994 The Anti-Politics Machine: "Development," Depoliticization, and Bureaucratic Power in Lesotho. Minneapolis: University of Minnesota Press.
—— 1996 Development. *In* Encyclopedia of Social and Cultural Anthropology. A. Barnard and J. Spence, eds. Pp. 154-160. London: Routledge.
Gordon, R. 1992 The Bushman Myth: The Making of a Namibian Underclass. Boulder: Westview Press.
Gosden, C., and Y. Marshall 1999 The Cultural Biography of Objects. World Archaeology: The Cultural Biography of Objects 31(2):169-178.
Hobart, M., ed. 1993 An Anthropological Critique of Development: The Growth of Ignorance. London: Blackwell.
Hodder, I. 2006 The Leopard's Tale: Revealing the Mysteries of Çatalhöyük. London: Thames and Hudson.
Ivison, D. 2002 Postcolonial Liberalism. Cambridge: Cambridge University Press.
Keane, W. 2003a Self-Interpretation, Agency, and the Objects of Anthropology: Reflections on a Genealogy. Studies in Society and History 45(2):222-248.
—— 2003b Semiotics and the Social Analysis of Material Things. Language and Communication 23(2-3):409-425.
Kuper, A. 2003 The Return of the Native. Current Anthropology 4(3):389-395.
Latour, B. 1991 We Have Never Been Modern. C. Porter, trans. Cambridge: Harvard University Press.
—— 1996 Petite réflexion sur le cultre moderne des dieux faitiches. Paris: Collection, Les Empêcheurs de Penser en Rond.
—— 2000 When Things Strike Back: A Possible Contribution of "Science Studies" to the Social Sciences. British Journal of Sociology 51(1):107-123.
—— 2004 Why Has Critique Run out of Steam? From Matters of Fact to Matters of Concern. Critical Inquiry 30(Winter):225-248.
Mamdani, M. 1996 Citizen and Subject: Contemporary Africa and the Legacy of Late Colonialism. Princeton: Princeton University Press.
Mbeki, T. 2004 Remarks of the President of South Africa, Thabo Mbeki, on the Occassion of the Celebration of National Heritage Day, Galeshewe, Kimberly, September 24, 2004.
Mbembe, A. 2000 At the Edge of the World: Boundries, Territorality, and Sovereignty in Africa. Public Culture 12(1):259-284.
—— 2001 On the Postcolony. Berkeley: University of California Press.
Meskell, L. M. 1999 Archaeologies of Social Life: Age, Sex, Class Etc. in Ancient Egypt. Oxford: Blackwell.
—— 2004 Object Worlds in Ancient Egypt: Material Biographies Past and Present. London: Berg.

—— Archaeological Ethnography: Conversations Outside the Kruger. Archaeologies 1:1.
—— forthcoming Trauma Culture: Remembering and Forgetting in the New South Africa. *In* Memory, Trauma, and World Politics. D. Bell, ed. Cambridge: Cambridge University Press.
Miller, D. 1987 Material Culture and Mass Consumption. Oxford: Blackwell.
—— ed. 1998 Material Cultures: Why Some Things Matter. Chicago: University of Chicago Press.
—— ed. 2005 Materiality. Durham: Duke University Press.
Miller, D., and C. Tilley 1996 Editorial. Journal of Material Culture 1(1):5–14.
Nuttall, S., and C. Coetzee, eds. 1998 Negotiating the Past: The Making of Memory in South and Africa. Cape Town: Oxford University Press.
Pels, P. 1998 The Spirit of Matter: On Fetish, Rarity, Fact, and Fancy. *In* Border Fetishisms: Material Objects in Unstable Places. P. Spyer, ed. Pp. 91–121. New York: Routledge.
—— 2002 "Materialism," "Spiritualism" and the Modern Fear of Matter and Materiality. American Anthropological Association, New Orleans, 2002.
Renfrew, C., C. Gosden, and L. DeMarrais, eds. 2005 Rethinking Materiality. Cambridge: McDonald Institute for Archaeology.
Sack, S. 2003 Poverty Alleviation. *In* Investing in Culture. Pp. 4–5. Pretoria: Department of Arts and Culture.
Scott, J. C. 1990 Domination and the Arts of Resistance: Hidden Transcripts. New Haven: Yale University Press.
Sellschop, S., W. Goldblatt, and D. Hemp 2002 Craft South Africa. Hyde Park: Macmillan.
Skotnes, P., ed. 1996 Miscast: Negotiating the Presence of the Bushmen. Cape Town: University of Cape Town Press.
Steiner, C. B. 1994 African Art in Transit. Cambridge: Cambridge University Press.
Tambiah, S. J. 1999 Magic, Science, Religion and the Scope of Rationality. Cambridge: Cambridge University Press.
Taussig, M. 1980 The Devil and Commodity Fetishism in South America. Chapel Hill: University of North Carolina Press.
Tylor, E. B. 1977 Primitive Culture: Researches into the Development of Mythology, Philosophy, Religion, Language, Art and Custom, vol. 1. New York: Gordon Press.
Wilmsen, E., S. Dubow, and J. Sharp 1994 Introduction: Ethnicity, Identity and Nationalism in Southern Africa. Journal of Southern African Studies 20(3):347–353.

2

Mastering Matters: Magical Sense and Apotropaic Figurine Worlds of Neo-Assyria

Carolyn Nakamura

Introduction: Magical Figures from the Past

When contemplating certain deposits unearthed during the excavations at Nimrud in the 1950s, Max Mallowan remarked, "this magical practice had an immensely long survival, as witness the nursery rhyme:

> Four corners to my bed,
> Four angels round my head,
> One to watch and one to pray,
> And two to bear my soul away." (1966:226)

Mallowan's commentary, rather typical of his time, concerned the discovery of numerous brick boxes encasing figurines made of sun-dried clay, found buried underneath the corners, thresholds, and central spaces of room floors, possibly where a bed once stood. Excavations during the late 1800s to mid 1900s located such deposits in residences, palaces, and temples at important political and religious capitals of the Neo-Assyrian Empire, including Nimrud, Assur, Nineveh, Khorsabad and at Ur in Babylonia under Assyrian rule; they first appeared during the reign of Shalmaneser III and generally persisted up through the reign of Sin-shar-ishkun (ca. 858–612 B.C.). One can imagine an excavator's delight in finding such deposits, and there was apparently considerable competition and excitement surrounding their discovery and unveiling (Oates and Oates 2001:253–254). But, locating such boxes did not always promise the discovery of figurines. Numerous "empty" brick boxes contained nothing more than a thick layer of sandy material, possibly remnants of decomposed organic matter such as wood or food. Deposits from Ur contained offerings of animal bones, remnants of grain and a pottery sherd along with the clay figures (Woolley 1926:692). And at Assur, some of the buried boxes entombed miniature bronze weapons (Rittig 1977). But perhaps the most curious finds were the figurines of "warrior" men, mythological fish- and bird-*apkallū* sages, human-beast hybrids, horned snakes, and other fantastical beings (Figure 2.1). Generally, such deposits comprised one, two, or seven figurines standing "at attention" in boxes facing in toward the center of the room. These deposits, not simply buried but concealed and contained, amounted to the discovery within a discovery, the revelation of an ancient secret or desire that had remained hidden for thousands of years.

Other archaeological findings, however, had already anticipated these discoveries: ancient texts preserved instructions for an apotropaic[1] ritual involving the burial of clay and wood figurines under room floors quite in the manner described above (Gurney 1935; Smith 1926; Wiggermann 1992). The name of one text explicitly pronounced its purpose: *šēp lemutti ina bīt amēli parāsu*, "to block the entry of the enemy in someone's house" (Wiggermann 1992:1); and the first twenty lines named the "enemy" to be almost any evil imaginable, from spirits, gods, and ancestors to disease, misfortune, Fate, and Death. The text guided a priest-exorcist through a choreography of very specific and often protracted ceremonies involving various objects, gestures, substances, and locations, leading up to the final installation of the magically protective figures entombed underground. Notably, another related text fragment, KAR 298, specifically detailed the making, function, character, number, and placement of the figurines (Smith 1926). The archaeological evidence proved to be remarkably consistent with these texts in terms of form and details of surface treatment, and to some extent, position and grouping of the figures. So the Neo-Assyrians themselves revealed the secret of the figurine deposits: they were magically powerful deposits that protected the individual and his house from sickness and evil. The protective figures served to "watch," "pray," and "bear souls away," as it were.

Figure 2.1 Apotropaic figurine deposit found in Room S57 of Fort Shalmaneser at Nimrud. Adapted from Curtis and Reade (1995:112)

Curiously, archaeological research has not fully exploited the evocative cooperation between text, iconography, material, and deposition in this apotropaic practice. Rather, it has been the art historical and Assyriological traditions that have provided the most thorough deliberations on the ritual. Iconographic analyses present detailed visual descriptions of the figurines (Klengel-Brandt 1968; Rittig 1977; Van Buren 1931), and trace out a visual typology of apotropaic images (Green 1993; Wiggermann

1993), while textual analysis investigates the symbolic logic of apotropaic prescription and the mythological identities of the figures (Wiggermann 1992). Two long-awaited volumes no doubt will provide further analyses of particular site assemblages (Green forthcoming) and the apotropaic figurines in general (Ellis forthcoming). Despite the richness of textual and archaeological data, an anthropological perspective is distinctly lacking; however, such research would considerably enrich our views of this remarkable ancient practice. Regrettably, studies of previously excavated materials have not exploited the diverse range of approaches afforded by modern social sciences. While previously excavated sites and materials admittedly do not often lend themselves to the analytical and interpretive techniques most favored by archaeologists, such data should not be omitted from modern reconsideration and inquiry simply because they present a special challenge for substantive interpretation (see Meskell 1999). There is, in fact, adequate data to perform detailed contextual and spatial analyses of the apotropaic practice at certain Neo-Assyrian sites.[2] Furthermore, I would argue that conventional interpretations in archaeology – still oriented toward explanation and meaning – fail to get at the most compelling aspects of ancient magic, exactly that which makes it *magical*. Magic surely presents something beyond the reach of representational or functional interpretations and thus demands a different perspective. What is required is an evocation of magic that aims directly at the caesura between meaning and matter and delves into the shadowy processes of materializing experience, belief, and value.

Perhaps it is not surprising that archaeology, with only material traces of human activity to work with, has left the critical study of magic to other disciplines. It is revealing that "magic" is generally invoked as an explanation for those slippery things, processes, and occurrences that our rational and linguistic varieties of logic can't quite master. From this vantage, magic has become something more suitable for explaining than for being explained. But as Mauss (1972) decisively observed in *A General Theory of Magic*, magic is as much a way of doing as a way of thinking. We should consider, then, not a logic but an *aesthetics* of magical practice, as a particular way of *making sense* (Gosden 2001). And this way of doing engages a radical materiality that not only enacts the mutual constitution of subjects and objects, but provides the condition for such discursive practices.

A consideration of materiality vis-à-vis magic, then, does not presume and continue the anthropological pursuit of finding *meaning in* matter, the well-rehearsed terrain of discovering how various cultures construct and inscribe meaning in their artifacts. What is magical or forceful in certain artifacts evades such fixed and flattened analyses since processes of abstraction do not account for the "untranscended materiality" or "plastic power" of the object that derives from the thing's materialness itself (Pels 1998:101). Impoverished attempts to discover the meaning or social context of a magical artifact, as it were, fall short not only because of an opacity of things, but also because our habituated ways of apprehending and constructing meaning threaten a veritable non-recognition of the things themselves.[3] This purifying analytical gaze effectively eviscerates matter of its very materiality – its innate capacity to continuously engage and enter into new relations. But recovering a recognition of things simply requires embracing the *thingness* of matter, namely, that insistent sensuousness of things that compels a confrontation with humans. This move does not return us to problematic theories of materialism, but rather engages a notion of materiality as a dialectic and supplemental aesthetic of *relating to*.

Humans mime the animate in the inanimate, and the ideal in the real, to create and transform the world around them, only to be created and transformed right back. Such is the reality of matter: it "strikes back" (Pels 1998:91). Within this framework I suggest that apotropaic figurine magic encompasses a process that enacts both a distinct mode of perception and a material event that renders a protected reality. This discussion converges specifically on two aspects of magic: first, how magic capitalizes on a tension between the social construction of meaning and the radical autonomy of matter, and second, how magical perception, in the way of poetic action, masters the unknown by recovering and performing a "derangement of all the senses."[4] From such a viewpoint, Mesopotamian magic neither constitutes nor opposes a "rational" mode of knowing the world, but rather moves alongside in tandem, as counterpoint in a polyphonic[5] system of knowledge. From this perspective, magic engages a sensuous metaphysics and grounds the possibility of a distinct socio-religious worldview.

Magic Presents More Than It Represents[6]

The magical object is nothing less than confounding; like Marx's table, it is "an apparition of a strange creature: at the same time Life, Thing,

Magical Sense and Apotropaic Figurine Worlds

Beast, Object, Commodity, Automaton – in a word, specter" (Derrida 1994:152). Like that other odd Table-thing, the magical object presents:

> the contradiction of *automatic autonomy*, mechanical freedom, technical life. Like every thing, from the moment it comes onto the stage of a market, the table resembles a prosthesis of itself. Autonomy *and* automatism, *but* automatism of this wooden table that spontaneously puts itself into motion, to be sure, and seems thus to animate, animalize, spiritualize, *spiritize* itself, but while remaining an artifactual body, a sort of automaton, a puppet, a stiff and mechanical doll whose dance obeys the technical rigidity of a program. (Derrida 1994:153)

Derrida's lucid description of the commodity provides an uncanny account of the magical object and its tendency toward unintelligibility. This opacity or resistance to meaning seems to extend from some perverse quality of thingness that precedes and exceeds reason and defies any empirical or semantic basis. While a magical work gathers meaning from the specific context of its production, it also produces a material intervention in the world that asserts a new force – like *mana* – that "always and everywhere, . . . somewhat like algebraic symbols, occurs to represent an indeterminate value of signification, in itself devoid of meaning and thus susceptible of receiving any meaning at all" (Levi-Strauss 1987:55). The condition of such opacity finds its origin not in a peculiar mental state as Levi-Strauss would have it, but in the promiscuous *materiality* of the work – the way in which it accommodates every relation it enters into, becoming spirit, idol, toy, or clay fabric G4 – such that it seems to defer and proliferate meaning. There is something unsettling in the way things simply *survive*, through and beyond meaningful human signification, by continual deferral and deference. This is the strange life of things, animated and constrained by invisible relations and yet defiantly autonomous in their discrete physicality. The allure of the thing lies in the way in which it can never be completed, never be fully or perfectly discovered; and it is always set in motion, propelled by human relations. In this way, the thing always exceeds its own narration.[7] And such authority in contingency, indeterminacy, and excess reveals an extra-semantic function of the magical object as the disclosure of powerful force in encounters of meaning and matter, life and death.

In this way, the magical object does not merely represent. It *presents*. This presentation, as not a reproducing or inventing but a *capturing*

(Deleuze 2003:48), conjures a force that exceeds the totality of the complex relations and ideas that produce it. Specifically, the magical event renders that which is not given over to meaning. Rather it vacillates between processes of signifier formation and the bare material potential of the world that is "superabundant beyond all understanding" (Menke 1998:69). In seeking the concrete, magic captures the intractable power of things that is forever inaccessible to human mastery: things in their capacity for such excess and autonomy present a possibility – if not a guarantee – of life in death since pure matter, as an energy unbounded and unqualified by organic life, asserts the force of an existence that can never be destroyed, only conserved. The obligation of death provides the very ground of life (Harrison 2003:70). And magic, as an event that disrupts the consensus (and what more final consensus can there be than death?), finds power in the bare possibility of presenting life as death, and meaning as matter. This is the power of a radical materialism that lies beyond rational or linguistic analysis and suspends an "irresolvable dialectic," a state of indeterminacy in the play between meaning and matter.[8] These human–thing transactions trace an economy of the present in the sense that they do not seek a reconciliation of opposites, but rather a preserving of disjunction (Spivak 1974:xlii). Within this ongoing movement, magic finds kinship with art and memory, unleashing a force as inscrutable to reason as it is captivating in our desire to control it.

The Sensuous Metaphysics of Magic: Mutual Constitution and Correspondence

> The representation of a wish is, eo ipso, the representation of its fulfillment. Magic, however, brings a wish to life; it manifests a wish.
>
> Ludwig Wittgenstein, *Remarks on Frazier's Golden Bough*
> (Miles and Rhees 1971)

Implicit in Wittgenstein's aphorism that magic "manifests a wish" is the notion that magic requires concrete demonstration: the fulfillment of the wish made real. At first glance, magic as both the manifestation of a wish and its fulfillment seems to pose a contradiction in this act of making real. But magic is an exchange that seeks synthesis, and such exchange, "as in any other form of communication, surmounts the contradiction inherent in it" (Levi-Strauss 1987:58). Mikhail Bakhtin (1984) surmised, "to *be* means to *communicate*" (287). And the movement of such exchange presumes a sensuous intimacy between the outside world and ourselves: "to be means to be for another, and through the other, for oneself. A person has no internal sovereign territory, he is wholly and always on the boundary; looking inside himself, he looks *into the eyes of another* or *with the eyes of another*" (Bakhtin 1984:287). This is the human orientation of being amidst the constant flux of the world that provokes our fear as much as desire, and discloses the condition for a way of knowing directly and sensuously.

Giambattista Vico (1999[1744]), a forward-thinking but marginalized philosopher of his time, implicated bodily sense in a critique of the Cartesian principle of *Cogito*; in response to the reductive logic of geometric certainty, he formulated the axiom: man can only know what he himself has made – "verum et factum convertuntur" – and to make is to transform oneself by becoming other (Vico 1999[1744]:160). The implication of this premise posits that human knowledge cannot be exhausted by rationality; it is also sensory and imaginative. Although Vico's project poses three progressive historical eras of man: the first ruled by the senses, the second by imagination, and the third by reflective reason, we now recognize that all three modalities of knowledge exist throughout human history albeit at different scales and intensities. From this perspective, magic, which embraces bodily imitation and play, is better viewed as a poetic reinterpretation of the concrete reality of human action rather than the discovery of an objective reality that presumes to regulate it (Böhm 1995:117).

Indeed it is our sensory faculties and not our rational faculties that better apprehend certain complexities of the magical realm: we know when we feel. In encounters with magic, we apprehend the apparent trickery of bodies, substances, and things. Our reaction to such events often betrays delight, horror, fear, disgust, attraction, and fascination simultaneously, and such disorientation is desired. Magic produces wonder, and in doing so returns us to a state of apprehending the world that short-circuits those automatic processes of intellection that discipline the senses. And wonder is central to a mode of understanding that is "capable of grasping what, in ourselves and in others precedes and exceeds reason" (Pettigrew 1999:66). Bodily sense is key here, since it can *know* something more than words express.⁹ The "trick" of magic, then, lies in attaining the unknown by disorganizing all the senses; in effect, it acts to deregulate relationships that are rigorously regulated by normative cultural forms. The aesthetic experience of magic seeks the recovery of correspondences between people, things, and places in their pre-differentiated unity, a unity that becomes obscured through "habitual modes of perception" (Harrison 1993:180).¹⁰ In this way, magic aims at the perceptual movements that continually render meaning rather than at meaning itself. In this intercalary register of experience, magic presumes a certain direct engagement with the world; specifically, it recalls a pre-differentiated world as an open possibility of interrelations constantly in flux.

Merleau-Ponty's (1968) notion of *intertwining* or *chiasm* between interior and exterior experience might provide a helpful ontological frame here. This bare movement of perception posits the emergence of various social worlds from the sensuous interchange between interior and exterior phenomena, namely, nodes of self-organization (perception) and the "chaos" of indeterminacy (being). There exists a necessary separation *and* continuum between the former and the latter as the very condition for perception, such that perceptual faith becomes a "strange attractor in the circulation of sense, in the interweaving of perceptual and material systems" (Mazis 1999:233). And Merleau-Ponty (1968) conceives of the bare notion of *flesh* as providing the substrate or condition for this movement. *Flesh* posits a world of indeterminate being connected by an essential openness to becoming completed by the world, things, others, qualities and interrelations (Grosz 1999:151). Such transactions are never "completed" per se, but rather engage in continuous exchange, in an ongoing process of becoming. This unity, therefore, conditions perception as "a communication or communion, the taking up or completion by us of some extraneous intention or, . . . the complete expression outside ourselves of our perceptual powers and coition, so to speak, of our body with things" (Merleau-Ponty 1962).

The notion of an original unity seems to inhabit a Mesopotamian worldview in which dreams, visions, abnormal events, internal organs, and entrails provided an "empirical" basis for reality. In this reality, interior events and natural and social phenomena were intimately and specifically related. One could argue that this worldview maintained a certain interpenetration or continuity between the interiority of the mind and the exteriority of the world. This notion is supported in the polysemic and polyphonic character of the Mesopotamian writing systems.[11] According to Asher-Grève and Asher (1998:39), the Sumerian language and vocabulary offers no evidence for the radical bifurcation of mind and body that is so fundamental to Western intellectual thought. They find support for this notion in the Sumerian word, šà, a holistic term that denotes the mind, body, and heart; the body and heart are the seat of the will, "it thinks, feels, has power over the limbs and is open to the influence of the deities" (1998:39). Moreover, they see the body as providing a fundamental point of reference in early Mesopotamia; Sumerians see the body as the total being, confirmed by the absence of a distinct Sumerian word for brain/mind (1998:40). In later times, ancient scribes and scholars exploited the flexibility of the Akkadian language evidenced in plays and puns on words (see Alster 2002). It is notable that the formation and development of the cuneiform script (created by Mesopotamians for Sumerian and adapted also to Akkadian), always allowed for a number of permutations and ambiguities to intervene, on the level of things indicated as well as on the level of signifying words (Bottéro 1992:94). This capacity for linguistic signs and phonemes to hold multiple and freely interchangeable values reveals an indeterminacy built into what Bottéro calls the concrete and polysemic character of a "script of things" (Bottéro 1992:100). In other words, linguistic thought also supports a material logic of correspondence.

Although Mesopotamians certainly made distinctions between various concrete and intangible phenomena – the supernatural and natural worlds were connected through a notion of divinity, but were not seen as the same – perhaps it was the potential for their connection or conflation that was significant in the context of magic. The reorientation of classical mind–matter, subject–object divisions within a relation of continuity and mutual implication sets up an ontological frame that might better approach an ancient Neo-Assyrian worldview (following Meskell 1999; 2002; 2004). Such a frame not only situates magic in a pre-discursive world of relations, but also grounds it in an aesthetics that discloses a powerful process of enacting correspondence. It should come as no surprise, then, to find mimetic work as a principle technique of magic, since the recovery of the world in its pre-differentiated unity provides the condition for the mimetic process of getting into the skin of an other (cf. Taussig 1993), that way of making which is the occasion of magic. If this unity becomes obscured by the habitual, purifying movements of social process, then magic seeks its recovery in secrecy, through the concrete work of mimesis.

Carolyn Nakamura

Bodily Sense: Magic's Perception and Performance

Mimesis asserts a gesture of expression that "retrieves the world and remakes it" (Merleau-Ponty 1973:78), and I am interested in how the Neo-Assyrian figurine deposits, as such gestures, retrieve and remake a protected world. Figurines, as miniature bodily forms petrified in clay or stone, are distinct works of wonder; in the way of poetic disclosure, they project an idealized past and more desirable future. Figurines fascinate as they confront our gaze with something familiar in the unfamiliar, real in the counterfeit. It is not only the object's form or physicality that we identify and relate to, but something of the mimetic gesture: the faculty to create and explore ourselves, to encounter and become other (Taussig 1993:xiii). Anterior to the organized knowledge of reflection, there is mimesis: this age-old and rather profound faculty that stands somewhere at the beginning of play, the beginning of language, and the beginning of self-making (Benjamin 1979). With mimesis, we already have a sense that reality, at some level, is simply a matter of relations. Walter Benjamin conceived of the mimetic faculty as producing "magical correspondences" between persons and things, objects and essences: "a child not only plays at being a grocer or a teacher, but also at being a windmill or a train" (1979:65). Relations forged through miming reveal remarkable correspondences between the material and immaterial; the copy assumes the power of the original, and a wish is "made real" in the material fabric of the world (Frazer 1957:55; Taussig 1993:47). The elegance of the mimetic process lies in the way in which it always renders an imperfect copy, and it is this very intervention of imperfection that locates and captures creative force.

If Neo-Assyrian apotropaic magic reenacts a circulation of sense – a reorientation of perceptual and material systems – to disclose the protection of space and being in time, how might we consider a notion of protection constituted in the material gesture of placing numerous figurine deposits under Neo-Assyrian room floors? Furthermore, what can we make of acts of burial, concealment, and containment in this context? Here, texts and archaeological materials considered together portray a remarkably detailed practice in the choreography of various mimetic acts.

Turning to the texts, we find they recount the exemplary life of these objects from creation to deposition. The ritual production of apotropaic figurines involved certain meaningful places, materials and gestures: one text instructs a practitioner, a high-ranking state *āšipu* (priest-exorcist) to go to the woods at sunrise to consecrate a *cornel* tree, recite the incantation "Evil [spirit] in the broad steppe" and then return to the city to make the figurines from the consecrated wood (see Text 1, 28–44 in Wiggermann 1992).[12] The crafting of clay figurines begins similarly, but what is notable here is the portrayal of the ritual scene that evokes a distinct sensory landscape in the enactment of certain requisite and standardized actions:

> when you make the statues, creatures of Apsû,
> in the morning at sunrise you shall go to the clay pit and consecrate the clay pit; with censer, torch and holy water you shall [purify] the clay pit,
> seven grains of silver, seven grains of gold, carnelian, *hulā*[*lu*-stone]
> you shall throw into the clay pit, then prepare the setting for Šamaš,
> set up a censer with juniper wood, pour out first class beer, kn[eel down,] stand up, and recite the incantation Clay pit, clay pit.
>
> Incantation: Clay pit, clay pit, you are the clay pit of Anu and Enlil,
> the clay pit of Ea, lord of the deep, the clay pit of the great gods;
> you have made the lord for lordship, you have made the king for kingship,
> you have made the prince for future days;
> your pieces of silver are given to you, you have received them;
> your gift you have received, and so, in the morning before Šamaš, I pinch off
> the clay NN son of NN; may it be profitable, may what I do prosper.
> (Text I, lines 144–57, Wiggermann 1992)

The appeal to the senses during this ceremony is striking.[13] The scent of the censer, heat of the torch, luster of the metals, flavor of the beer, and sound of spoken words together invite and gather the human, natural, and divine worlds to a feast of sensory correspondence. This demonstration accomplishes a sort of dazzling synthesis that deregulates the faculties – of imagination, outer sense, inner sense, reason, and understanding (Deleuze 1998:33) – and seeks communion through the apprehension of the world. The result effectively gathers and binds spirit with matter to forge a unity of being as divergence or noncoincidence. It is a matter of "capturing and befriending" insensible forces by embracing the strife in which the perceptible and imperceptible, sensuous and non-sensuous belong to each other. Through this performance, the clay pit as divine material is reenacted in a demonstrative process of making sense, and the sensual or aesthetic enactment of a certain understanding of the world discloses power in the *process* of re-forming meaning: "in the process of mimetic reenactment, we reach behind the already formed figurines of meaning, back to the dynamics, force and energy of their formation" (Menke 1998:97–98).

After this "enlivening," the *āšipu* then molds this clay into various figures of power and protection, in effect reenacting the divine creation of humans from the clay of the *apsû*, the primordial underground freshwater ocean.[14] And this mimetic act doubles back, for at the end of the incantation the *āšipu* invokes the creative utterance of Enki (Ea) and incants himself into the picture;[15] here he blurs his position as both mime and mimed other: "in this way, as both chanter and person chanted about, as demonstrator and demonstrated, he creates the bridge between the original and copy that brings a new force, the third force of magical power, to intervene in the human world" (Taussig 1993:106). And it is the *āšipu*'s body that provides the ligature of this bond:

> O Ea, King of the Deep, to see . . .
> I, the magician am thy slave.
> March thou on my right hand,
> Be present on my left;
> Add thy pure spell unto mine,
> *Add thy pure voice unto mine,*
> *Vouchsafe (to me) pure words,*
> *Make fortunate the utterance of my mouth,*
> Ordain that my decisions be happy,
> Let me be blessed wherever I tread,
> Let the man whom I (now) touch be blessed.
> (Utukki Limnuti, III/VII:260ff.
> Thompson 1903–04:27–29, added emphasis)

It is bodily sense – initiated by the *āšipu*'s voice, movement, and touch – that forges a correspondence between the natural and the divine. Through the mimetic faculty, magical craft and performance invites a direct and sensuous relation with the open world capable of recuperating a pre-organized state of sensation and perception. This visceral presentation of the self-becoming-other and spirit-becoming-substance, reproduces the original fold of being that encompasses divine, human, and natural worlds. The Mesopotamian world was indeed enchanted, and humans, always already engaged in such a world, needed only to feel or sense in order to retrieve such unity.

I have dwelled upon the bodily aspects of practice – namely, those gestures of relating and transforming through incantation, touch, and movement – to underscore magic as a technique, as a knowing and producing that choreographs a dis/re-organization of worldly relations. Magical performance amounts to a mimetic demonstration of vital correspondences between ideas, essences, and things in the processual enactment of an ideal made real. The affective force of such bodily techniques arises from the kinetic communication and experience of the performance; but how are we to make sense of the power or force of ideal protection *made real* through the burial of miniature figurine deposits? Most commonly, scholarship has approached this ritual practice and material assemblage by considering certain symbolic and conceptual linkages to Neo-Assyrian ritual, religion, and culture, for instance, the common terrain shared by myth and iconography (see Green 1983; 1993; Wiggermann 1992; 1993). While such critical analyses get at important aspects and processes of ancient intellection, they ultimately fail to consider the devastatingly material logic of magic that often subverts (only to reinforce) such discursive productions of meaning. To redress this imbalance, I presently examine this concrete logic and how it discloses apotropaic power.

Mastering Matters

In the material register, Neo-Assyrian figurine assemblages present a physical gesture of miniaturization, hybrid form, and concealment. I have intimated that such material gestures disclose a magic technology as a symbolic and sensual logic that conspires with and against conventional value-producing forms. The question now becomes one of how this material reality *presents* protection. I would suggest that in the context of apotropaic performance, a material economy that produces a miniature, hybrid, and hidden reality anchors and accomplishes an experience of human mastery. Furthermore, this suite of gestures skillfully sustains the belief in divine power and order through a cunning reversal. The collision of Neo-Assyrian socioreligious beliefs with this material making engenders a force that cannot be contained or mastered by narrative closure. This resistance to such mastery, in effect, secures magic's very power. Magic does not seek the restoration of balance or the resolution of contradiction (Taussig 1993:126), rather it renders such contradiction immaterial, and in doing so, masters the system which defines the conditions of its disclosure. The slippage between meaning and matter, belief and practice, enshrouds magic in secrecy that is at once opaque and transparent. As both contingent and autonomous, the magical object secretes indeterminacy into the structure that conceives it, holds it at a distance and thereby masters it.

Artifacts congeal processes of making – the simultaneous forging of objects, selves, relations, cultures, and worlds – in a gesture of becoming. To make is to transform, and such transformation derives from the human enactment of both the self and the world. If we accept Bakhtin's idea that to be means to communicate, then figurines are self-creating works that specifically address communications among various beings, human, animal, divine, and supernatural. They provide the material site for the human action of creation which moves back on the human creators themselves (Scarry 1985:310), and this reverse process acts in complicit as much as disruptive, subversive, and obfuscating ways. Notably then, the process of material creation discloses a certain "mimetic excess" (cf. Taussig 1993) whereby reproduction amounts to metamorphosis, self-amplification to self-effacement, and divergence to unity.

The Neo-Assyrians crafted protective figurines as clay or stone copies of various mythological and supernatural beings. Their form as miniature, portable, durable, free-standing, three-dimensional objects confronts humans within a distinct relationship; namely, this material choreography reproduces powerful beings in a reality that assumes an anthropocentric universe for its absolute sense of scale (following Stewart 1984:56). The materiality of the figurine thereby discloses the authority of humans over the copy, and hence over the original. Here, the production and reception of the copy itself becomes a "dramatic form of (social) experience" (Jenson 2001:23), namely, that of human mastery. Whether deity, double, ancestor, spirit, or animal, the "original" comes to inhabit a material reality of human design. As petrified and choreographed "life," the figurine recreates the human as master in this relation, a relation whereby humans, as all-powerful giants, assert and play out their desires within the diminutive tableau of the figurine. The specific "bundling" of material properties of the figurine provides an enduring frame and anchor for the various ways in which other subjects relate to it thereafter. As a thing, the petrified miniature object will always encounter and constitute subjects as vigorous, gigantic masters with the capacity to possess, manipulate, command, and destroy.

Through this production of figurines, Neo-Assyrian apotropaic rituals trace out complex, and even disorienting, relations between humans, deities, and various supernatural beings in space and time. Throughout the ritual, the *āšipu* priest creates protective beings in a perpetual mode of dedication to important deities who are the "creators" of humankind. I have previously argued that these acts of dedication constitute a giving that takes back (Nakamura 2004); here, dedication is a demand for protection, a dialectic of giving that gives back more in return. Protection then arises from the "mimetic slippage" that exacts a brash assertion of human mastery over divine power, masked through a posed reality of servitude. Apotropaic rituals enact a radical synthesis of material work and belief that configures a force capable of surmounting contradiction. The durable material gestures of miniaturized scale, hybrid form, and concealment inscribe the subterranean landscape, effectively preserving a desired past for the future. In this way, an idiom of protection arises in the material enactment of memory.

The miniature

The creation of powerful supernatural beings in diminutive clay form mimes the divine creation of being from primordial clay. But this figurine work enacts an idealized relation between the human and divine such that the mimetic act establishes a double appropriation. Through mimesis, the *āšipu* appropriates the divine power of creation by making copies of protective beings that assume the powers of the original. In addition, his material relation to the figurine manifested in relative size also embodies a divine relation to humans. The diminutive size of the figurine renders humans giant in comparison. The *āšipu*, as creator and master of the figurines, becomes creator and marshal of the divine power of protection, who then fashions, commands and deploys a small army of protective spirits. This cunning reversal amounts to a self-realizing request for protection made possible by the exposure of a secret: that humans make up the gods who make them.[16] But this exposure finds certain cover in the opacity of the figurine object, which presents itself to the world as a small, doll-like object made of clay, as a king in beggar's clothes, as it were.

This "auto-affection" enacted through the creation of objects galvanizes power in mimesis as idealized repetition; in Derrida's words, "[it] gains in power and in its mastery of the other to the extent that its power of repetition *idealizes itself*" (1974:166). And repetition does not produce the same; rather it magnifies difference masked by the similarity it bears to the original. The miniature figurine then provides a locus for the human enactment of a variety of desires and actions that animate the being it represents; in the Neo-Assyrian case, humans control, protect, contain, and command powerful deities and spirits in this spatial and material production of simulacra. The scale of the miniature invites activities of play and fantasy. According to Roger Caillois, play, as "pure form, activity that is an end in itself, rules that are respected for their own sake, constitutes an area of "limited and provisional perfection," in which one is the master of destiny" (2001:157). In the realm of play, humans are free to "master" any relation, being, reality, or power, immune to any apprehension or consequence regarding their actions; this is especially true when such play is circumscribed by human–object relations. The tableau of the miniature solicits a relation of human mastery through an idiom of play that thrives on transgressive maneuvers of inversion and appropriation.

The hybrid

The magical power of the *āšipu* also allows him to identify certain mythological and supernatural beings appropriate for the task of protection; these are ancient sages (*apkallū*), warrior deities and monsters, associated with civilized knowledge and the formidable forces of life, death, peace, and destruction of divine will and rule (Green 1993; Wiggermann 1993). These figures take on different protective attributes depending on the nature of the represented being; the *apkallū* act as purifiers and exorcists to expel and ward off evil forces, while monsters, gods, and dogs tend to the defense of the house from demonic intruders (Wiggermann 1992:96–97). All of these figures find some association either with the underworld or the freshwater ocean under the earth (*apsû*) which was the domain of Enki, the god associated with wisdom, magic, incantation, and the arts and crafts of civilization (Black and Green 1992:75), and notably, all but the *laḫmu* portray composite human–animal physiognomies (Figure 2.2).

Such forms manifest a communion of things generally held to be opposed to each other. The blending of humans and animals in this context might capitalize on the tension between Mesopotamian conceptions

	APKALLU SAGES				LOWER GODS			ANIMAL
Type	Bird-*apkallu*			Fish-*apkallu*	Ninšubur	Smiting-god?	Latarak	Dogs
Attributes	cone & bucket	staff	branch & bucket	branch? & bucket	gold foil staff		flail	
Form	bird-human (plaque)	bird-human (plaque)	bird-human (plaque)	fish-human (figurine)	god (figurine)	god (figurine)	god in lion pelt (figurine)	quarduped (figurine)
Representation								
Type Number	Ia	Ib	Ic	II	III	IV	V	VI

	TIAMAT'S CREATURES: MONSTERS & DEMONS							
Type	Six-curled *laḫmu*			*Bašmu*	*Mušḫuššu*	*Ugallu*	*Kusarikku*	*Kulullû*
Attributes	spade	staff	spear	copper axe in mouth				
Form	human (plaque)	human (plaque)	human (figurine)	snake (figurine)	snake-dragon (figurine)	lion-demon (figurine)	bull-human (plaque)	fish-man (figurine)
Representation								
Type Number	VIIa	VIIb	VIIc	VIII	IX	X	XI	XII

Figure 2.2 Apotropaic figures with associated features. 1. Drawing after Richards in Black and Green (1992:65). 2. The identification of the *laḫmu* figure is controversial; it names both a cosmogonic deity and one of Tiāmat's creatures (Wiggermann 1992:155–156), and may also represent an *apkallu* sage (Ellis 1995:165; Russell 1991:184, fn. 27)

of a structured, civilized human world and a chaotic, untamed natural world (Bottéro 1992). Hybrids materialize a unity of self and other, human and animal as a strange being that is at once knowable and controllable and unknowable and incontrollable. As beings in-between, hybrids embody potential, transition, and similarity in difference. Such liminality is often associated with dangerous power, a power that obeys the apotropaic economy of the supplement, since it terrifies and yet provides the surest protection against that terror (Derrida 1974:154).

By miming such beings in clay figurines, the *āšipu* brings forth their active life and force in petrified form. Capitalizing on the apotropaic logic of defense, this gesture captures self-defeating force and suspends it in space, material, and time. Many of the figurine types are depicted in movement with hands gesturing and a foot forward to suggest forward movement. Following Susan Stewart (1984:54), I submit that the force of animated life does not diminish when arrested in the fixity and exteriority of the figurine, but rather, is captured as a moment of hesitation always on the verge of forceful action. The apotropaic figurine is a magical object – what Michael Taussig calls a "time–space compaction of the mimetic process" – doubled over since its form and matter, creation and presentation capture certain inherent energies that humans desire to control. The magical object, which encounters the unknown by presenting its form and image "releases a force capable of vanquishing it, or even befriending it" (Deleuze 2003:52). But as ritual texts and archaeological deposits confirm, it was not just the images themselves that rendered power, but something in the process of their creation. While such apotropaic figures appear in grand scale and idealized form on wall reliefs flanking entrances of kingly palaces purifying all who passed through the gates, the figures standing guard in floor deposits performed an additional task.[17]

The buried and enclosed

The multiple layers of concealment in this Neo-Assyrian figurine ritual suggest a play on the hiding and receiving powers of the earth. In Mesopotamia, burial constituted a pervasive and important ritual idiom; people buried valuables, sacrifices, foundation offerings, caches of various materials, and their dead. Such diverse practices surely supported an equally diverse range of meanings. But in a basic sense, burial can mean to store, preserve, and put the past on hold (Harrison 2003:xi). This concept of burial holds purchase in the way in which protection relates to memory. By burying figurines of powerful beings, the *āšipu* preserves an expressed belief in a present reality of supernatural power, mythological origin and divine order. Burial keeps things hidden and protected such that preservation binds memory to a specific locality, from which it can be retrieved in the future as a given past. And this preservation of the future configures protection as survival. It is interesting to mention here a temporal particularity in the Akkadian language that designates the "past" as lying before and the "future" as lying behind (Maul 1997:109), a stark reversal of our modern notions. Mythology also seems to corroborate the notion that Mesopotamians "proceeded with their backs to the future," as it were. Berossos' *Babyloniaka* presents the primordial sage Oannes as having taught humans all the arts of domestic and cultural life. Other myths regard this knowledge of the civilized arts as a gift from the god Enki (Ea). What is striking in both of these accounts is that the Mesopotamians believed that all cultural achievements – be they architecture, writing, healing, metalwork, carpentry, etcetera – were endowed to humans at the *beginning of time*, and this notion locates the ideal image of society in a primordial and mythological past rather than in a hopeful future (Maul 1997:109).

Furthermore, the figurines were not only buried, but also placed appropriately *under* the earth, in the space of the Netherworld and the *apsû*, the primordial freshwater ocean.[18] Numerous sources locate the underworld in the ground, beneath the surface of the earth (Black and Green 1992:180; Bottéro 1992:273–275).[19] This idea follows from a traditional Mesopotamian conception of a vertical and bipolar universe where the earth, inhabited by living humans, separated the Heavens (*šamú*) from the Netherworld (*erṣetu*) (Bottéro 1992:273). And the borders of these domains were permeable, as entry to the Netherworld could be gained by way of a stairway leading down to the gate, while spirits could access the human world through a cracks and holes in earth's surface. But importantly, the prevailing worldview of this time held that every being occupied a proper space in the world, with the lower hemisphere, symmetrical to the upper heavens, providing a discrete space and residence for the dead and other supernatural beings. In this context, the burial of figurines of creatures from the underworld and *apsû* might constitute a mimetic gesture of placing or commanding such beings to their proper place in the world. This ritual practice not only reflects but reenacts the notion of an underworld located underground. Furthermore, the strategic placement of the figurine deposits under certain architectural and household features may act to channel and focus the protective power of the beings, since they dwell in their "proper" realm. The fact that the figurines were encased in boxes is also evocative of the important gesture of providing a "house" for the deities, and there could be no greater service rendered to a divine being than the building of his or her house (Frankfort 1978:267).

Additionally, the "immateriality" of a buried geography as an invisible, powerful presence is itself provocative. The figurines, so installed, become effectively removed from the sensuous sphere of human–object relations. In this register of experience, they are "completed," no longer engaging in processes of mutual constitution and becoming. But the materiality of the figurine deposit endures and is powerful in this capacity to survive, virtually unmolested, performing its original duty;[20] cut off from human relations, mute, blind, and restrained, they no longer strike back at human subjects, but can only direct their force to fighting off evil spirits in the Netherworld, as instructed by the *āšipu*. There is a sense here of Derrida's (1994) autonomous automaton, the animate puppet with a will of its own that yet obeys some predetermined program. By containing, concealing, and hiding these magical figures, the priest has made his mastery of their power complete.

Conclusion

> An obscure memory of cosmic perturbations in the distant past and the dim thought of future catastrophes form the very basis of human thought, speech and images.
>
> M. Bakhtin, *Rabelais and His World*

This obscure memory and dim thought of humankind vividly inhabited Neo-Assyrian mythologies, religious values, and social practices. In Mesopotamian thought, dichotomies did not provide a fundamental way of organizing experience. Rational thought was neither dominant nor lacking in their system of knowledge; the medical use of plants, social ordinances and laws, city planning, and other cultural forms certainly exhibited strains of deductive reasoning. But Mesopotamian thought also embraced the various shadows, symmetries, torsions, syncopations, ruptures, and reversals that punctuate the rich texture of human experience.[21] Magic traces a mode of thinking that is layered, reticular, and corporeal, rather than linear and abstract, and this mode provided the ground for Mesopotamian social and religious life in both its logical and sensory depth. Magic, then and now, enchants us not with the truth, but with the possible made real.

Neo-Assyrian magical figurine work conjures and materializes a primordial secret: if apotropaic magic names that which wards off and turns away evil, then evil is nothing other than the insidious reality that humans themselves create their own creators and make their own world. But the exposure of this secret, which would seem to threaten the very dissolution of the religious belief and tradition at the core of Assyrian social life, instead serves to *preserve* these beliefs and traditions (cf. Taussig 1999). In this way, the apotropaic device recalls that perverse disposition of the supplement: "a terrifying menace, the supplement is also the first and surest protection against that very menace" (Derrida 1974:153). Figurine deposits secure the protection of the present by giving a future to the mythological past, a past in which the gods and spirits ground the condition for human social life. This mimetic production does not reproduce the same, but discloses a new life through the figures of repetition, transfiguration, and burial; as such, it constitutes the processual enactment of a memorial gesture whereby a particular Neo-Assyrian mythohistory preserves its future in the material memory of itself. The gods and spirits, like the dead, become our guardians, "we give them a future so that they may give us a past. We help them live on so they may help us go forward" (Harrison 2003:158). As an art of doing, magic capitalizes on this strife between meaning and matter, life and death, past and future, and in it, grounds the authority of a desired social order.

Acknowledgments

First and foremost I want to thank Lynn Meskell for her unfailing vision and support for this project. I also want to thank all of the Santa Fe short seminar participants for their helpful and constructive comments on an earlier draft and Norman Yoffee for his comments, especially with respect to certain details concerning the Mesopotamian languages and materials. The Wenner-Gren Foundation and Getty Research Institute have provided generous funding for this research. Finally I want to thank Tom Aldrich for his patient readings and invaluable critiques of this chapter throughout its various phases. All standard disclaimers apply here.

Notes

1. "Apotropaic" means that which wards off evil.
2. My dissertation undertakes such research (Nakamura In prep).
3. Merleau-Ponty (1968:162) identifies and critiques this non-recognition of things as the condition of Western positivism arrived at by the refusal of entering "into the interrogative and involving nature of experience" (Mazis 1999:238).
4. Arthur Rimbaud (1967) frames poetry as "reaching the unknown by the derangement of all the senses" (302). Also see Deleuze (1993).
5. Polyphony here is meant to evoke Bakhtin's (1984) sense: "*a plurality of consciousnesses, with equal rights and each with its own world*, combine but are not merged in the unity of the event" (6, original emphasis).
6. This idea takes from Deleuze's (2003) discussion of the image as that which "presents more than it represents."
7. Clark Lunberry (2004:648–650) poses the city in these terms, but I take these qualities as arising from the city's materiality: the city is perhaps "*too much* of a thing for it to be finally fixed, to be fully said" (650).
8. Notably, Lunberry (2001:641, n. 20) points out that Robert Hobbs (1981), when speaking of Robert Smithson's art as engaging an "unresolvable dialectics," remarks that Smithson "strives to achieve a state of indeterminacy in which meanings are produced as much as cancelled out" (23). Something extra is captured in this "non-dialectical" movement such that contradiction vanishes or becomes the force behind magical logic.
9. In the formulation of an anthropology of the body, Blacking (1977) states, "My knowledge is both generated and restricted by the perceptions and cognitive processes of my society, but through my body I can sometimes understand more than I know through my own or another's society because I have more experience than society labels" (5–6). His concern for the body rests on the conviction that feeling as bodily knowledge forms the basis for mental life (4).
10. See also Levi-Strauss (1987); in his critique of Mauss' conception of *mana*, he claims that, "all magical operations rest on the restoring of a unity; not a lost unity (for nothing is ever lost) but an unconscious one, or one which is less completely conscious than those operations themselves" (59).
11. See Glassner (2003) for a thorough discussion of the development of the cuneiform script and Sumerian language.
12. No examples of such wooden figurines have been published (but see Oates and Oates 2001:148).
13. Notably, this ceremony recalls certain aspects of the *pīt pî* ("washing of the mouth") ritual that "enlivened" statues and images such that they could smell, drink, and eat like the deities that came to indwell in them.
14. Similar narratives of the creation of humankind reiterate a trope of the divine formation of being from clay. In the *Atrahasis* epic (Tablet I, lines 210–213) humankind is born from the mixing of primordial clay and the blood of a

slain god, and in *Enki and Ninmah* (lines 24–26) humankind is made from this clay only.

15 One creation myth (of many) also poses Enki (Ea) as taking on the organization of the entire universe and accomplishes this feat solely in the creative power of his word (Black and Green 1992:54).
16 See Michael Taussig's discussion of the "public secret" in *Defacement* (1999). Especially compelling here is his deliberation on the economy of revelation and concealment that preserves the secret: the secret is revealed so as to conserve it (51, 93).
17 Wall reliefs were found at Nimrud (Mallowan 1966), Nineveh (Botta and Flandin 1849–50) and Khorsabad (Loud et al. 1936).
18 The Netherworld became more or less confused with the *apsû*, also located underneath the earth (Bottero 1992:274).
19 Although most sources locate the underworld below the earth, some references associate the underworld with the desert, the far West, and the mountains, essentially inaccessible regions of the earth (Black and Green 1992:180). These ambiguities may be symptomatic of merging cosmologies in late Mesopotamia; by the Neo-Assyrian period, rulers in the north were known to have made active attempts to appropriate Babylonian mythologies into their own (Black and Green 1992:38).
20 However, at Nimrud it is interesting that some figurines were apparently reused for the same purpose (see Green 1983:89; Oates 1961), and also found smashed and discarded in a long-barrack room (SE 5) of Fort Shalmaneser at Nimrud (Green 1983:89; Oates and Oates 2001:256).
21 This characterization draws upon Barton's (2001:14–17) similar description of and approach to Roman experience.

References

Alster, Brendt 2002 il awlum: we-e i-la, "Gods : Men" versus "Man : God" Punning and the Reversal of Patterns in the Atrahasis Epic. *In* Riches Hidden in Secret Places: Ancient Near Eastern Studies in Memory of Thorkild Jacobsen. T. Abusch, ed. Pp. 35–40. Winona Lake, IN: Eisenbrauns.
Asher-Grève, Julia M., and A. Lawrence Asher 1998 From Thales to Foucault. *In* Intellectual Life of the Ancient Near East: Papers Presented at the 43rd Rencontre assyriologique internationale Prague, July 1–5, 1996. J. Prosecky, ed. Pp. 29–40. Academy of Sciences of the Czech Republic Oriental Institute. Prague: Academy of Sciences of the Czech Republic Oriental Institute.
Bakhtin, Mikhail 1984 Problems of Dostoevsky's Poetics. C. Emerson, trans. Minneapolis: University of Minnesota Press.
Barton, Carlin A. 2001 Roman Honor: The Fire in the Bones. Berkeley: University of California.

Benjamin, Walter 1979 Doctrine of the Similar (1933). New German Critique 17(Spring):65–69.
Black, Jeremy, and Anthony Green 1992 Gods, Demons and Symbols of Ancient Mesopotamia. London: British Museum Press.
Blacking, John 1977 Towards an Anthropology of the Body. In The Anthropology of the Body. J. Blacking, ed. Pp. 1–28. London: Academic Press.
Böhm, Winfried 1995 Theory, Practice and the Education of the Person. A. L. Richards, trans. Washington D.C.: Organization of American States.
Botta, P. E., and E. Flandin 1849–50 Monument de Nineve, découvert et décrit par M. P.-E. Botta et dessiné par M. E. Flandlin. 5 vols. Paris: Imprimerie Nationale.
Bottéro, Jean 1992 Mesopotamia: Writing, Reasoning and the Gods. Z. Bahrani and M. Van De Mieroop, trans. Chicago: University of Chicago.
Caillois, Roger 2001 Man and the Sacred. M. Barash, trans. Urbana and Chicago: University of Illinois Press.
Curtis, John E., and Julian E. Reade 1995 Art and Empire: Treasures from Assyria in the British Museum. New York: Metropolitan Museum of Art.
Deleuze, Gilles 1993 On Four Poetic Formulas That Might Summarize The Kantian Philosophy. In Essays Critical and Clinical. Pp. 27–35. London: Verso.
—— 1998 On Four Poetic Formulas That Might Summarize The Kantian Philosophy. In Essays Critical and Clinical. Pp. 27–35. London: Verso.
—— 2003 Francis Bacon: The Logic of Sensation. D. W. Smith, trans. Minneapolis: University of Minnesota Press.
Derrida, Jacques 1974 Of Grammatology. G. C. Spivak, trans. Baltimore and London: Johns Hopkins University Press.
—— 1994 Specters of Marx, The State of the Debt, the Work of Mourning and the New International. P. Kamuf, trans. New York and London: Routledge.
Dick, Michael B. 1998 The Relationship Between the Cult Image and the Deity. In Intellectual Life of the Ancient Near East. J. Prosecky, ed. Pp. 111–116. Prague: Academy of Sciences of the Czech Republic Oriental Institute.
Ellis, Richard 1995 The Trouble with "Hairies." Iraq 57:159–165.
—— forthcoming Domestic Spirits: Magical Figurines in Mesopotamian Buildings.
Frankfort, Henri 1978 Kingship and the Gods: A Study of Ancient Near Eastern Religion as the Integration of Society and Nature. Chicago and London: University of Chicago Press.
Frazer, James George 1957 The Golden Bough: A Study in Magic and Religion I–VIII. 12 vols. London.
Glassner, Jean-Jacques 2003 The Invention of Cuneiform: Writing in Sumer. Z. Bahrani and M. Van De Mieroop, trans. Baltimore, MD: Johns Hopkins University Press.
Gosden, Chris 2001 Making Sense: Archaeology and Aesthetics. World Archaeology 33(2):163–167.
Green, Anthony 1983 Neo-Assyrian Apotropaic Figures: Figurines, Rituals, and Monumental Art, with Special Reference to the Figures from the Excavations of the British School of Archaeology in Iraq at Nimrud. Iraq 45:87–96.

―― 1993 Mischwesen B. *In* Reallexikon der Assyriologie und Vorderasiatischen Archaologie. D. O. Edzard, ed. Pp. 246-264, vol. 8, Meek-Mythologie. Berlin and New York: Walter de Gruyter.
―― forthcoming Neo-Assyrian Apotropaic Figures.
Grosz, Elizabeth 1999 Merleau-Ponty and Irigaray in the Flesh. *In* Merleau-Ponty, Interiority and Exteriority, Psychic Life and the World. D. Olkowski and J. Morley, eds. Pp. 145-166. Albany: State University of New York Press.
Gurney, Oscar Reuther 1935 Babylonian Prophylactic Figurines and Their Rituals. Annals of Archaeology and Anthropology 22:31-96.
Harrison, Robert Pogue 1993 Forests: The Shadow of Civilization. Chicago: University of Chicago Press.
―― 2003 The Dominion of the Dead. Chicago and London: University of Chicago Press.
Hobbs, Robert 1981 Smithson's Unresolvable Dialectics. *In* Robert Smithson: Sculpture. R. Hobbs, ed. Ithaca: Hacker Art Books.
Jenson, Deborah 2001 Trauma and Its Representations: The Social Life of Mimesis in Post-Revolutionary France. Baltimore and London: Johns Hopkins University Press.
Klengel-Brandt, Evelyn 1968 Apotropäische Tonfiguren aus Assur. Forschungen und Berichte 10:19-37.
Levi-Strauss, Claude 1987 Introduction to the Work of Marcel Mauss. F. Baker, trans. London: Routledge & Kegan Paul.
Loud, Gordon, Henri Frankfort, and Thorkild Jacobsen 1936 Khorsabad, Part I: Excavations in the Palace and at the City Gate, vol. 38. Chicago: University of Chicago Press.
Lunberry, Clark 2004 So Much Depends: Printed Matter, Dying Words and the Entropic Poem. Critical Inquiry 30(3):627-653.
Mallowan, Max E. L. 1966 Nimrud and Its Remains I, II. 2 vols. London: Collins.
Maul, Stefan M. 1997 Die altorientalische Hauptstadt – Abbild und Nabel der Welt (The ancient middle eastern capital city – reflection and the navel of the world). *In* Die Orientalische Stadt: Kontinuität, Wandel, Bruch. 1. Internationales Colloquium der Deutschen Orient-Gesellschaft (The eastern city: continuity, change, rupture. 1. International Colloquium of the German Oriental Society), 9.–10. Mai 1996 in Halle/Saale. G. Wilhelm, ed. Pp. 109-124. Saarbrücker: SVD Druckerei und Verlag.
Mauss, Marcel 1972 A General Theory of Magic. New York: W.W. Norton & Company, Inc.
Mazis, Glen A. 1999 Chaos Theory and Merleau-Ponty's Ontology. *In* Merleau-Ponty, Interiority and Exteriority, Psychic Life and the World. D. Olkowski and J. Morley, eds. Pp. 217-241. Albany: State University of New York Press.
Menke, Christoph 1998 The Sovereignty of Art: Aesthetic Negativity in Adorno and Derrida. N. Solomon, trans. Cambridge: MIT Press.
Merleau-Ponty, Maurice 1962 Phenomenology of Perception. C. Smith, trans. London: Routledge.
―― 1968 The Visible and the Invisible. Evanston: Northwestern University Press.

―――― 1973 The Prose of the World. J. O'Neill, trans. Evanston: Northwestern University Press.
Meskell, Lynn 1999 Archaeologies of Social Life: Age, Sex, Class Etc. in Ancient Egypt. Oxford: Blackwell.
―――― 2002 Private Life in New Kingdom Egypt. Princeton, NJ: Princeton University Press.
―――― 2004 Object Worlds from Ancient Egypt: Material Biographies Past and Present. Oxford: Berg.
Miles, A. C., and Rush Rhees 1971 Ludwig Wittgenstein's Remarks on Frazier's *Golden Bough*. The Human World 3(May 1971):28–41.
Nakamura, Carolyn 2004 Dedicating Magic: Neo-Assyrian Apotropaic Figurines and the Protection of Assur. World Archaeology 36(1):11–25.
―――― In prep The Matter of Magic: Materiality, Representation and Space in Neo-Assyrian Apotropaic Figurine Rituals. Ph.D. dissertation, Columbia University.
Oates, Joan, and David Oates 2001 Nimrud: An Assyrian Imperial City Revealed. London: British School of Archaeology in Iraq.
Pels, Peter 1998 The Spirit of Matter: On Fetish, Rarity, Fact and Fancy. *In* Border Fetishisms: Material Objects in Unstable Places. P. Spyder, ed. Pp. 91–121. New York: Routledge.
Pettigrew, David E. 1999 Merleau-Ponty and the Unconscious: A Poetic Vision. *In* Merleau-Ponty, Interiority and Exteriority, Psychic Life and the World. D. Olkowski and J. Morley, eds. Pp. 57–68. Albany: State University of New York Press.
Rimbaud, Arthur 1967 Letter to Georges Izambard, 13 May 1871. *In* Rimbaud: Complete Works, Selected Letters. Pp. 302–305. Chicago and London: University of Chicago Press.
Rittig, Dessa 1977 Assyrisch-babylonische Kleinplastik magischer Bedeutung (Assyrio-Babylonian magical figurines). Munchen: Verlag Uni-Druck.
Russell, John Malcolm 1991 Sennacherib's Palace without Rival at Nineveh. Chicago and London: University of Chicago Press.
Scarry, Elaine 1985 The Body in Pain: The Making and Unmaking of the World. New York and Oxford: Oxford University Press.
Smith, Sidney 1926 Babylonian Prophylactic Figures. Journal of the Royal Asiatic Society 1926:695ff.
Spivak, Gayatri Chakravorty 1974 Translator's Preface. *In* Of Grammatology. Baltimore and London: Johns Hopkins University Press.
Stewart, Susan 1984 On Longing: Narratives of the Miniature, the Gigantic, the Souvenir, the Collection. Baltimore, MD: Johns Hopkins University Press.
Taussig, Michael 1993 Mimesis and Alterity: A Particular History of the Senses. London: Routledge.
―――― 1999 Defacement: Public Secrecy and the Labor of the Negative. Stanford: Stanford University Press.
Thompson, R. Campbell 1903–04 The Devils and Evil Spirits of Babylonia: Being Babylonian and Assyrian Incantations Against the Demons, Ghouls, Vampires,

Hobgoblins, Ghosts, and Kindred Evil Spirits which Attack Mankind. 2 vols. London: Luzac & Co.

Van Buren, E. Douglas 1931 Foundation Figurines and Offerings. Berlin: Hans Schoetz & Co. G.M.B.H.

Vico, Giambattista 1999[1744] New Science: Principles of the New Science Concerning the Common Nature of Nations. D. Marsh, trans. London: Penguin.

Wiggermann, Frans A. M. 1992 Mesopotamian Protective Spirits: The Ritual Texts. Groningen: Styx.

—— 1993 Mischwesen, A. *In* Reallexicon der Assyriologie und Vorderasiatichen Archaologie (Encyclopedia of Assyriology and Near Eastern Archaeology). D. O. Edzard, ed. Pp. 222–245, vol. 8, Meek-Mythologie. Berlin and New York: Walter de Gruyter.

Woolley, C. Leonard, and Sidney Smith 1926 Babylonian Prophylactic Figures. Journal of the Royal Asiatic Society 1926:692–713.

3

The Social Life of Rock Art: Materiality, Consumption, and Power in South African Heritage

Lindsay Moira Weiss

Introduction

This chapter examines the relationship between consumption, materiality, and sites of heritage practice. My questions will follow the turbulent history of a rock art site known as Wildebeestkuil, situated in the Northern Cape of South Africa. Today, the regional landholders, the !Xun and Khwe San, provide local tours of Wildebeestkuil and other members of their community have come to produce goods for tourists that recreate the engraved images of the rock art on such unlikely surfaces as t-shirts, fabrics, mugs, batiks, and even in the paintings produced by their local art cooperative. Though the community is originally from Namibia and Angola, and therefore not likely descendants of the creators of Wildebeestkuil, they have nonetheless come to objectify Wildebeestkuil as a source of discourse on their own contemporary national and San heritage. Sites like Wildebeestkuil have become potent material loci of community identity formation. Ineluctable to this process of making a site their own is their appropriation and objectification of the site, which allows them to "consume" heritage in ways that positively refashion potentially alienating notions of cultural authenticity. My use of consumption derives from the work of Danny Miller. Miller has taken the Hegelian notion of material objectification and loosened it from its more pessimistic and narrow conceptualization within Marxist social critique. As Miller sees it, the practice of consumption is also a process of formulating material significance, which occurs within a much more complex and nuanced interplay of personal agency and market forces (Miller 1987). I would like to extend Miller's insights from the more traditional realm of cultural studies to the heritage industry, in order to understand the mechanism that drive the consumption of heritage more generally as they come to interact with the specific colonial history of Wildebeestkuil.

Most would agree that contemporary heritage practices surrounding the Wildebeestkuil site exist at a fundamental rupture from a more seemingly authentic period during which shamanic rituals would have been practiced. Nonetheless, I am interested to pursue the potential for conceiving of historical continuities at sites like Wildebeestkuil, particularly with regard to the site's navigation of powerful regional shifts in dominant modes of consumption and political economies. Therefore, this chapter moves from the contemporary site to a consideration of colonial-era conceptualizations of Wildebeestkuil, when the settler economy came to collide with the last of the /Xam San responsible for the first symbolic rock engravings.

The conceit of many archival settler accounts of expansion throughout the interior of Southern Africa is a sense of deep removal and superiority over the autochthonous political economies operating throughout the interior landscapes (Mudimbe 1988). However, in the diamondiferous region surrounding Wildebeestkuil, the intense clash of the settler economy and the /Xam San spiritual economy did not always unfold according to familiar legislative and archival narratives. By tracing a region's history from the materially situated site of the rock engravings, I hope to momentarily marginalize archival narratives in order to excavate their tacit ordering of knowledge and history – an ordering that compels us to consider contemporary practices at such sites and the history of such sites as profoundly unrelated projects (Foucault 1972). Frequently marginalized, I propose the material and sensual aspect of the rock art site – as related to bodily practice as well as mythical landscapes – to be instrumental to a complete historical narrative of Southern Africa. Their central presence forces us to frame settler narratives in light of the *Lebenswelt* of the San, just as it also forces more traditional historical narratives to duly grant rock art and shamanic practitioners their historical legitimacy as major players in the colonial story (Marks 1972).

In tracing the seemingly immobile materiality of the rock face, a perspective on the turbulent interface of these two divergent regimes of valuation is gained – a perspective that avoids either simplistic economic determinism or mere ethnographic analogy. An enormous amount of literature examines the significance of rock art with respect to shamanic beliefs and practices, but comparatively little of this research successfully bridges a tacit discursive rupture between South African historical studies and narratives of San belief systems (though see Blundell 2004). In no small part the biases of the archives tend to reproduce themselves in the settings of contemporary disciplinary boundaries. Alternative readings of the past require efforts to pursue alternative conceptual categories than those forged in the colonial archives. Therefore, pursuing the material site as an analytical anchor in a historical study creates the possibility of considering the profound alterity with which political forms might have been conceived in the past (Appadurai 1990; Meskell 2004). To understand the materially grounded conceptualization of political and spiritual sovereignty among San shamans[1] also allows us to expand a political understanding of materiality from hyper-deterministic or traditional materialist perspectives.

Materiality and Consumption

Miller's work centers on the material world in its own right as a source of understanding of ephemeral and often confounding modes of social practice. This work diverges profoundly from traditional North Atlantic culturalist approaches to material studies such as Boasian particularlism or Tylor's evolutionism (Stocking 1985). Material culture studies continues today largely under the signs of circulation and consumption and emerges in the wake of the disintegrating conceptual rift between the Maussian gift and Marxian commodity (Appadurai 1986). Returning ethnography from the tropics, Miller sought to examine how consumption practices in his own communities, far from reducing the consumer to a state of alienation, actually enabled a positive sense of overcoming of social rupture (Miller 1995:2); he states, "observations of industrialized societies reveal a search by the mass population for other instruments which might act directly to negate the autonomy and scale of these historical forces, and turn to advantage certain aspects of the very materiality of the object world in consumption" (Miller 1987:217).

Central to his optimistic tack on the process of objectification through consumption is a very un-Marxian take on the Hegelian notion of objectification. Miller repeats throughout his work that what had originally been intended by Hegel as a positive moment in a process of self-actualization, has received a vastly delimited and pessimistic reading in its subsequent political offshoots as alienation, reification, and the notion of capital's fetish developed by scholars from Marx through Lukács to Adorno (Adorno 1978; Lukács 1971; Marx and Fowkes 1977).[3]

Miller's anthropologically-minded thinking about consumption opens up the discussion of modernity in a very crucial way that goes beyond postmodern tropes posing as either remedies or unmaskings of the travails of late modernity – and does so in a way that is not irrelevant to those, like members of the Frankfurt school, who wished to induce greater self-awareness of the citizen and also to improve overly-dogmatic readings of Marxism. Fixing sites of materiality as one's analytical framework and one's anthropological site for the production of culture, offers to elude essentializing and inadequate a priori theoretical assumptions about the relations between material culture and consumers or materiality and culture more generally. More importantly, thinking with what are often transnational and unexpected vectors of material circulation allows the researcher to avoid the construction of bounded localities that capture only fragmentary understandings of material practices, and finally, this allows the possibility of articulating political cultures that do not always align along the same seams as the nation-state (Latour 1999; Trouillot 2003:127).

Consumption and Heritage

Miller's notion of objectification confers a certain understanding to processes at work in the heritage industry, certainly no less a site of consumption than any other rapidly expanding market of material culture (Mitchell 2002:200), albeit one typically infused with the aura of history and all the moralizing rhetoric that such a medium inevitably entails (Brown 2001:30–44). The object of heritage, in my thinking, in many ways conceals the same social inequities as those concealed by Marx's fetish – and both intersect with the state in remarkably similar ways. The heritage "thing" (or site) carries just the same aporia; specifically its promissory failure resides in the differential between the state's egalitarian promises of equal "shared heritage" for all, and its inevitably unequal deliverance of such goods on the ground. Following in this Marxian vein, one could proceed to point out how such heritage sites tend to effectively alienate those who feel their own daily activities and vernacular sense of heritage practice to be at a disconnect with the national experience conveyed by the heritage site. One could read the high-impact heritage tourist site as analogous to a factory specializing in the production of the past. However, if we take seriously the understanding that consumption and related material practices around heritage sites also prove to be a more positive site of objectification, a problematization of this narrative is forced.

The daily life of heritage is a much more nuanced and ambiguous sphere in all its vernacular incarnations, particularly as a site of consumption as well as a site of production – and not only consumption performed by the tourist. The epistemic horizon of the heritage site must be liberated from the discursive limits of "authenticity" and other such suspicious hermeneutics, because heritage consumption is not merely about discursive framing of the past, but has become an integral aspect of identity-making particularly in the multicultural state, where community consumption of the past is seldom coterminous with state production of the past, and the individual is even more likely to fashion their consumption of the past differentially than national rhetoric might prescribe.

Over two decades ago, in an article entitled "The Past as a Scarce Resource," Appadurai suggested that even the most agonistic debates about the past "are subject to the same normative framework" (Appadurai 1981:217) determining the very debatability of the past. To what extent can we take Appadurai's understanding to frame the seemingly ceaseless contemporary invention at immobile landmarks, monuments, and the stuff of the South African past? In post-apartheid South Africa where the task of historical revisionism seems to be more vigorously and politically mandated than perhaps anywhere else in the world at the moment (Comaroff 2004), a complete understanding of heritage politics requires an interrogation of the discursive boundaries of this production. On the one hand, there emerges the push to tear down the valorizing monuments of those figures of apartheid terror and oppression and to undo the tradition of museumization of indigenous groups and to counter "a history of pathologizing objectification"(Coombes 2003:242). On the other hand, there is the consumption side of heritage in which "new cultural villages are positioning themselves for tourism virtually every day" (Rassool 2000:10) and "instead of guns, these tourists came armed with cameras, seeking to capture an image of 'Timeless Africa' to adorn their walls like animal trophies" (Rassool 2000 cited in Coombes 2003). But do these two moves truly participate in discrete discursive realms, or do they in fact, share the same set of limits that frame their very debating of the past, as Appadurai suggests? I believe that the proper answer to this question resides in the space between specific day to day interactions and the discursive horizons of the field more broadly (Hacking 2004), but I would add that this space must be anchored in the realm of the material – and steadfastly pursue the changes that this material undergoes through time, if our discussion of the production of the past is not to be waylaid by debates over cultural and historical authenticity.

Wildebeestkuil Rock Art Site

The San have always been linked to a history of ethno-commodification because they have always been a source of fascination for Europeans, from the earliest missionary reports, to the time that philologist Wilhelm Bleek first systematically studied /Xam San language and folk tales in the late 19th century, to present-day ethnographic research. The San rock art site of Wildebeestkuil is firmly imbricated in the cultural politics of the "Bushman Myth" (Gordon and Sholto-Douglas 2000), a myth that carries a special currency for the tourist as Elizabeth Garland illustrates:

> In visiting Bushmen, tourists seek – and indeed often claim to find – much needed redemption for the alienation and fragmentation of their modern lives... tourists gain reassurance that they are themselves worthy and whole; through exposure to the authentic Other, the Self shores up a sense of its own authenticity. (Garland and Gordon 1999:272)

This redemptive signification has come to figure prominently within the state rhetoric of unity in diversity; San paintings have even been inserted in the new South African national coat of arms (Smith et al. 2000). This appropriation of San identity and heritage within the state's unifying rhetoric fits well within Appadurai's notion of a normative framework that always preemptively delimits new readings around heritage sites, often silencing contesting readings to the margins of the heritage sphere. However, I would like to suggest that a closer look at the material site points to other readings or consumptive practices that fall outside of the dominant discursive framework – enabling contestation though nonverbal material practice that subverts archive-oriented narratives while concomitantly reproducing these traditional narratives. When we consider daily practices at heritage sites and museums, could our consumption and production of historical sites entail a much more expansive discursive framework?

The Wildebeestkuil site is located on a slightly elevated andesite boulder outcropping; its rocks are covered in over four hundred ancient pecked images. Such sites, because of their elevated location and Wildebeestkuil, because of its proximity to a water pan, were most likely significant on the landscape as rain-making sites (Deacon 1988; 1997). Wildebeestkuil is today near the city of Kimberley in central South Africa, and falls within the land grant of Platfontein, where the !Xun and Khwe from Angola and Namibia are newly enfranchised South African citizens, who act as custodians and local guides to the rock art thought to have been made by the /Xam San spanning a period from a few hundred to possibly a few thousand years ago (Beaumont and Vogel 1989; Morris 1988). Although the !Xun and Khwe come from distinct traditions and different parts of the world from the creators of Wildebeestkuil, community leaders and some members of the community present these rock engravings to visitors as if also created by their own ancestors (Morris et al. 2001). Other members of the community have begun to produce artwork – paintings, ceramics, and batiks – much of which reproduce of motifs and images found in the local rock engravings and are geared for tourist consumption. While some would choose to read such adoption of a site's history and the creative tours and art-making that has sprung up around it as nothing more than another instance of "apartheid-infected" strategic essentialism (Garland and Gordon 1999), I would suggest that this marks the objectification of a heritage site and heritage more generally, and this objectification can be considered a crucial mode of self-making in a multicultural state, but perhaps more importantly of citizen-making by a previously disenfranchised people.

The recent history of the !Xun and Khwe groups living in Platfontein involves much difficulty, violence, and displacement. Having fought on behalf of the apartheid-era South African defense force (SADF), this group was offered citizenship in South Africa upon the independence of

MATERIALITY, CONSUMPTION, AND POWER

Namibia and Angola. While this move was intended to protect this group of soldiers and their families from potential difficulty with their fellow countrymen, the fact of their historical alliance with the apartheid government continues to be the cause of community resentment in the Kimberley area (Becker 2003). Considering their recent history of transnational displacement and the negative perceptions that the surrounding communities have of this group, then, one comes to understand that something more profound is occurring than simply strategic choices, but that also these forms of identity (re)construction perhaps are what allow some members of the group to express not only a sense of belonging and new citizenship, but also and perhaps more importantly, the construction of improved memories and historical narratives. Considered in this light, the objects for sale that one sees at this heritage site, the adoption of local motifs, the vague intimations of ancestral links with the site, point to a much more valuable function of local heritage practice:

> In such contexts the act of making and objects themselves can become an insurance against forgetting and thus against the loss of personhood through reinstating – particularly in the case of whimsical manufacture – the capacity for fantasy. By invoking the personal, the naive, and the fantastic despite the grim context of political suppression and resistance, these objects signal the complexity and contradictions of sustaining the self while also seeking membership in the ideal of political community. (Coombes 2003:9)

This is not, of course, to naïvely suggest that this community has somehow overcome or is even resisting their aggrieved situation. To a large extent, their modes of heritage production and consumption operate well within the same webs of power and global flows of capital that have structured their own political choices. However, at the same time, it is important to recognize that such practices often operate along multiple levels of power. I feel that this is an important facet of heritage practice, one which unfolds on a non-discursive level, the fashioning of one's national identity, and even a sense of sovereignty within one's locality. In a sense, !Xun and Khwe practices have come to appropriate, reformulate, and objectify the site on numerous levels, some of which can be interpreted as playing into their role of autochthonous bearers of the rainbow nation or an African renaissance (Douglas 1997) and some of which are distinctly operating according to a much more radically personal and identity building conceptualization of what the site means, and often in ways that appear to operate according to intimate and non-universal modes of thinking about their own histories. It is in examining latter such practices that an expanded sense of objectification provides a useful way to understand that, although heritage certainly has difference-flattening tendencies, materially situated and frequently non-discursive practices would seem to present a more complex composition for the micro-physics of power (de Certeau 1984). I would like to examine how material levels of self-making intercalate with broader categories of identity such as nationalism. Such sites are not an extra-constitutional resting spot for the disaffected citizen, but provide the opportunity for novel discursive modes of citizen participation; the novel ways in which the physicality of the site is consumed, reproduced, or even disassembled, points to the radical possibility for heritage to become a site of multiple modes of positive objectification and a radical refashioning of dominant (and often ethnoracist) modes of citizen making (Mbembe 2004:404).

The radically diverse nature of the !Xun and Khwe community has recently been illustrated in events that have come to reveal members of the community as practicing sorcery (Vorster 1993). There are many instances in South Africa in which a rock art site has been co-opted into contemporary spiritual practices and it has even been the case that non-San groups have come to practice the objectification of rock art sites within contemporary rain-making rituals (Ouzman 1995). Flake scarring, and other non-visual use of the rocks may come to comprise another historical turn at this site, as the rocks are still considered to contain potency of some form. What is particularly interesting in the instance of Wildebeestkuil is the extent to which this community has come to objectify the site in the face of much wider community ambivalence to their presence. There is an important sense in which the community's proximity to the rocks, their disassembling of the imagery and reassembling of said imagery on the surfaces of mugs, t-shirts, and other consumer items tends to evoke a counter-discourse undertaken in the material medium, one that also powerfully articulates a sense of belonging and possessing. This is not only articulated in a private sense, but I would argue that these kinds of material practices also articulate more broadly within national and state networks of power. Indeed, it is when viewed in light of the aporias of national heritage rhetoric that such practices may even come to resonate with a form of post-apartheid self-fashioning for which heritage sites have come to provide an especially fecund location. Essential to such practices is the very material and tangible form of such sites. As Gaonkar and Povinelli discuss, the demanding environment of things and their movement seems to provide a supra-semiotic promise; "they entail, demand, seduce, intoxicate and materialize rather than simply mean" and they argue that it is, in fact, also at such levels that politics of (mis)recognition occur – different groups not only practice "translation" but in fact, also "transfiguration" (Gaonkar and Povinelli 2003:396). Considered in this light, Ouzman's discussion on a rock-engraving site where similar flake removal scars are evident comes to take on a less seemingly idiosyncratic significance. Ouzman states, "I suggest that these cynosuric rock engravings were sought out and flaked by people wishing to possess a piece of potent place" (Ouzman 2001:250). This phenomenon transforms a rock art site's locus of potency, from a single fixed point on the landscape to a portable piece of this point; it becomes necessary to consider Miller's observation that sites of material practice have proliferated to such an extent that a single "material ideology" might prove inadequate to a comprehensive understanding of the contemporary significance of such sites (Miller 1987:163). So what does the proliferation of media by which we come to practice heritage imply more broadly for the multicultural state?

The contemporary attitudes toward such rock engravings, and indeed their potency, do not solely exist within strata of spiritual or ritual practices. The Platfontein community, granted a citizen status rendered somewhat marred as a result of their collusion with the apartheid-government SADF, practicing an historical iconicity entirely ruptured from local histories due to their foreign origins, seem to emblematize the modern contradictory state of contemporary political membership; they simultaneously exist within the rhetorical promise of equality for all citizens and experience exclusion or at least unequal access to an authentic sense of membership or belonging on the ground (Agamben 1998). Balibar concludes that one of the main outcomes of the inability of national rhetoric to concretize its promises for all individuals is that it,

> unleashes a permanent process of displacement and escape. You need more nationalism. You need a nationalism which is, so to speak, more nationalistic than nationalism itself: what I would call in the language of Bataille an *excess* of nationalism, or in the language of Derrida a *supplement* of nationalism *within* nationalism itself. (Balibar 1994)

Balibar understands this supplement to occur along lines of racial or cultural purity – that the construction of such narratives seeks to resolve and ultimately defer the puzzling aporia created by ideal of nationalism. In the postcolonial multicultural state, such narratives have been torn down, and it is arguably in this discursive wake that the universalizing language of world heritage, and national heritage – and the material realm of heritage sites – enters into. Considered in this light, the variety of material practices around heritage sites, such as the destruction of the giant Buddhas at Bamiyan, powerfully evoke the ways in which objectification of material objects – particularly those that have entered into the realm of heritage – can effectively articulate in non-discursive ways, perceptions of nationally fostered inequities concealed by heritage rhetoric (Bernbeck and Pollock 2004; Meskell 2002). It is equally provocative to consider the unorthodox and "inauthentic" material practices around Wildebeestkuil as a necessary supplement to a historical narrative primarily concerned with ethnic origins – the timeless time of the "Bushman Myth." The community has literally refashioned the icon of the origins of San culture in a way that simultaneously reflects the violence of this imposed identity and asserts a power over a material source of such narrative.

Colonial-Era Wildebeestkuil

Before its present day incarnation, Wildebeestkuil was associated with the turbulent history of the resident /Xam San, who refused to fit into the "savage slot" designated for them by the rush of diamond miners who came to the area in the late 19th century. A comment made to Péringuey by missionary Westphal refers to the last Khoesan occupants of the site being Scheelkoos and his family; he notes "in the neighborhood of the[ir] dwelling-places were the most numerous and the best chippings" (Péringuey 1909:411). Such engravings attracted G. W. Stow, who became the first geologist to record the engravings at Wildebeestkuil and who also recounted the story of the savage genocide unleashed by the Boers on the /Xam San group described as "Scheelkoos and his followers." Stow spoke of the systematic stock theft and eventual uprising led by Scheelkoos, who sought to regain lands that David Dantzer, son of a lesser chief, had been induced to sell to the Boer prospectors and farmers for one riding horse and 70 fat-tailed sheep – a sale that even colonist Stow decried as "a premium for fraud and forgery" (Stow

1905:394–395). Scheelkoos had rallied a commando that continually raided the Boer farms and was killed along with his followers by a Burgher commando in 1858. Some colonial agents, it seemed, had more than a passing awareness of what these rock art sites suggested in terms of San claims to the landscape and their sovereignty more generally. Stow writes, "these rude works of art are the ancient title-deeds of their race to the wide-spread plains around them, which had been occupied not only by themselves, but by their remote ancestors" (Stow 1905:297). Furthermore, when he sent rubbings of the rock engravings to Wilhelm Bleek, the foremost philologist studying /Xam languages and folklore in Cape Town, Bleek replied to Stow that he was sure that general knowledge to be gained from these images would permanently and fundamentally shift the public perception of the "Bushmen" as savages (Bleek 1875). In much of the late 19th-century colonial literature about the Khoesan, the landscape is constantly referred to as a silent index of San identity. Dr Atherstone, who identified the first diamond from Kimberley, wrote of the frequent stories of murdering "Bushmen" who lived around the diggings. While listening one story, writes Atherstone, a settler expressed anxiety about the sinfulness of such massacres; "'Maar het die schepsels toch *zielen?*' shouts one of the listeners – can they have souls? The wild rocks answer back, echoing – 'They *have souls*'; but it finds no echo in the heart of the Boer" (Robinson 1978:144). Indeed it would seem unlikely that "wild" rocks would have had no effect on the settlers and colonists; while they could not translate the precise meanings with clarity, they seemed to haunt their recordings of the San genocide and their attempts to understand who these people were. In the 19th century, local rocky outcrops such as Wildebeestkuil were commonly known to be inhabited by /Xam San – natural scientists like Péringuey were puzzled by the inhabitation of the Wildebeestkuil and other hills with rock engravings given the fact that it was an extremely dangerous spot due to the frequent lightning strikes, emphasizing that "most of the rock-engravings have been split through their agency" (Péringuey 1909:411). Despite misunderstanding their significance, the fact that these rock engravings were significant would have been doubtlessly recognized.

In light of these observations, it is quite interesting, then to discover that about thirty years after the murder of Scheelkoos and his followers, arrangements to remove several of the engravings from the Wildebeestkuil site were quietly undertaken. The engravings joined a larger group of items, reorganized, labeled, classified, and displayed during the Colonial and Indian exhibition in London in 1886, several of which remains in the British museum today (Fock and McGregor 1965). According to prominent British curators of colonial exhibitions at the time such as Henry Balfour, rock art as "graphic art" was considered more complex than the more three-dimensional "plastic art" from other parts of Africa. Such complexity could only lend to the underlying motives for collecting such art – motives that Annie Coombes terms "trophy art." Such art, particularly when coupled with the eradication of a group of people associated with the traditions that produce such material culture, lent an added valence to the objects which came to serve "as a signifier of 'capture' and 'conquest'" (Coombes 1994:198). This is important to consider in light of the fact that rock art sites were directly observed to be connected with anti-colonial violence in the records of Arbousset and Daumas, which indicate that the shamanic "dance" of blood was ritually enacted before confrontations with white settlers, hence "the paintings associated with these clashes were implicated in the power struggles and conflict generated within Bushman society, as well as between Bushmen and their enemies" (Arbousset et al. 1846:253 cited in Lewis-Williams 1994:220). One may conclude, then, that the materiality of these rock arts sites was very much at the interstices of colonial and autochthonous regimes of power, and the colonial appropriation of such physical landmarks could not have been read as anything other than a modes of power-taking that is articulated within the realm of "things." For Foucault, this is the most fundamental state of governmentality, which

> in no way refers to territory: one governs things. But what does this mean? I think this is not a matter of opposing things to men but, rather, of showing that what government has to do with is not territory but, rather, a sort of complex composed of men and things. The things, in this sense, with which government is to be concerned are in fact men, but men in their relation, their links, their imbrication with those things that are wealth, resources, means of subsistence, the territory with its specific qualities, climate, irrigation, fertility and so on; men in their relation to those other things that are customs, habits, ways of acting and thinking and so on . . . (Foucault and Faubion 2000:209)

These material objects seem to provide foundations for building relationships of power between Africans, not as sites of semiotic or symbolic representation, but sites that enable these very sorts of representations

Materiality, Consumption, and Power

of power — a sort of ancient and dispersed panopticon. The delicate elaboration of the microphysics of colonial struggle requires precisely the excavation of such sites — as they sit on the frontier of the violent transfiguration between settler ideology and San *Lebenswelt* — which involves a profoundly different cosmology. Colonial era attempts to understand the cosmology of the San, if they could even be termed that, were — it goes without saying — deeply inadequate, and yet these accounts do in rare instances, record instances of courageous defiance by the San (Marks 1972). Crucial here is the very important theme of death as it applies to the divergent ideologies of the San and the settler — because it is most clearly under the sign of death — a death that applies to the other race, that sovereignty comes to ultimately concretize (Foucault 2003:256). In the genocidal slaying of sometimes up to one hundred "Bushmen" a day by Boer commandos in the late 18th century, there were inevitably displays of resistance and revolt. Missionary John Philip records how a group of "Bushmen" were told to lead a commando to where their fellow countrymen were in hiding; they were told that if they did not comply they would be killed. Philip records that,

> The Bushmen, resolved not to betray their countrymen, fell upon the ground, and on being commanded to rise, *behaved as if they were dead*. When no answer could be obtained from them, blows were inflicted, but as their determination was inflexible, and the invaders could not remove them, they slew them on the spot. As the Bushmen were fully aware of the consequences of their resolution, their conduct was an instance of patriotism not surpassed by any thing in ancient or modern history. (Philip 1969:47, emphasis added)

Writing in 1834, roughly 30 years before Wilhelm Bleek was to conduct his interview with incarcerated /Xam San in Cape Town, Andrew Smith notes in his diary that "the Bushman wherever he is found is imbued with a degree of pride and courage far superior" and further, that "he delights in comment upon the existence or non-existence of courage and is most acute in discovering the proportion of it possessed by various natives..." (Smith 1975:129–130). Bleek, who was primarily engaged with imprisoned /Xam San in his home in Mowbray, Cape Town, was never to visit these landscapes as part of his philology project; it was only his daughter who was to finally have the chance to travel to territories farther north. Observations from outside the canonical Bleek archive – and the material examination of rock art sites such as Wildebeestkuil – lend perspective to the Bleek interviews; while of course all archival documents were presumably operating under a very powerful set of discursive constraints, it is doubtlessly in the constant shifting of the locus of these recordings that an interrogation of those very constraints are best achieved (Guenther 2001).

Delving further back into the history of Wildebeestkuil, archaeological excavations of stone circles identified by Stow indicate that the site has been intermittently occupied for thousands of years; LSA assemblages were associated with radiocarbon readings of 1790±60 B.P. and 1230±80 B.P. (Beaumont and Vogel 1989). During this time period, it is likely that this site was used in relation to the shamanic practices of rain-making both for /Xam San as well the local agropastoralists.[4] Shamanic practices, such as rain-making, healing, and visiting parties in distant locales, were known to be performed by and for members of a San group, although they have been known to be performed on behalf of non-San clients upon contact with African agropastoralists – in such instances the shaman performs a sort of "symbolic labor" in return for cattle or some other form of payment by the clients. Thomas Dowson has utilized both the rock art record and recent ethnographic material in order to more fully demonstrate the historically determined transformations undergone by the San shamans as a result of contact with African agropastoralists and subsequently settler farmers[5] (Dowson 1994a; 1994b; Dowson 1998:336; Lewis-Williams and Dowson 1989). Dowson's work is especially concerned to engage the physical rock face as an active material signifier, emphasizing that the rock itself was "intimately implicated in developing social relations and the reproduction and transformation of social forms" (Dowson 1998:336). Because the African farmers were as dependent on the rain as the San, and the San were recognized as custodians of the land, the symbolic labor of rainmaking came to be a valuable commodity of sorts for San shamans. Rain-making typically involves a shaman entering trance, then traveling out-of-body to a water hole and leading a water animal back from a water hole, mountain, or kloof across the veldt, killing it, and then letting its blood or milk fall across the parched earth. Images of this process in the rock art record tend to be quite varied; however, the basic motifs would include those generally attendant to scenes of shamanic trance, importantly featuring the water-bull (Deacon and Deacon 1999:173; Lewis-Williams and Dowson 1989:92–100).

MATERIALITY, CONSUMPTION, AND POWER

Rock art sites in the late nineteenth century not only had the potential to signify and historicize the process of rural hybridity, but the potential to convey this sense of hybridity to all those who inhabited the landscape – Africans and Europeans alike. Indeed, in a 21st-century interview with "M," cited as one of the "last surviving southern San," Lewis-Williams relates how "M" "demonstrated the way [shamanic] dancers turned to face the paintings when they wanted to intensify their power. As they looked at the paintings and raised their arms, power flowed from the paintings to them" (Lewis-Williams 1986:11).[6] Yet, what significance does this religious symbolic labor of the shamanic ritual have when considering the encroachment of agropastoralists and eventually colonial settlers? I would argue that rock art sites could easily have held a double significance; ostensibly, their significance resided in the story created by the figures superimposed on the panel, but the meta-signification was the slippage itself that constitutes San cosmology – between the mundane inequities of everyday life and the dream-like animals and therianthropes of myth.

> The artist places his animal and his human subjects within, respectively, a natural and social setting; settings both pervaded with the flavor of concrete, present-day reality. It is a reality, however, that is capable of becoming altered and alternate, as happens when the artist depicts trance and transformation images, thereby changing his creative mode and idiom from the mundane to the numinous. (Guenther 1994:260)

But when important rocks are engraved and painted with images of this cosmology, there is arguably a reification of the ritual itself, so that the sacred contouring of the land that might otherwise be "no more than implicit networks, smoky trails, manifested but indirectly in the cracks, dreams and jokes of everyday life" (Taussig 1986:203) becomes a source of power in its own right, one that emblematizes what came to be the challenge to the dominant settler vision of the landscape. Deacon's exploration of the topophilic aspect of San cosmology opens up the investigation of South African rock art sites as constructing what Taussig has termed "moralized topography" in which the cosmological disorder as well as inequity brought about by settler invasion is sublated within the eminent domain of the shaman – signified in rock art sites scattered across the landscape.

Without question, rock art sites "named the landscape" with the recorded memories of shamanic activities and stories, importantly reifying and underscoring their powers – while continually mediating the present and subsequently reformulating the significance of these shamanic practices (Hallam and Miller 2001). Images of shamanic trance necessarily underscored the preeminent power of a group's shamanic realm – something that, in some instances has been suggested to have provoked counterclaims to a site's power, made in the form of a differently styled art painted over shamanic imagery (Hall and Smith 2000). The emphasis of the dying eland, in most therianthropic depictions of the San shaman, present the inhabitants of the landscape with a material constitution of sorts, a declaration of sovereignty in the sense that "the sovereign is he who is as if death were not" (Bataille 1988:222). The shamans' skillful negotiation of the dying that occurs as part of the trance was reified through countless depictions on the rock outcrops of the landscape. Echoing this, the landscape was literally then imprinted on the newborn San; according to George Stow, "the child would be named either from the place where it was born, a cave, river etc." (Hewitt 1986:30).[7] The /Xam San did not appear to feel that the different lifestyles of the settlers exempted them from this same existential relationship with the land. When Bleek collected stories of beliefs of life after death, he recorded, "one informant described how the spirit of a dead person traveled along an underground path leading from the grave to a vast hole where it then lived. The spirits of all San went to this place, so did the spirits of the animals and the spirits of the Afrikaners" (Hewitt 1986:42). One can infer from this sort of assumption that the average /Xam San's superior attunement to the environment and its ancestral inhabitants more generally would have led them to consider themselves in a very good position to vie with the settler for dominion over the landscape. The sites of rock art, though radically untranslatable into the *Lebenswelt* of the settlers, could not have failed to carry some form of political salience in terms of this very untranslatability. Viewed in contradistinction to the practices and indeed emergent landscape of the settlers, the full message of rock art radically underscored the presence of the settler as partial and inadequate to the San cosmology and relegated the settler in no small sense to the "outsider" or the *homo sacer* to the San cosmology.

The settler, carrying no ancestral rights, who often killed the ostrich without reason or need, and took water without rights, participated in a form of excess that came to also constitute their very connectedness and indebtedness to their neighbors. This is the pivotal assumption of Bataille's notion of the general economy; "the immense travail of recklessness, discharge and upheaval that constitutes life could be expressed by stating that life starts only with the deficit of these systems . . . It is only by such subordination – even if it is impoverished – that the human race ceases to be isolated in the unconditional splendor of material things" (Bataille 1985:128). This same economy of excess is embodied in the death that was necessary to enter through the rock veils into the shamanic world. Importantly, these rock art sites signified the plenary power bestowed by the San cosmology – whose "general economy" encompassed and surpassed the more restricted practices and knowledge of the settlers; if this preeminence included the occasional sacrificing of the settler's "accursed share" (read cattle), understood within the general economy of the San rather than the restricted economy of the settler, it was not theft, but the equalizing and restoring force of the general economy – a mitigation of the obvious excesses of the settlers (Bataille 1988).

In much the same way that missionary Moffat records some San groups as claiming the sacred power of the Tswana divining bones (*morimo*), groups of the Northern frontier might have also appropriated the 19th-century Sotho-Tswana belief that the ox was "a European sacred animal" and have subsequently appropriated this animal and its image into their own panoply of power (Chidester 1996:198). But most importantly, the shamanic world was one in which the shaman fully dies and enters the trance *and returns* to the world being appropriated by the settlers. In light of this – the appropriating of settler livestock is but one symbolic action – but what is most profoundly translated, through images of nasal hemorrhaging and therianthropic figures is the *death* of the shaman-eland. In this sense, the rock art sites convey most forcefully of all their transcendence of the world of things, for "a thing is identical in time, but man dies and decomposes and this man who is dead and decomposes is not the same thing as that man who lived. Death is not the only contradiction that enters into the edifice formed by man's activity, but it has a kind of preeminence" (Bataille 1988:213). The site of this entry and exit, and reentry to the preeminent domain of dying and trance, would certainly pose as a powerful site of sovereignty, a veil that is inlaid with the potent evidence of shamans who were, above all, familiar with death.

Conclusion

In a sense, rock art sites have come to and will continue to be read much more broadly than merely the reminders of "timeless time" of the San. Or perhaps it is the notion of timeless time that will be reread to constitute a much more fundamental interrogation of the settler cosmology and economy. Imbued with historical context, it becomes clear that the material anchor of the rock-engraving site is a much more unstable and unlimited signifier than the archive alone would indicate. When situating the shamanic practices surrounding rock art sites within regional histories and contemporary politics, it becomes clear that it is impossible to limit what sorts of symbolic and economic regimes of value these sites may have engaged with at any one period. It becomes apparent that when we situate our historical gaze from the rocks themselves rather than the archivally mandated interpretation of these images, a much broader and more nuanced sense of how these beliefs and practices came to engage historical change and shifts of power can emerge. Perhaps what the contemporary site has come to signify is a tradition of defiant subversions of Western economies. Central to this understanding is recognition of the positive transformations to be gained from maintaining awareness of the power and variety of forms by which the cultural project of consumption has been and continues to be reflexively refashioned within the medium of materiality. The colonial project was waged primarily in words, texts, laws, and census reports that sought to reduce the very landscape of South Africa to a sort of grammar, that the state could "read" or "see" (Scott 1998). The rock art site, in all its historical incarnations, was simply not classifiable or alignable to this grid, and confounded even the most basic conceptual certainties of the settler project. The site of Wildebeestkuil emerges today as a site that continues, in no small sense, to confound colonial-era assumptions of what constitutes a culture-bearing or ethnic citizen. The material site of the rock engravings itself has not merely persisted in the wake of the colonial project, it profoundly de-centers and disassembles the very conceptual categories by which systems of rule have historically attempted to arbitrate such fundamental categories as ethnicity, death, and sovereignty.

MATERIALITY, CONSUMPTION, AND POWER

Notes

1 While in South American usage the word shaman is contested politically, it is more a more broadly accepted term when describing the regionally diverse and temporally shifting practices historically connected with rock art sites in South Africa (e.g. Klein et al. 2002).

2 Of course, this is only insofar as this moment was not abstracted from the greater Hegelian *telos* – and Miller admits that this is somewhat problematic but also points out that Marx picked and chose from Hegel's theory in much the same way.

3 Miller does acknowledge Marx's positive valuation of objectification in the context of production under the aegis of the communist state. Miller's positive conceptualization of objectification represents the fascinating "untapped potential" of Frankfurt School thoughts on the commodity structure of mass culture (Jameson 2000, though see Olsen 2003). Many Frankfurt scholars could be described as having a nostalgic attitude for the liberal phase of early capitalist development as it emerged from the bondage of pre-bourgeois European society, though they knew that it would be impossible to return to this state of classic liberal capitalism without ultimately arriving at the inevitable overtaking by the politics of fascism and industry-driven mass culture. Andrew Arato points out that frequently confusion arises because some Frankfurt scholars named certain aspects of liberal capitalist society as part of the process of human emancipation "to be preserved or remembered – for the sake of a liberated future" (Arato and Gerhardt 1977:9). While Miller's research moves within a *Kulturindustrie* anathema to Adorno and Benjamin, it is instructive to keep in mind that these theorists were not limited to "critical theories of the status quo" (Miller 1987:216), but that, in fact, "the Frankfurt critique of liberal capitalism could confront ideal with reality . . . and individuality as self-development [read: Miller's objectification] with individuality as self-preservation (i.e. individualism as a step in human development) with individualism as an ideological veil masking the new atomization and functionalization of concrete individuals) [read: alienation]". Miller's materialist reading of objectification as self-development, and his vision of a political future that is neither defined in contrast to capitalism nor enchanting commodity practices with Maussian notions of pre-market exchange (e.g. Appadurai 1986), might not be entirely at odds with some Frankfurt scholars.

4 This is evidenced by the emergence of ceramics in the Cape interior at roughly the same period, although it may have been a later date that agropastoralists came to this region (Sealy and Yates 1994).

5 This idea was first put forward by David Lewis-Williams – but in a way that has been critiqued as being structural–Marxist (e.g. Lewis-Williams 1981:103–116). Dowson, by contrast, situates his social interpretation of rock art as stemming from a more Giddens-like notion of structuration, in which emphasis is placed

on the constructive agency of the knowledgeable individual artist as well as the system of symbolic labor. Dowson also derives his theory from C. Campbell's unpublished MA thesis at the University of the Witwatersrand: "Art in Crisis: Contact Period Rock Art in the South-eastern Mountains."

6 Though see Willcox (1984) for a critique of what he considers unreflexive ethnographic inquiry.
7 Though eventually, this "little name" would be dropped for an adult name.

References

Adorno, Theodor W. 1978 Minima Moralia: Reflections from Damaged Life. New York: Schocken Books.
Agamben, Giorgio 1998 Homo Sacer: Sovereign Power and Bare Life. Stanford, CA: Stanford University Press.
Appadurai, Arjun 1981 The Past as a Scarce Resource. Man 16(2):201–219.
—— 1986 The Social Life of Things: Commodities in Cultural Perspective. Cambridge: Cambridge University Press.
—— 1990 Disjunction and Difference in the Global Cultural Economy. Public Culture 2(2):1–24.
Arato, Andrew, and Eike Gerhardt 1977 The Essential Frankfurt School Reader. New York: Urizen Books.
Arbousset, Jean Thomas, Francois Daumas, and John Croumbie Brown 1846 Narrative of an Exploratory Tour to the North-East of the Colony of the Cape of Good Hope. Cape Town: Robertson.
Balibar, Etienne 1994 Masses, Classes, Ideas: Studies on Politics and Philosophy Before and After Marx. New York: Routledge.
Bataille, Georges 1985 The Notion of Expenditure. *In* Visions of Excess: Selected Writings 1927–1939. G. Bataille, ed. Pp. 116–129. Minnesota: University of Minnesota Press.
—— 1988 The Accursed Share: An Essay on General Economy. New York: Zone Books.
Beaumont, Peter B., and John Vogel 1989 Patterns in the Age and Context of Rock Art in the Northern Cape. South African Archaeological Bulletin 44:73–81.
Becker, Heike 2003 The Least Sexist Society? Perspectives on Gender, Change and Violence among Southern African San. Journal of Southern African Studies 29(1):5–23.
Bernbeck, Reinhard, and Susan Pollock 2004 The Production of Heritage in the Middle East. *In* The Companion to Social Archaeology. L. Meskell and R. Preucel, eds. Pp. 335–352. Oxford: Blackwell.
Bleek, Wilhelm 1875 Bushman Researches. Parts 1 and 2. Cape Monthly Magazine 11:104–115;150–155.
Blundell, Geoffrey 2004 Nquabo's Nomansland: San Rock Art and the Somatic Past. Ph.D. dissertation, Uppsala University.

Brown, Wendy 2001 Politics Out of History. Princeton, NJ: Princeton University Press.
de Certeau, Michel 1984 The Practice of Everyday Life. Berkeley, CA: University of California Press.
Chidester, David 1996 Savage Systems: Colonialism and Comparative Religion in Southern Africa. Charlottesville: University Press of Virginia.
Comaroff, Jean 2004 The End of History, Again? Pursuing the Past in the Postcolony. *In* Postcolonial Studies and Beyond. S. Kaul, A. Loomba, M. Bunzl, A. Burton, and J. Esty, eds. Durham: Duke University Press.
Coombes, Annie E. 1994 Reinventing Africa: Museums, Material Culture, and Popular Imagination in Late Victorian and Edwardian England. New Haven: Yale University Press.
—— 2003 History After Apartheid: Visual Culture and Public Memory in a Democratic South Africa. Durham, NC: Duke University Press.
Deacon, H. J., and Janette Deacon 1999 Human Beginnings in South Africa: Uncovering the Secrets of the Stone Age. Walnut Creek, CA: Altamira Press.
Deacon, Janette 1988 The Power of a Place in Understanding Southern San Rock Engravings. World Archaeology 20(1):129–140.
—— 1997 "My heart stands in the hill": Rock Engravings in the Northern Cape. Kronos 24:18–29.
Douglas, Stuart 1997 Reflections on State Intervention and the Schmidtsdrift Bushmen. Journal of Contemporary African Studies 15(1):45–66.
Dowson, Thomas A. 1994a Hunter-Gatherers, Traders and Slaves: The "Mfecane" Impact on Bushmen, Ritual and their Art. *In* The Mfecane Aftermath: A Revolution in Thinking about Nineteenth-Century "Bantu Africa." C. Hamilton, ed. Pp. 51–70. Johannesburg: Witwatersrand University Press.
—— 1994b Reading Art, Writing History: Rock Art and Social Change in Southern Africa. World Archaeology 25(3):332–345.
—— 1998 Like People in Prehistory. World Archaeology 29(3):333–343.
Fock, Gerhard, and Alexander McGregor 1965 Two Rock Engravings from South Africa in the British Museum. Man 65:194–195.
Foucault, Michel 1972 The Archaeology of Knowledge: The Discourse on Language. New York: Pantheon Books.
—— 2003 Society Must be Defended: Lectures at the Collège de France, 1975–76. M. Bertani, A. Fontana, F. Ewald, and D. Macey, trans. New York: Picador.
Foucault, Michel, and James D. Faubion 2000 Power. New York: New Press.
Gaonkar, Dilip Parameshwar, and Elizabeth A. Povinelli 2003 Technologies of Public Forms: Circulation, Transfiguration, Recognition. Public Culture 15(3):385–397.
Garland, Elizabeth, and Robert J. Gordon 1999 The Authentic (In)Authentic: Bushmen Anthro-Tourism. Visual Anthropology 12:267–287.
Gordon, Robert J., and Stuart Sholto-Douglas 2000 The Bushman Myth: The Making of a Namibian Underclass. Boulder: Westview Press.
Guenther, Mathais 1994 The Relationship of Bushman Art to Ritual and Folklore. *In* Contested Images: Diversity in Southern African Rock Art Research. T. A.

Dowson and D. Lewis-Williams, eds. Pp. 257–275. Johannesburg: Witwatersrand University Press.

—— 2001 Attempting to Contextualize /Xam Oral Tradition. *In* Voices from the Past: /Xam Bushmen and the Bleek and Lloyd Collection. J. Deacon and T. A. Dowson, eds. Pp. 77–99. Johannesburg: Witwatersrand University Press.

Hacking, Ian 2004 Between Michael Foucault and Erving Goffman: Between Discourse in the Abstract and Face-to-Face Interaction. Economy and Society 33(3):277–302.

Hall, Simon, and Ben Smith 2000 Empowering Places: Rock Shelters and Ritual Control in Farmer-Forager Interactions in the Northern Province. South African Archaeological Society Goodwin Series 8:30–46.

Hallam, Elizabeth, and Daniel Miller 2001 Death, Memory and Material Culture. Oxford: Berg.

Hewitt, Roger L. 1986 Structure, Meaning and Ritual in the Narratives of the Southern San. Hamburg: Helmut Buske Verlag.

Jameson, Fredric 2000 Reification and Utopia in Mass Culture. *In* The Jameson Reader. M. Hardt and K. Weeks, eds. Pp. 123–148. Oxford: Blackwell.

Klein, Cecelia, Eulogio Guzman, Elisa Mandell, and Maya Stanfield-Mazzi 2002 The Role of Shamanism in Mesoamerican Art: A Reassessment. Current Anthropology 43(3):383–419.

Latour, Bruno 1999 On Recalling ANT. *In* Actor Network Theory and After. J. Law and J. Hassard, eds. Pp. 15–25. Malden, MA: Blackwell.

Lewis-Williams, David 1981 Believing and Seeing: Symbolic Meanings in Southern San Rock Paintings. London and New York: Academic Press.

—— 1986 The Last Testament of the Southern San. The South African Archaeological Bulletin 41:10–11.

—— 1994 Aspects of Rock Art Research: A Critical Retrospective. *In* Contested Images: Diversity in Southern African Rock Art Research. T. A. Dowson and D. Lewis-Williams, eds. Pp. 201–222. Johannesburg: Witwatersrand University Press.

Lewis-Williams, David, and Thomas Dowson 1989 Images of Power: Understanding Bushman Rock Art. Johannesburg: Southern Book Publishers.

Lukács, György 1971 History and Class Consciousness: Studies in Marxist Dialectics. Cambridge, MA: MIT Press.

Marks, Shula 1972 Khoisan Resistance to the Dutch in the Seventeenth and Eighteenth Centuries. Journal of African History XIII(I):55–80.

Marx, Karl, and Ben Fowkes 1977 Capital: A Critique of Political Economy. New York: Vintage Books.

Mbembe, Achille 2004 Aesthetics of Superfluity. Public Culture 16(3):373–405.

Meskell, Lynn 2002 Negative Heritage and Past Mastering in Archaeology. Anthropological Quarterly 75(3):557–575.

—— 2004 Object Worlds in Ancient Egypt: Material Biographies Past and Present. London: Berg.

Miller, Daniel 1987 Material Culture and Mass Consumption. Oxford: Blackwell.

—— 1995 Introduction: Anthropology, Modernity and Consumption. *In* Worlds Apart. D. Miller, ed. Pp. 1–22. London: Routledge.

Mitchell, Timothy 2002 Heritage and Violence. *In* Rule of Experts: Egypt, Techno-Politics, Modernity. T. Mitchell, ed. Pp. 179–205. London, UK: University of California Press.

Morris, David 1988 Engraved in Place and Time: A Review of Variability in the Rock Art of the Northern Cape and Karoo. South African Archaeological Bulletin 43:109–121.

Morris, David, Sven Ouzman, and Gabriel Tlhapi 2001 Tandjesberg San Rock Painting Rehabilitation Project: From Catastrophe to Celebration. South African Archaeological Society: The Digging Stick 18(1):1–4.

Mudimbe, Valentin Y. 1988 The Invention of Africa: Gnosis, Philosophy, and the Order of Knowledge. Bloomington: Indiana University Press.

Olsen, Bjornar 2003 Material Culture after Text: Re-Membering Things. Norwegian Archaeology Review 36(2):87–104.

Ouzman, Sven 1995 Spiritual and Political Uses of a Rock-Engraving Site and Its Imagery by San and Tswana-Speakers. South African Archaeological Bulletin 50:55–67.

—— 2001 Seeing is Deceiving: Rock Art and the Non-visual. World Archaeology 33(2):237–256.

Péringuey, Louis 1909 On Rock Engravings of Animals and the Human Figure, Found in South Africa. Transactions of the South African Philosophical Society 18:401–420.

Philip, John 1969 Researches in South Africa: Illustrating the Civil, Moral, and Religious Condition of the Native Tribes, Including Journals of the Author's Travels in the Interior, Together with Detailed Accounts of the Progress of the Christian Missions, Exhibiting the Influence of Christianity in Promoting Civilization. New York: Universities Press.

Rassool, Ciraj 2000 The Rise of Heritage and Reconstitution of History in South Africa. Kronos: Journal of Cape History 26:1–21.

Robinson, A. M. Lewin 1978 Selected Articles from the Cape Monthly Magazine: (new series 1870–76). Cape Town: Van Riebeeck Society.

Scott, James C. 1998 Seeing Like a State: How Certain Schemes to Improve the Human Condition have Failed. New Haven, CT: Yale University Press.

Sealy, Judith, and Royden Yates 1994 The Chronology of the Introduction of Pastoralism to the Cape, South Africa. Antiquity 68:58–67.

Smith, Andrew 1975 Andrew Smith's Journal of his Expedition into the Interior of South Africa, 1834–36: An Authentic Narrative of Travels and Discoveries, the Manners and Customs of the Native Tribes, and the Physical Nature of the Country. Cape Town: Published for the South African Museum by A. A. Balkema.

Smith, Benjamin, David Lewis-Williams, Geoffrey Blundell, and Christopher Chippendale 2000 Archaeology and Symbolism in the New South African Coat of Arms. Antiquity 74:467–468.

Stocking, George W. 1985 Objects and Others: Essays on Museums and Material Culture. Madison, WI: University of Wisconsin Press.

Stow, G. W. 1905 The Native Races of South Africa. London: Swan Sonnenschein.

Taussig, Michael T. 1986 Shamanism, Colonialism, and the Wild Man: A Study in Terror and Healing. Chicago, IL: University of Chicago Press.

Trouillot, Michel-Rolph 2003 Global Transformations: Anthropology and the Modern World. New York: Palgrave Macmillan.

Vorster, Louis P. 1993 The !XU of Schmidtsdrift and Sorcery. *In* Speaking for the Bushmen. A. Sanders, ed. Pp. 101–115. Vol. Papers from the 13th International Congress of Anthropological and Ethnological Sciences. Gabarone: The Botswana Society.

Willcox, Alex 1984 The Motives in San Rock Art. South African Archaeological Bulletin 39(139):53–57.

4

With a Hint of Paris in the Mouth: Fetishized Toothbrushes or the Sensuous Experience of Modernity in Late 19th Century Bogotá

Felipe Gaitán Ammann

> But who, even among the most educated of us, doesn't have his own fetish?
>
> Jean-Baptiste Boussingault, *Memoirs*, 1892

Among the ascending republican elites of late 19th-century Bogotá, refined bourgeois manners were adopted as distinctively modernizing features that, paradoxically enough, also contributed to the reproduction of a stubbornly colonial order. While they often claimed an American cultural heritage as a major justifier for their political independence from the Spanish Crown, urban upper classes strove to bend to the increasingly standardized and hygienized European ways defining a performative domestic border within which modern materiality vouched for the maintenance of an oligarchic status quo. Archaeological and firsthand historical data both suggest that elite groups in republican Bogotá experienced modern concepts of civility and urbanity as materially tangible phenomena that, more often than not, were intimately linked with their consumption and display of luxurious imported goods. In this chapter, I will explore how the process of fetishization of a seemingly innocuous item such as a toothbrush evolved as an inescapable outcome of the long-distance trade webs that supplied 19th-century Bogotá with expensive manufactured novelties. However, rather than simply focusing on how the sacralization of a modern artifact could be seen as an inevitable consequence of its cultural, geographical, or chronological decontextualization, I propose to trace some more subtle facets of what might have been the life history of the first archaeological toothbrush recovered in Colombia. The exploration of the multi-sensuous performative possibilities entangled in the materiality of this archaeological toothbrush is an experiment that will take us from its semi-industrial carving in 1870s Paris to its recent incorporation to the permanent collection of one of Latin America's most cherished museums.

The Bride's Teeth

Bogotá, April 1864

Everyone at the Vélez's house quivered in excitement as young Miss Pilar's wedding day swiftly approached. And yet, evading the bridal turmoil for a while, Pilar's elder sister, Mrs. Paula Arango de Vélez, sat down at her writing table, opened her accountancy book and started reckoning all the expenses she had incurred since she had become the tutor of her younger sibling. She tallied every single boarding cost, the laundrywoman's and the ironer's wages and the exorbitant tuition paid to Doña Sixta Pontón for the time Pilar spent at her Young Ladies' School.[1] She recalled Dr. Vargas' charges for the medicines and care that Pilar had received when she contracted measles, and reviewed the bill for her convalescence trip to the neighboring village of Serrezuela. Last but not least, she added young Pilar's contribution to the cost of the many masses she had ordered to be said for the eternal rest of their mother's soul. Indeed, more than 1,500 pesos were to be deducted from the total assets hoarded in the dowry Pilar would soon be bringing to her future husband. In stylish handwriting on fancy pale blue writing paper, Mrs. Vélez built up a sober financial report, denoting her keen sense of domestic organization. Far from betraying any feeling of sisterly love, she methodically performed a list of all the corsets, crinolines, chemises, petticoats, and gowns fashionably tailored out of fine European woolens, chintzes, muslins, and silks that she had acquired for her younger sister. Pilar had taken possession of some eighteen pairs of ankle boots and shoes, at least a dozen pairs of cotton stockings, several linen handkerchiefs and embroidered collars, a woolen shawl, a pair of golden earrings, two ivory combs and, quite exceptionally, a silk mantilla embellished with velvet flowers that she could proudly display every day at church. Following their mother's death in early 1861, young Pilar had been given her own bed, and a ewer and basin enameled tin set to perform her daily ablutions in the privacy of her bedroom. Furthermore, since she was placed under the guard of her sister, Pilar had used a substantial amount of fine grooming items: three fine soap bars, one little glass flask of rose-essence and, noblesse oblige, two little French bone toothbrushes with which she occasionally cleaned her mouth in the same convenient manner prescribed in her manual of bourgeois *savoir-vivre*. After all, unlike the majority of the 50,000 people crammed in late 19th-century Bogotá, Pilar was part of the happy few who knew how it felt to have a hint of Paris in her mouth.

Out of the Bone Bag

Slowly ripened among dusty notarial documents preserved in Colombia's National Archive,[2] Mrs. Vélez's scrupulous list and price of each purchase on behalf of her orphan sister has become a most wonderful object lesson. Crystallized in time by the means of written words, young Pilar's troves can now stand up as an indexical – and sensuously iconic – clue to the materiality in which Bogotá's 19th-century emerging bourgeoisie was willing to invest its rising economic capital. Ultimately, Mrs. Vélez gave away the price – this is, the exchange value – of being a respectable young lady in republican Bogotá. What else could we add on young Pilar's account? Not much indeed. We know that, by 1864, she lived at her sister's place in a good enough neighborhood of the dour capital city of what, in those days, was officially named the United States of Colombia. We have had the chance to pry into her wardrobe and her material daily life at the time of her marriage. As evocative as it may seem to our minds, the list that Mrs. Vélez finally presented before the notary-public in hope of a quick and fair rebate is no more than an accidental outcome, a suggesting opening capable of adding some

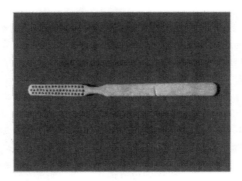

Figure 4.1 The fetishized toothbrush (courtesy of the Casa Museo Quinta de Bolivar – Bogotá, Colombia)

contextual, magical gleam to the tale of a particular toothbrush that came back to life on a famous museum's ground (Gaitán 2003; In press). In fact, the toothbrush I am writing about might not have been very different from those regularly used by young Pilar in order to, consciously or not, reify her gentrified sense of distinction. Our museum's toothbrush and hers might have been carved by the same people in the same place and, most certainly, followed the same path up to chilly heights of Bogotá. They might even have been stored in the same shop, have been sold by the same shopkeeper and have been purchased for the same price within less than a decade's time. Yet, our museum toothbrush still keeps a particular *something* that most 19th-century toothbrushes referred to in historical accounts have inevitably lost: our museum toothbrush displays the wholesome materiality through which, in the end, the commodity can become a fetish.

Colombia's first archaeological toothbrush (Figure 4.1) came back to life at the Quinta de Bolivar, a late-colonial villa nested on Bogotá's tutelary hills and enshrined by Colombian government as a tribute to its most illustrious occupant: General Simon Bolivar. By the end of the 1990s, Bolivar's favorite residence was being given a complete architectural rejuvenation when, to the astonishment of many, some forgotten remains of Bogotá's republican bourgeois consumption unexpectedly showed up, buried in the backyard of the house. In striking contrast to the reverence with which the Quinta was architecturally restored, most of the historical objects forming part of its domestic landscape, gradually accumulated in an ancient cistern nearly 50 years after Bolivar's death, were disrespectfully drawn out of the soil. Left to the rapid desecrating movement of the masons' spades, archaeological artifacts were smashed, scrambled, and hastily piled up in refuse bags that would eventually be handed over to archaeologists. It was then, in the context of its profane recovery, that a splintered toothbrush was mistaken for an ordinary bone and thrown into a bone bag. However, a bagful of soiled cow bones may now seem a quite fitting setting of cultural resurrection for an object actually made out of bone. One could hardly find a more evocative situation to mimic the toothbrush's birth in a Parisian brush-making store in which, back in the 1870s, cattle bone and boar bristle were carved and imbued with a modern cultural identity.

When studied as historical artifacts, archaeological objects from the recent past tend to be unequivocally identified with the practical, and yet social, function that their physical appearance may betray. This is especially true of the highly standardized commodities that have flooded the modern world since the rise of the Western industrial revolution (Hall 2000; Shackel 1993). In modernized social contexts where consumption may be seen as an inevitable outcome caught in the rationale of a worldwide capitalistic market, materiality is understood as merely standing for the technical and psychical needs of a person, of a group, of a class. When does the tracing back of an object's material trajectory become more than methodological fetishism and embody the artifact with a fetishized aura (Taussig 1993) per se? This is an essential question for archaeologists wanting to be true to the artifacts they study. Further, contributing to the release of the latent power accumulated in objects' sheer materiality may eventually constitute both a remembrance lesson on social life in the past and, paraphrasing Miller (1998), a sensuous explanation of why some of things in our daily life matter.

The particular relish that biographical approaches on ancient things always seem to produce in archaeologists (Gosden and Marshall 1999; Meskell 2004) is not unrelated to our pervasive desire to control the settings in which material remains of the past can be found. Quite similarly, when it is put at play in the context of ethnographic collections (e.g. Legêne 1998; Seip 1999), the biographical approach looks like an attempt to repossess things culturally alien to the West with what they were denied in enlightened taxonomic systems (Dupré 1993; Foucault 1966), with an ontological right to transcend classificatory rules, to bear as many names as their materiality would stand throughout social space and time. Both in anthropology and in archaeology, the biographical approach challenges the fragmentation of social life in independent, functionally articulated, theoretically discrete, spheres (Latour 1991). It evokes a practical and functional dimension entangled with a social component of sensuous meaning that has often been concealed by what Miller calls the "humility of objects" (1987:87), an overly utilitarian idea of the role that objects play in social life. Yet, the biographical potential of an ancient, ethnographical, or archaeological object is still utterly dependant on the fortuitous unreeling of present eventualities.

The cultural biography of objects – an analytical scope inaugurated by Kopytoff (1986) – is thus an extremely useful scholarly tool closely linked to the paramount concept of materiality. This approach also seems to have been used as an amorphous methodological asset comfortably fitting quite different theoretical views on the role that material things can play in the shaping and reproduction of social life. While it was originally used to illustrate the problematic process of commoditization and singularization within the context of exchange (Kopytoff 1986), it has also been employed in order to enhance the metaphorical role of things in the process of reproducing social relations (Davis 1997; Edwards 2001; Hoskins 1998). The biographical approach is also a way of tracing back the social history of particular kinds of objects that certain cultural taxonomies classify as spiritually significant (O'Neill 1999; Saunders 1999; Seip 1999). However, it is striking that most of the literature addressing the biography of objects as a central topic never focuses on things as materially pervasive meaningful entities per se. In that sense, most of this scholarly production is engaged into what Appadurai (1986) has called "a methodological fetishism," a posture that has recently been widely criticized for overlooking the cultural possibilities of objects' materiality (Pels 1998).

One could argue that archaeological practice necessarily resorts to methodological fetishism in its attempt to seize the logics of ancient cultural systems through the intermediacy of the objects these systems once produced. However, at this point, one can see there is usually a salient difference between the ethnographical and the archaeological research contexts that makes it difficult to compare the way in which they might both surrender to a methodological fetishism. As Hoskins (1998) has eloquently shown through her own work in Melanesia, objects-in-use can often retain the cultural clue the ethnographer may need in order to decrypt a richly metaphorical living language. Once it has been unlocked through the means of, let us say, a betel bag, this language may be accessed and can therefore admit the possibility of a cultural translation. From the moment one has captured the code needed to perform ethnographic interrogations the material character of the betel bag seems to lose any cultural relevance. The object seems nothing but an empty shell having shed all of its symbolic layers. The problem for archaeologists is that we simply cannot move away from the material domain. In that sense, the only way for us to eschew the conceptual limitations of a fetishistic methodology is to embrace the notion of materiality as a theoretical anchoring point, to acknowledge that there is an essential material identity in any archaeological object. Paradoxically, this has been underestimated in spite – and yet, also, because – of the analytical efforts of archaeologists seeking to understand "the material aspects of technology and to interrogate the cultural logics that underlie choice and ultimately transform society" (Meskell 2004:1–2). Thus, it seems clear that archaeologists are in a privileged position to truly address the social biography of objects as interpretative accounts of the different life stages of their materiality.

The biographical approach toward things has been more rigorously explored in ethnographic contexts and it would seem as if archaeologists had only recently succumbed to the rich potential of biography as an analytical strategy. However, this development is actually quite unexceptional in archaeology and has frequently been employed by archaeologists in order to highlight the particular cultural power that certain types of artifacts may gain according to the social context in which their materiality is ultimately activated (e.g. Holtorf 2002). As for historical archaeologists, although many of them may not specifically refer to their scholarly work as biographical performances (e.g. Yentsch 1993), their unique possibility to contrast archaeological material with historical texts is a methodological asset (Andrén 1998; Leone and Potter 1988; Shackel 1993; Yentsch 1993) allowing them to develop particularly detailed outlooks on the historical trajectory of singular objects.

It is clear from a theoretical perspective that ethnographic perspectives on biography tend to be diametrically opposed to archaeological ones. First, some ethnographers' explicit or tacit assertion that only a distinctive kind of artifact – addressed as biographical objects (Hoskins 1998) – can be endowed with the personal characteristics of their owners is particularly opposed to archaeological views understanding the biography of artifacts as the life history of their materiality. Materiality ought to be understood as an ontological character which is not restricted to special kinds of artifacts. Second, in archaeological contexts, the distinction between a singularized biographical object and a public commodity (Kopytoff 1986) in archaeological contexts can be extremely problematic. How could archaeologists refuse to singularize the physical remains of past commodities? To skip over the biographical potential of apparently innocuous, discardable commodities would be precisely to overlook the relevance of materiality as a conceptual framework challenging preceding approaches on the social life of things. Third, the biographical approach to things has often been related to ethnographic views on specific societies within which the circulation of objects has been considered to be the symbolic basis for the process of personhood-constructing (e.g. Strathern 1988). This perspective still allows the objects' materiality to be literally absorbed by the circulation performance itself: insofar as a material exchange succeeds in establishing a vital completion and accumulation of movable, interchangeable parts of personhood (Hoskins 1997:10), it doesn't really matter what the exchanged object actually is, what it looks like, and for what it can practically be used. And yet archaeologists are compelled to focus on these very physical characteristics of things, those they can effectively attempt to retrieve in the archaeological record. Thus it is essential for archaeologists to recognize that, although the wide scope of metaphorical significations that some artifacts can demonstrate in ethnographic milieus may most probably remain silent in archaeological contexts, the materiality of both ancient and present-day objects is still assessable through the performative possibilities they can reveal, either in terms of the technical efficiency they display, of the social prestige they award, or of the psychic stability they confer (Csikszentmihalyi 1993).

Archaeologists working on historical periods are particularly aware that, even though our perception of an ancient artifact's present-day appearance might seem thoroughly disconnected from the social meanings its materiality was once endowed with, those meanings can sometimes be recaptured through written texts. It sounds quite appropriate for historical archaeologists to argue that, following Kopytoff (1986), a biographical approach implies the contrasting of particular data with ideal life models that have been historically constructed, either for persons or for things. The most seductive aspect of the biographical approach appears to be the opportunity it gives us to link the material world as thought and the object world as lived in a succession of singular social settings. What are the cultural possibilities of change given to a thing or to an individual in specific social, economic, and historical conditions? This is a question worth asking in relation to the biographical toothbrush that came out of a bone bag.

Consuming Class on Tormented Grounds

The wars of Independence (1810–19) marked the beginning of a long period of political, social, and economic instability in what now constitutes the Republic of Colombia (Bushnell 1996). The most salient evidence of this pervasive unsteadiness is the fact that the official republican name of the former viceroyalty of New Granada was modified five times throughout the 19th century. These recurring changes in designation obviously came hand in hand with some more radical transformations in the political and legal framework within which local ruling classes intended to consolidate a modern nation-state. By the time our biographical toothbrush might have been used in the bucolic setting of the Quinta de Bolivar, the country was undergoing the most radically liberal phase of its recent history. From the second half of the 19th century onwards, Colombian rulers bowed to the political and economic pressures exerted by international powers seeking to incorporate young South American republics in their transatlantic commercial networks. Thus, from 1845 on, many government officials actively supported free trade policies that eventually transformed New Granada into a strong exporter of raw materials and an avid consumer of European and North American manufactured goods (McGreevey 1982; Nieto Arteta 1975; Tirado Mejía 1988). At this time, most classical liberal ideas regarding political economy were popular among local young generations, particularly sensitive to the printed propaganda announcing the countless virtues of Western modernity (Jaramillo Uribe 2001). Still, complex political tensions brought into opposition different social sectors of the national population, according to the source of their revenues and to their political affiliations. Internal conflicts also frequently resulted from more subtle discords based on regional pride and religious beliefs.

In 1863, under the name of United States of Colombia, the country was divided into nine sovereign states, each one enjoying virtually unlimited juridical and legal liberties. This period, extending from 1863 to 1889 and suggestively known in local history as the Radical Olympus, is a time during which both modern civil rights and traditional moral precepts were constantly challenged on the basis of the most classical liberal principles. Broadly matching this period, a boom in tobacco exports to Europe inflated the acquisitive power and political influence of traditional landlords and tradesmen whilst also reinforcing the economic dependence of peasants, the hardship of local artisans, and the misery of lower urban classes (Nieto Arteta 1975).

Although the redefinition of class identities in late 19th-century Colombia could occasionally brave some preexisting social schemes founded on ethnic and genealogical traits, it often reproduced an oligarchic social order based on the accumulation and the codified material display of economic capital (Gaitán 2003). Now, retracing the life story of an archaeological bone toothbrush that may have contributed to defining the republican boundaries of social class necessarily leads us to explore the way in which the concept of class can be understood in terms of material consumption and daily practice (Wurst and Fitts 1999).

Despite recent critiques on the validity of Bourdieu's theoretical framework as an analytical tool allowing archaeologists to address the issue of the material expressions of social agency (Dornan 2002), I still believe that the seminal notion of *habitus*, and the related concept of *doxa* (Bourdieu 1979; 1990), constitute extremely useful elements in understanding consumption patterns and their relation to the definition of social classes in 19th-century Bogotá. As it has often been pointed out, Bourdieu conceived *habitus* as a structured and structuring system of cultural dispositions that is gradually built on the base of experience. The particularities of this system are expressed by the means of individual practices. Although *habitus* is basically determined by the socioeconomic context in which it is originally generated, its social sense can only be perceived when it is enacted in practice and within a determined social field. This is why the social signification of one particular practice may change significantly according to the social environment in which it is performed. In addition, *habitus* may seldom be perceived in everyday life as a body of social conditionings that are *learned* and *nurtured* according to a specific social origin; rather, it is likely to be experienced as a function of conscious, free, and independent individual choices.

The practices in which *habitus* is expressed are normally understood by social agents as being of a supra-social nature that is inherent to every individual. Even though *habitus* might be described as a conglomerate of institutionalized practical dispositions that bind individual actions to a limited number of social choices, it still leaves open the possibility of actually performing agency through the active and personally-oriented shaping of the meanings of every human practice. Finally, Bourdieu (1979:190) asserts that *habitus* does not only allow people to perform practices with a distinctive social meaning, but that it also enables them to classify them according to a basic system of class division. He argues that "the practices of all the agents of a same class have a style affinity that makes of each one a metaphor of the others" (1979:234, my translation). This attraction between similar habits encourages the generation of distinctive lifeways, which can be seen as direct expressions of class identities that converge in the social world.

Following Bourdieu, we can consider class as an expression of *habitus*, a matter of lifestyle not unrelated to economic capital, but also relying on cultural and symbolic factors that may ultimately be independent of mere wealth. Mrs. Vélez did not spend much on Miss Pilar's pair of brushes. She could have bought fifty of them with the money she invested on her sister's mantilla and more than a dozen with the cash she paid for her recovery weekend in the countryside. The price of a toothbrush was roughly equivalent to the cost of two average-size river fish or of two wild ducks, while two of them might have been worth the same as an English canned plum cake (see Carnegie-Williams 1882). After all, owning a toothbrush might not have been so much a matter of price as it was a question of taste (cf. Kirshenblatt-Gimblett 1998). However, the toothbrush was clearly inscribed only in the *habitus* of the highest local gentry, and found its consumption locus only in those individuals whose modernized sensitivity was expressed by the adoption of increasingly regularized grooming behaviors that betrayed their desire to engage in a performative membership of the modern civilized world.

A Modern Tooth-Brushing World

The historical transition towards a modern, civilized, and teeth-brushing world can be seen as an evolutionary process that eventually endowed human beings with the cultural apparatus required to escape the dishonoring yoke of nature. From the end of the Middle Ages, European court societies guided the course of the civilizing process and made clear attempts to manipulate all its expressions in order to promote themselves in the eyes of the social sectors they intended to dominate. In its dazzling physicality, the elite material culture of the Renaissance stood for those ancient lineages whose legitimacy was at stake because the construction of a political and economic modern order was strongly influenced by bourgeois sectors. As Elias (1973; 1974) has convincingly shown, the shaping and display of new and highly regulated ways in courtly milieus was a protective reflex intended to defend the social hegemony of Western traditional aristocracies. The development of such mechanisms of social distinction thrusts dominant sectors in a feverish consumption that, in time, spurred the modernization of the Western world. Thus, the first signs of a modern behavior were deeply rooted in avatars of courtesy and etiquette, often associated with the employment of new instances of material culture (e.g. forks, napkins, clocks, and toothpicks), that fell into the hands of a disempowered nobility who cultivated a fantasy of the God-given character of their socioeconomic privileges.

It is ironic to see how the mask of privilege is made evident through one of the most effective modernizing tools developed in the Renaissance – the courtesy treaties and etiquette manuals – which scrupulously describe appropriate behaviors in a coercive tone. These treaties, intended to normalize and naturalize the objectification of an aristocratic power, actually kept in their pages the secret of social ascendancy. They testified to a process in which aristocracy sought to shelter in the sphere of taste, luxury, and refinement. After the 17th century, constantly harassed by the expansive bourgeois concept of respectability, courtly manners fell into the hands of European high bourgeoisies who adopted and redefined them according to their own necessities. Insofar as the mere concept of courtesy was vulgarized and lost its distinctive power, it was gradually replaced by the notions of civility and civilization.

It was in educated bourgeois circles that elite behavior like brushing the teeth seems to have survived the downfall of the aristocratic Ancien Regime. In the 18th and 19th centuries, the middle classes were enhanced by increasing their control over the capitalist system that was rapidly spreading throughout the world. Although bourgeois sectors continued to perceive the display of luxurious and highly specialized objects as the most evident instrument of distinction, the socially accepted ways of integrating distinguished manners into daily life were radically transformed (Elias 1974). While a sumptuous material life was previously deemed inherent to the aristocratic condition, it gradually began to be seen as a legitimate outcome of the gradual accumulation of economic and cultural capital (Bourdieu 1979). Probably more than ever, Western bourgeoisies were conscious that the behavior ruling social differentiation was nothing but an arbitrary set of norms that could be learnt and assimilated, but also questioned and modified.

The gentrification of good manners, within which teeth-cleaning always played a primary role, seems to be closely related with the rise of *urbanity* as a term designing not only the behavior of a good courtesan but also that of a good citizen. More than the notions of courtesy and civility preceding it, this concept is morally (Goffman 1990:37) and Christianly inflected (Pedraza 1999). This is particularly true in conservative societies in which religious authorities had been undermined by the rise of republican regimes. Indeed, within the context of late 19th-century Bogotá, members of the high bourgeoisie tended to present themselves as the standard bearers of Christian morality in order to justify their monopoly of the principles of modern civilization. Local upper classes perceived their capacity to assume the social norms contemplated in urbanity manuals, written by bourgeois for members of the bourgeoisie, as being endowed with a virtuous character not unlike the divine right sustaining the power of court societies. Thus, the artifacts through which such morally-charged behaviors could be performed would also have the potential to acquire a sacrosanct gleam embedded in their specific, exotic, and luxurious materiality. The fetishization process evoked by this mystic association between modern artifacts and their modernly codified use in the confines of Western civilization may be clarified as we delve into the unique social history of the modern toothbrush.

The Sleeping Fetish

The toothbrush concept seems to be a very old one (Mattick 1998:9). As with so many objects exerting a fetishistic fascination over Western minds, its origins are related to the mythical figure of an ancient Chinese emperor, a mighty personification of the exotic *other* so perfectly synthesized in Borges' enchanting classification (Foucault 1966; Meskell 2004). The exact way in which the basic Western design of the toothbrush emerged in Europe since the end of the 18th century is still unclear, though it is worth noting that its basic form has remained essentially unchanged up to the present. Even though toothbrush manufacturing centers developed in England, France, the United States, and Japan throughout the 19th century, toothbrushes were kept in the preserve of the upper classes until, by the late 1870s, the rise of mechanization reached the sphere of brush production. The time in which our biographical toothbrush was most probably carved and used corresponds to a period in which the reduction in the exchange value of this particular type of item contributed to spread its consumption to Western middle classes. Interestingly enough, this period also matches the moment in which Pasteur's scientific research contributed to publicize the image of an invisible, murderous bacterial horde constantly besieging the healthiness of the human body. Brushing the teeth, previously perceived as a mere matter of discipline and convenience intended to enhance the natural elegance of distinguished people, began to be seen as a wholesome habit by which people could also preserve their health. By the turn of the 20th century the toothbrush was engaged in a defetishizing pathway, into a commodification route that would necessarily compromise its original elitist character. Although mechanization is said to have been tenaciously resisted by brushmakers (Mattick 1998:11), machines were eventually incorporated into the toothbrush manufacturing process, resulting in a standardizing, homogenizing, and multiplying movement. Up to the 1880s, toothbrushes such as ours still bore a hint of uniqueness in their shape as the unevenness of bristle holes drilled on their head betrayed a semi-industrial manufacturing process in which singularity may have been perceived as a shortcoming. Yet once the bleached boar bristles had been drawn and tied into the brush stock, there was little that could discriminate one toothbrush from another, were it not for the conspicuous variations in size, shape, and softness that differentiated one model from the others. After they were safely packed and shipped from Paris to the ports of Le Havre, Nantes, or Saint-Nazaire, after they were stored in docks, passed through the customs officials' expertise and loaded in the holds of the *Ville de Bordeaux*, the *La Fayette*, the *Louisiane* or another transatlantic steamer, the fetishes-in-the-brushes lay asleep while waiting to be dispatched from their French motherland. Torpid as they might have seemed, every toothbrush was then, indeed, a powerful object waiting to be purchased by someone willing to worship its material individuality as an icon of modern happiness and class (Pinch 1998). Why and how could that primal encounter happen in late 19th century Bogotá?

Seeking Modern Class in a Hybrid City

In the early 1800s Prussian naturalist Alexander von Humboldt visited the moribund viceroyalty of New Granada within the framework of one of the greatest scientific enterprises of his time. Following him, a good number of foreigners, mostly British, French, and American, traveled throughout the Neogranadine territory for diplomatic, scientific, or commercial reasons. Back in their homelands some of them wrote and published extensive accounts of their adventurous trips to the very edge of the civilized world. Most of these records oscillate between a romantic fascination for luscious tropical landscapes virtually untouched by human hands and the deep cultural shock that barbaric ways imposed on modern, educated selves. Many of these 19th-century chronicles actually testify to the impressive analytical skills of some of the authors who cast their imperial glance (Pratt 1992) on the rusticity of Neogranadine customs. These foreign transcripts remain some of the major sources of information on daily life in early republican Colombia until the emergence (typically after 1850) of an artful manners literature in which local educated classes humorously showed off their disregard for popular social sectors (e.g. Cordovez Moure 1978).

Whether foreign or locally based, historical descriptions of republican Bogotá are frequently disdainful, occasionally sympathetic, and rarely appreciative of the scanty charms the remote capital could offer to its visitors. Thus both literate travelers and educated locals usually referred to Bogotá as a hybrid city (cf. Dean and Leibsohn 2003), moving toward modernity in the face of poverty and isolation. It is within this context that, by the mid 19th century, some scientifically based classificatory projects attempted to define discrete human types among the Neogranadine population (e.g. Deas 1989; Rozo 1999). These taxonomic endeavors oversimplified the way in which ethnic and socioeconomic categories were locally permeable and overlapping from countless generations of biological and cultural miscegenation (Gutierrez and Pineda 1999). Insofar as ethnic identity could be difficult to apprehend in a city such as late 19th-century Bogotá, the material expressions of particular lifestyles gained increasing relevance in defining the limits of respectability (cf. Stallybrass 1998) (Figure 4.2). By the time our biographical toothbrush might have reached the capital city of the United States of Colombia, the local bourgeoisie had fallen under the enchantment of

Figure 4.2 Bogotanos at Choachí. From Holton (1857) New Granada: Twenty Months in the Andes. New York: Harper & Brothers

modern materiality. Yet while this nobility revered modern goods that might lend them insight into their desired lifestyles, urban upper classes also celebrated the uniqueness of indigenous material cultures, seizing the materiality of vernacular traditions only to the extent in which this reified the prominence of their social position. Thus, when owned by the elites, wide straw hats, striped woolen blankets, and ocelot skin chaps frequently outlawed the normal trajectories of this popular kind of objects. In the hands of the local bourgeoisie, these artifacts became fetishized as they captured an unsettled, burgeoning national feeling that swung back and forth between a positive notion of what was picturesque and a derogatory one of what was primitive (Spyer 1998). For the republican elites of 19th-century Bogotá, daily consumption was frequently ruled by what Bourdieu (1979) described as the *elective asceticism* of the bourgeoisie. While their economic status virtually gave them an unlimited access to the material offerings of the modern world, local upper classes often chose objects of refined simplicity rather than publicly displaying excessively luxurious modern items. But now, how does a modern artifact such as our biographical toothbrush fit in a republican social scheme shaped by the logics of temperance?

The Sensuous Experience of Modernity

Up the Hills and Down the Dump

Cradled by the ocean throughout their two-week-long transatlantic voyage, the toothbrushes reached the sandy coasts of the New Granada. Under the humid heat of the Caribbean tropics, they were put ashore to be taxed by the national port authorities at Cartagena, Sabanilla, or the soaring Barranquilla. Then, along with other burdens of the most varied origins and kinds, they were loaded onto one of the flat-bottom boats navigating their way through the treacherous sandbanks and whirlpools of the Magdalena River. Their upstream journey would last for an uncertain number of days, mostly depending on the capricious moods of both the river and its bargemen. As long as they remained on their intended track, the toothbrushes were no more fetishes than the hairbrushes, the soap bars, the rose essence flasks, or the ivory combs that shared the exiguity of their hay-filled wooden case. Indeed, all these objects had absorbed the aura of long-distance trade and of rarity. They had all become fetishes of distinction.

As the simple, plain designs of most of the 19th-century toothbrushes suggest, these grooming artifacts were not made to be visually worshiped. They were carved smooth and soft to be felt in the hands and, most importantly, in the mouth; furthermore, as ventilation holes appearing on toothbrushes after 1890 suggest (Mattick 1998:30), they could have even been conceived as objects to be smelt. Artifacts of their kind could still behave as *domesticated fetishes* insofar as the sensuous possibilities of their materiality did not challenge the classificatory order of modern capitalistic consumption. And yet it is wonderful to discover how some toothbrushes made this transition. Their materiality was allowed to develop all its fetishistic power, breaching planned routes and hegemonic taxonomies, invading other sensuous realms than the ones originally addressed in their physicality. In 19th-century New Granada, as in any borderland of the modern world, toothbrushes could literally be consecrated, and transformed into the representation of the unearthly, of the awesome, of the spiritually powerful (Keane 1998); they could be taken away from taste, touch, or smell and be seized by a different sphere of human perception: the visual (cf. Seremetakis 1996). The uncontrolled toothbrush, then, left the realm of action and entered the one of contemplation. It was, truly, on its way to becoming an accomplished fetish.

The metamorphic process through which a modern artifact could acquire a fetishized, pre-modern identity was certainly one of the most puzzling observations that civilized explorers could behold in the frontiers of the modern world. It is not surprising then to come across the fabulous allusion once made by French naturalist Jean-Baptiste Boussingault to the material power of a bone toothbrush. Appointed by the local government to run the first school of mining and engineering to be established in the newborn Republic of Colombia, Boussingault fell to the temptation of tracing particularly sharp critiques of the Neogranadine society. Published in Paris after his death, in 1887, Boussingault's memoirs compile some incredibly perceptive observations such as the quote opening this chapter. In the same witty style that characterizes the narration of his exploratory trips throughout the early 19th-century New Granada, Boussingault portrayed the curious toothbrush theft of which he was once the victim while camping in the wild:

> Among my property, I had an officer canteen with all one could need to cook and dress the table at camp: a marmite, a teapot, some glazed dishes and liquor flasks, etc. and an object of which I was particularly fond, a set of brass candlesticks, quite portable for they would fit together as a snuffbox: they were a real jewel. The next day, as we were about to take off, I missed my brass candlesticks. I then realized someone had pinched my red, Indian silk scarf and my toothbrush as well. (J. B. Boussingault [1892]1994:176, my translation)

At this point, nothing could have predicted the fate of the stolen toothbrush. Indulging himself in the pleasures of storytelling, Boussingault leads his readers into a nearby chapel where they eventually witness a truly staggering sight:

> As I stepped into the church, I found my candlesticks on the altar, next to a wooden image of Our Lady. The Immaculate Virgin wore my red scarf as a mantle and held my toothbrush pressed against her heart. I took back my candlesticks but I didn't want to deprive Our Lady of her mantle; I also left her in possession of my toothbrush, as it was clear to me that the thief had acted with a saintly good intention. (J. B. Boussingault [1892]1994:176, my translation)

The holy destiny of Boussingault's fetishized toothbrush may have actually been shared by many other modernized and modernizing artifacts reaching New Granada throughout the 19th century. Sadly, most material examples of such a fetishization process do not survive the passage of time. While earlier I suggested that modern paraphernalia may have gained a sacred aura through their codified consumption in the borderlands of the modern world, there is little reason to think that, once the modern possibilities inscribed in their materiality had been exhausted, consumed fetishes would end their useful life elsewhere than in a domestic dump. It is within this context that archaeology allows us to delve into Colombian republican life through the recovery of a past materiality not treasured in glass cases as a special acknowledgment of the fineness of its manufacture. It allows us to address the deceptive categorization of what is discardable and what it is not, of what is archaeological and what is not. This differentiation is particularly meaningful in the context of historical archaeology, covering a period of time characterized by soaring production and consumption of an increasingly specialized and segregating materiality, and where the symbolic frontiers of social life were being constantly redefined.

Our biographical toothbrush is part of some past elitist trifles whose material power has been reactivated by means of archaeology. The useless has become priceless; the disposable has been turned museum-worthy. Once it had been washed, once the soil had been wiped away from its tortured surface by the ironical means of an old plastic toothbrush, the three-piece-broken bone toothbrush revealed its sensuous forms. Its restored physicality bore the mark of the cause of its discard; yet, it also showed some evidence of its irreverent recovery. The first, triggered by wear, was the wound that put an end to the life of the modern fetish; the other, induced by desecrating spades, was the scar of its rebirth.

Clean and reconstructed, the toothbrush undertook its first material re-identification. Thanks to archaeologist and historian Barbara Mattick's deep knowledge of 19th-century bone toothbrushes (see Mattick 1998), the brush was given a typological name, a potential origin, and a range of age. It was slowly permeated with a renewed identity that enhanced its fetishized value and made the shades of its patina perceivable. In spite of their artificial arbitrariness, these are categories capable of revealing the force of the fetish to contemporary eyes. Hence, Barbara Mattick's technical diagnostic on the toothbrush's materiality sounds briskly powerful to us:

From my typology, the brush would be an England Type, Maryland variety. Its character-defining attributes are its rounded square head, rounded square base, and the fact that it is flat. The number of rows, shape of the neck, and method of inserting the bristles in the stock also fits this type/variation. The brush appears to have been trepanned since no slits for a wire-drawn brush are visible, and bits of thread are still visible in one of the holes. The broad date range for this kind of brush is 1870–1920, with a mean date range of 1890–1901. Because some of the holes are unevenly drilled, this brush probably dates before 1880. Therefore, my date estimate would be ca. 1870–1879. These brushes were made in England, France, and Japan, but were often unmarked as to place of manufacture. I could not see any imprint anywhere. (Mattick, personal communication on November 2 2000)

The Quinta de Bolivar now offers a juncture where the biography of the toothbrush meets the life story of its owners. Some notarial transcripts kept in Colombian National Archives indicate that, between 1870 and 1880, the Quinta belonged to Don Diego Uribe, a provincial self-made man who had rapidly succeeded in amassing a considerable fortune (see Gaitán In press). An elderly couple by the time they moved to the countryside, Don Diego and his wife, Doña Maria Antonia Restrepo de Uribe, undoubtedly longed for the invigorating air of the Quinta's famed pastoral setting. Moreover, moving away from the polluted vapors of republican Bogotá could have only enhanced the health of their youngest son, Juan Crisóstomo. Sadly, as Don Diego himself wrote in his will,[3] the last of his six children was "thoughtless or mad, absolutely deprived of his mental faculties and sunk in a state of total idiotism." Assuming their fate in the most decorous and temperate way, Don Diego and his wife provided all their care and affection to their beloved son, for they thought that the acceptance of their child's unfortunate fate could only substantiate the firmness of their Christian faith.

Indeed, a sacralized bone toothbrush was no more an out-of-place commodity in Diego Uribe's bedroom than it was a superfluous item in young Pilar's trousseau. Yet even in the clearly gentrified environment in which the Uribes lived, their toothbrush was unique. In the cesspool that was temporarily used as their household's dump, the toothbrush stood out as the only item of its kind among more than forty earthenware pots and jars, nearly thirty whiteware plates, and some twenty cups made of white ironstone or immaculate French porcelain. Perhaps even at the time when we may presume it was used for its original purpose, the toothbrush's singularity defied the unstable border between the commodity and the fetish.

And it Read Extra Fine, Paris

Little more than a century has been enough to stabilize the toothbrush's identity. By September 2000, there is no doubt that the bone brush had fully accomplished its gestation as a fetish. It became the showpiece of the first public archaeology project to have been initiated in Bogotá. It has been the talk of the cultural elite of the city and was featured in the cultural sections of both print and broadcast media. The visitors to the House Museum Quinta de Bolivar, mostly schoolchildren, crowded by the gate of the dark and narrow room where an improvised archaeological lab had been installed. Casting a glance at this very special thing was, for them, a multi-sensuous experience, mixing an exciting expectancy for the unusual with some awe for the ancient and a little condescendence for the pre-modern. Some people even risked touching the fetish, so as to get a more intimate contact with its materiality: it felt cold, smooth, and nice, they said. And it is to the general public that the toothbrush gave away its ultimate secret. As it circulated from hand to hand on a clear October afternoon, the sun illuminated the unnoticed birthmark that the brush bore on its handle; it read EXTRA FINE PARIS.

A few months after the revelation – collapsing historical categories and chronological exactitude – the toothbrush invaded Simon Bolivar's bedroom as it became part of the permanent collection of the Museum through which Colombia pays a tribute to the memory of its liberator. Since then, it has stood on a small red wooden pedestal suggesting to visitors that this odd piece of bone is somewhat different from the other objects in the room. From its privileged position the toothbrush seems to be mocking its once better-off companions standing on Bolivar's English acajou commode – the silver ewer and basin, the fine cologne water flask, and the blue rimmed porcelain soap case. Although it is now broken, although its bristles are now gone, its material power is greater than it ever was; this toothbrush is now a fetish and will not be forgotten anymore.

Acknowledgments

I would like to thank Lynn Meskell for encouraging me to contribute to this publication. My gratitude also goes to Meredith Linn, Lizzie Martin, Jessica Striebel McLean, Elena Uprimny and, especially, Nan Rothschild for their insightful comments on earlier drafts of this chapter. Many thanks to Barbara Mattick for allowing me to include some of our electronic conversations in this chapter. Finally, thanks to Daniel Castro and to all the staff in the Casa Museo Quinta de Bolivar for their support throughout this project.

Notes

1   Mrs. Sixta Pontón was the widow of General Francisco de Paula Santander, first president of the Republic of New Granada. She was considered to be one of the most distinguished, intelligent, and virtuous ladies of her time and, in 1852, she became one of the first women to receive voting rights in the American continent. Her school was utterly selective and admitted a very small number of students. Mrs. Pontón's institution was known to impart a very strict discipline on young ladies; it offered courses on Catholic religion, Castilian grammar, arithmetic, accountancy, geometry, geography, physics, astronomy, history, Italian, French, English, morals, music, painting, and singing (Londoño 1996).
2   Archivo General de la Nación, Sección Notarías. Notaría 2a de Bogotá volumen 307. Folios 93–95.
3   Archivo General de la Nación, Sección Notarías, Notaría 2a de Bogotá volumen 498. Folios 607r–616 (1884).

References

Andrén, A. 1998 Between Artifacts and Texts: Historical Archaeology in Global Perspective. New York: Plenum Press.
Appadurai, A. 1986 Commodities and the Politics of Value. *In* The Social Life of Things: Commodities in Cultural Perspective. A. Appadurai, ed. Pp. 3–58. Cambridge NY: Cambridge University Press.
Bourdieu, P. 1979 La Distinction. Critique sociale du jugement. Paris: Les Editions de Minuit.
—— 1990 The Logic of Practice. Stanford: Stanford University Press.
Boussingault, J-B. 1994[1892] Memorias. Bogotá: Banco de la República.
Bushnell, D. 1996 Colombia, una nación a pesar de sí misma: de los tiempos precolombinos a nuestros días. Santafé de Bogotá: Planeta.

Carnegie-Williams, R. 1882 A Year in the Andes or A Lady's Adventures in Bogota. London: London Literary Society.

Cordovez Moure, J. M. 1978 Reminiscencias de Santafé y Bogotá. Biblioteca Básica Colombiana. Bogotá: Instituto Colombiano de Cultura.

Csikszentmihalyi, M. 1993 Why We Need Things. *In* History from Things: Essays on Material Culture. S. Lubar and W. D. Kingery, eds. Pp. 20–29. Washington DC: Smithsonian Institution Press.

Davis, R. 1997 Lives of Indian Images. Princeton: Princeton University Press.

Dean, C., and D. Leibsohn 2003 Hybridity and its Discontents: Considering Visual Culture in Colonial Spanish America. Colonial Latin American Review 12(1):7–35.

Deas, M., E. Sánchez, and A. Martínez 1989 Types and Customs of New Granada: The Collection of Paintings Made in Colombia by Joseph Brown Between 1825 and 1841 and the Journal of his Excursion to Girón, 1834. Bogotá: Fondo Cultural Cafetero.

Dornan, J. 2002 Agency and Archaeology: Past, Present, and Future Directions. Journal of Archaeological Method and Theory 9(4):303–328.

Dupré, J. 1993 The Disorder of Things. Metaphysical Foundations Of The Disunity Of Science. Cambridge, MA: Harvard University Press.

Edwards, E. 2001 Raw Histories: Photographs, Anthropology and Museums. New York: Berg.

Elias, N. 1973 La civilisation des moeurs. Paris: Calman-Lévy.

—— 1974 La société de cour. Paris: Calman-Lévy.

Foucault, M. 1966 Les mots et les choses: Une archéologie des sciences humaines. Paris: Gallimard.

Gaitán, F. 2003 Recordando a los Uribe: Memorias de higiene y de templanza en la Bogotá del Olimpo Radical. Revista de Antropología y Arqueología 13(1):125–146.

—— In press Expresiones de Modernidad en la Quinta de Bolívar: Arqueología de la alta burguesía bogotana en tiempos del Olimpo Radical (1870–1880). Bogotá: Universidad de los Andes – CESO.

Goffman, E. 1990 The Presentation of Self in Everyday Life. New York: Doubleday Anchor Books.

Gosden, C., and Y. Marshall 1999 The Cultural Biography of Objects. World Archaeology: The Cultural Biography of Objects 31(2):169–178.

Gutiérrez de Pineda, V., and R. Pineda Giraldo 1999 Miscegenación y cultura en la Colombia colonial, 1750–1810. Bogotá: Conciencias, Universidad de los Andes.

Hall, M. 2000 Archaeology and the Modern World: Colonial Transcripts in South Africa and the Chesapeake. London: Routledge.

Holtorf, C. 2002 Notes on the Life History of a Pot Sherd. Journal of Material Culture 7(1):49–71.

Hoskins, J. 1998 Biographical Objects: How Things Tell the Stories of People's Lives. New York: Routledge.

Keane, W. 1998 Calvin in the Tropics: Objects and Subjects at the Religious Frontier. *In* Border Fetishisms: Material Objects In Unstable Places. P. Spyer, ed. Pp. 13–34. New York: Routledge.

Kirshenblatt-Gimblett, B. 1998 Destination Culture: Tourism, Museums and Heritage. Berkeley: University of California Press.

Kopytoff, I. 1986 The Cultural Biography of Things: Commoditization as Process. In: Appadurai (ed.), The Social Life of Things: Commodities in Cultural Perspective. A. Appadurai, ed. Pp. 64–91. Cambridge: Cambridge University Press.

Latour, B. 1991 We Have Never Been Modern. Cambridge: Harvard University Press.

Legêne, S. 1998 From Brooms to Obeah and Back: Fetish Conversion and Border Crossings in Nineteenth-Century Suriname. *In* Border Fetishisms: Material Objects In Unstable Places. P. Spyer, ed. Pp. 35–59. New York: Routledge.

Leone, M., and P. Potter 1988 Issues in Historical Archaeology. *In* The Recovery of Meaning. Historical Archaeology in the Eastern United States. M. Leone and P. Potter, eds. Pp. 1–22. Washington: Smithsonian Institution Press.

Londoño, P. 1996 Educación de la mujer en la joven República. Boletín Cultural y Bibliográfico del Banco de la República 31(37):n.a.

Mattick, B. 1998 Bone Toothbrushes of the 19th & 20th Centuries: A History and a Typology Based on Brushes from the Roberts Collection. MA thesis, Department of Anthropology, Florida State University.

McGreevey, W. 1982 Historia económica de Colombia. 1845–1930. Bogotá: Ediciones Tercer Mundo.

Meskell, L. 2004 Object Worlds in Ancient Egypt: Material Biographies Past and Present. London: Berg.

Miller, D. 1987 Material Culture And Mass Consumption. Oxford: Blackwell.

—— 1998 Material Cultures: Why Some Things Matter. London: UCL Press; Chicago: University of Chicago Press.

Nieto Arteta, L. E. 1975 Economía y cultura en la historia de Colombia. Bogotá: Editora Viento del Pueblo.

O'Neill, T. 1999 The Lives of the Tibeto-Nepalese Carpet. Journal of Material Culture 4(1):21–38.

Pedraza, Z. 1999 En cuerpo y alma. Visiones del progreso y de la felicidad. Bogotá: Universidad de los Andes.

Pels, P. 1998 The Spirit of Matter: On Fetish, Rarity, Fact, and Fancy. *In* Border Fetishisms: Material Objects in Unstable Places. P. Spyer, ed. Pp. 91–121. New York: Routledge.

Pinch, A. 1998 Stealing Happiness: Shoplifting in Early Nineteenth-Century England. *In* Border Fetishisms: Material Objects in Unstable Places. P. Spyer, ed. Pp. 122–149. New York: Routledge.

Pratt, M. L. 1992 Imperial Eyes: Travel, Writing and Transculturation. London: Routledge.

Rozo, E. 1999 Naturaleza, paisaje y sensibilidad en la Comisión Corográfica. Revista de Antropología y Arqueología 11(1–2):71–116.

Saunders, N. 1999 Biographies of Brilliance: Pearls, Transformations of Matter and Being, c. A.D. 1492. World Archaeology: The Cultural Biography of Objects, 31(2):243–257.
Seip, L. 1999 Transformations of Meaning: The Life History of a Nuxalk Mask. World Archaeology: The Cultural Biography of Objects 31(2):272–287.
Seremetakis, C. (ed.) 1996 Senses Still: Perception and Memory as Material Culture in Modernity. Chicago: University of Chicago Press.
Shackel, P. 1993 Personal Discipline and Material Culture. An Archaeology of Annapolis, Maryland, 1695–1870. Knoxville: The University of Tennessee Press.
Spyer P. 1998 The Tooth of Time, or Taking a Look at the "Look" of Clothing in Late Nineteenth-Century Aru. *In* Border Fetishisms: Material Objects in Unstable Places. P. Spyer, ed. Pp. 150–182. New York: Routledge.
Stallybrass, P. 1998 Marx's Coat. *In* Border Fetishisms: Material Objects in Unstable Places. P. Spyer, ed. Pp. 183–207. New York: Routledge.
Strathern, M. 1988 The Gender of the Gift: Problems with Women and Problems with Society in Melanesia. Berkeley: University of California Press.
Taussig, M. 1993 Mimesis and Alterity: A Particular History of the Senses. New York: Routledge.
Tirado Mejía, A. 1988 Introducción a la historia económica de Colombia. Bogotá: El Ancora.
Wurst, L., and R. Fitts 1999 Introduction: Why Confront Class? Historical Archaeology, 33(1):1–6.
Yentsch, A. 1993 Legends, Houses, Families, and Myths: Relationships Between Material Culture and American Ideology. *In* Documentary Archaeology in the New World. M. Beaudry, ed. Pp. 5–19. London: Cambridge University Press.

5

Faith in Objects: American Indian Object Lessons at the World in Boston

Erin Hasinoff

> There are some caravans laden with rich gems and spices, with all manner of curious and precious things, which only enter Mansoul by way of Eyegate.
> Pilgrim's Progress, *Handbook and Guide to the World in Boston*, 1911

This chapter is a synthesis of the fragmentary missionary and anthropology archived texts describing the World in Boston (April 24 to May 20, 1911), "America's first great missionary exposition" (New York Times 1911). I provide a first glance at the large-scale late 19th- and early 20th-century North American missionary expositions, adding to a vast literature on the exhibition history of World's Fairs, and ethnological and natural history museums (Conn 1998; Jacknis 1985; Kirshenblatt-Gimblett 1990; Rydell 1984). I propose the idea that in the late Victorian frenzy of the visible (Pels 2003:263), object lessons were the principal pedagogy of the day. In considering the didactic nature of "things," I push the boundary of this literature into discussions of materiality, or how we appropriate the material character of the world around us, and the various ways we materialize social being (Buchli 2002:18; Graves-Brown 2000:1). I treat materiality as an objectifying discourse, a sleight of hand that evokes wonder and instantiates change.

With the advent of the World in Boston, the widely popular English phenomenon of the missionary exhibition took root in the United States.

American Indian Object Lessons at the World in Boston

The Young People's Missionary Movement (YPMM)[1] borrowed the idea of the exhibition from the well-publicized and attended Orient in London (1908). In keeping with the Orient in London, material culture was choreographed and exhibited in Boston as visible proof of the expansion of Protestant Christendom to the far reaches of the world: the Americas, Africa, "Mohammedan Lands," Japan, China, and India. The exposition's object world fabricated a dual relationship; one that both enchanted future missionaries and educated America's polyglot population about the progress of evangelism.

The objects displayed in Boston mediated between those remote peoples and the more "advanced Christians" whose mandate it was, under the doctrine of Manifest Destiny, to spread the Gospel to them. In the United States those remote peoples were, above all, American Indians; "Our foreigners at home" (see Jonaitis 1992:46; The World in Boston 1911:46). The exhibit underscored the assimilative progress of the Indians from "lowly aborigines" to "civilized Christians" under the Board of Home Missions (BHM) of the Presbyterian Church of America.[2] As an introduction to the exposition, the American Indians section summarized the success of the missions in spreading Christianity to American Indians and from them to the unenlightened world in general. In this way, the work of the home missions was introduced as an object lesson for which subsequent Christianization abroad could follow.

Ethnological artifacts, on loan from the American Museum of Natural History (AMNH), and missionary objects contributed by participating Protestant missionary boards were assembled in the exhibition hall to cover the whole world. In the American Indians section, artifacts from the AMNH appear to have provided the necessary scientific legitimacy that underscored the social evolutionism illustrated by the World in Boston. The exhibition's exegetical aim was scientifically validated, and anthropological theory in turn disseminated. American Indian handwork sold at the Foreign Sales Stalls provided visible proof of the nascent potential of converts as producers of objects that conformed to non-Native material worlds and tastes. In this way, exhibition organizers presented pre-Christians as having the potential for social progress and moral reform through missionary intervention, coupled with Christian education and handicraft production.

Erin Hasinoff

Object Lessons

Protestantism was self-represented as a religion of the Word and was accordingly seen as being antagonistic to matter, materiality, and materialism (Keane 1996; 2002; 2005; and see Meyer 1997). And yet, recognizing the efficacy of the Roman Catholic Mass as a potent object lesson in portraying the sufferings of Christ, American Protestant denominations sought Catholicism's objectifying discourse. During the first part of the 20th century, a surplus of Christian books appeared incorporating the term "object lessons." Reverend W. H. Woolston, "The Object Man" and "Gospel Illustrator for the Common People," asked in a book entitled, *Seeing Truth: A Book of Object Lessons with Magical and Mechanical Effects*; "If Catholics can do so much by the use of objects with only a half truth, how much more can we, as Protestants do with the whole truth?" (1910:197). The powers of words and objects were recognized as being completely and mutually dependent, and consequently, truth was effectively material.

Object teaching was presumed to be a mighty propaganda which set forth through objects and actions the Holy truth. The justification that Woolston gave for object lessons was that they conjured up the scriptures and were not in any crude opposition to Protestant Christianity's evasion of the material world. He argued the Bible was full of visible illustrations, and it was also the best primer on object teaching the world had ever known. And so Woolston articulated that Jesus, the "Greatest of Teachers," used this method constantly in His teachings: "He compares his precious body to broken bread and His Holy Blood to the fruit of the vine, two of the common objects of the common people" (1911:197).

Woolston (1911:15) writes that we need not hesitate to use the common objects of everyday life. Christ used the most common objects of everyday life to teach the highest and most holy lessons of the High life and God. In Woolston's teaching, "sin" could be effectively materialized in a Sunday school lesson with "three colored handkerchiefs and a rubber band," or deeds that multiply through a "multiplying plate." Object teaching, however mundane, was considered to be God's method, and therefore supremely dignified and divinely correct. It could not be considered disparaging to those who employed it, or a lowering of the high function of the pulpit. The object and the Word were conflated.

Object lessons provided direct access to the scriptures; "truth made shining and as clear as crystal" (Woolston 1911:197).

The World in Boston drew on the popularity of such objectifying discourse as that of Woolston. In entertaining and instructing the largest possible public in evangelism, "the triumph of the teachings of Christ over the Pagan religions and the moral darkness of the Heathen world" was substantiated (London Missionary Society 1908:80). The exposition effectively materialized the spread of the Gospel. Evangelism was presented not as it was but as it was envisioned, underscoring the imaginative geography of Christianity. Salvation was presented as being freely available, and efficacious for all non-Christians. Consequently, and paradoxically, the materiality of the exhibition was apprehended as being congenial to the core of a fundamentally immaterial Protestant Christianity.

The American Indians

The American Indians section was located to the right side of the main entrance of the exhibition hall (Figure 5.1). It was the aim of the exhibition organizers "to avoid the purely spectacular and Wild West features so widely exploited" during this time. With the invention of Buffalo Bill Cody's Wild West Show in 1882 stereotypes of Indianness came to be inscribed with unprecedented vividness and reached unparalleled numbers of people (Phillips 2001:31). Instead, exhibit organizers lent themselves to "truthfully portraying the manner of life, habitations, and dress of American Indians and the work being done for them" (WIB 1911:62). And yet, the exhibition amounted to a material spectacle of the Wild West, though in a Christian context and with a scientific tone.

The enormous diversity of Indian tribes in language, customs, and costumes was underscored as restricting the extent to which each group could be dealt with in the exhibit. The aim was to portray the most central features that could be adequately represented in a limited scope. So as to permit the most complete coverage of the continent possible within the exhibition space, the American tribes were grouped broadly and manageably into a four-fold classification: the Indians of the Southwest, Indians of the Plains, Indians who live in the woods, and Alaskan Indians (WIB 1911:62).

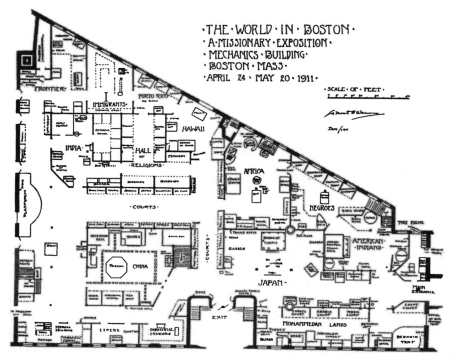

Figure 5.1 Floorplan of the World in Boston. Handbook and Guide to the World in Boston, 1911

Particular attention was given to exhibiting and reproducing the dwellings of the four regions as close to their natural size as space permitted. The structures were presented as being iconic of the North American Indian tribes. However only the "rude structures" (the hogan, tepee, and lodge) were reconstructed in the section's three corners, while the more "advanced houses" (pueblo and stone and mortar) were depicted on the exhibit's walls (WIB 1911:61–66).[3] The stone and mortar construction of the "cliff dwellers," a "former race" unrelated to the historically known and living Native Americans exemplified the latter more permanent structures (WIB 1911:63).

In this way, the cliff dwellers were situated in a distant and remote past, discontinuous with the destitute present of contemporary North American Indians. To apply Edward B. Tylor's (1896:xix) notion of degeneration to the exhibit, traces of the remote ancestral culture were thought only to be kept up in scanty and perverted memory as "survivals" of the foregrounded tribes degraded from the far nobler state which formed a background to the American Indians section. However connected Native Americas were to these structures, their presumed lack of ancestral memory and purported lack of skill effectively removed them as descendants, consequently validating the missionaries' role of intervention (cf. Fine-Dare 2002:37–39). Like other ranked forms of material culture, the dwellings were not only a visible illustration of the prehistoric state of progress reached, or inscribed in a particular hierarchy, but also of the necessity for missionaries to uplift their inhabitants from their sullied contemporary state.[4]

The most conspicuous structure in the American Indians section was the "Indian Christian Chapel" situated at the center of the exhibit. According to the floorplan to the WIB, it was constructed over four times the size of the Native American dwellings. The Chapel, modeled after the John Eliot Chapel in Tucson, Arizona, was presented as typifying the Christian missions to the North American Indians. Its interior testified to the advancement of Christianity with photographs of Indian missions and missionaries, Indian pastors, and church members from across the country displayed on its walls (WIB 1911:66).

The Chapel established distance between the backward Indian tribes of America's frontier and Christian civilization, set against the smaller scale, rudimentary, and impermanent dwellings of the four regions. While the dwellings were installed to represent regional disparateness, the Chapel characterized the civilizing force of Christianity in its material and symbolic assimilation of all Indians under one God and one church roof. The structure provided an object lesson of Christianity's successful expansion and the movement of Native Americans toward civilization (WIB 1911:66). Conversion was reinforced by the distance between the dwellings and the Chapel, giving public testimony to the ontological change that had transpired.

Notes for Stewards in the North American Indian Scene

Stewards gave talks to small groups of visitors about the exhibit and the work done for Indians in the Board of Home Missions of the Presbyterian Church in proselytizing Native American societies. Congregation members of the Presbyterian Church were selected for this role and were trained according to a guide entitled, *Notes for Stewards in the American Indians Scene* (Missionary Education Movement in the United States and Canada 1911). Topics included in the guide covered a wide range, from "the reservation system and land in 'severalty'" to "ancient industries and arts, their implements, games, folk-lore music and religion" (Humphrey 1912:12).

Prior to the opening of the World in Boston, seven hundred stewards organized themselves into informal weekly classes where they met to study American Indian life and domestic mission work outlined by the guide, and supplemented by missionary literature (Humphrey to Wissler, February 25, 1911).[5] In presentations to the public, the stewards discussed the various phases of mission work with visitors while "giving out copious information about the life conditions and religion in North America" (YPMM 1911:4). The talks appear to have helped to verify that the congregations' dollars had been well spent, and publicized the domestic mission's success in the field, thereby attracting new subscriptions for the cause (Altick 1978:299; Cannizzo 1998:166; Corbey 2000:59).

The organizing society, the Young People's Missionary Movement, specified that stewards had the most important role as interpreters. Costumed in the attire of Native Americans from "the plains and woods," they represented pre-Christian Indians attending to their domestic duties while answering visitors' questions about their activities (WIB 1911:66). In demonstrating the condition of the peoples among whom work was being done, the stewards provided insight into the labor of the various mission fields, thereby elucidating the overarching message of the expansion of Christianity. The stewards, inserted into the object world of the Native Americans, brokered its physical presence. The performance of Indianness gave material form to identities which were usurped by Protestant Christianity, affording a foundation for subsequent pursuits of a Christianized national identity (cf. Deloria 1998:7). Without the stewards, the YPMM (1911:4) feared that the exhibition would become mere show and that the promise of Christianity, revealed by the way the objects were presented in the exhibition, would be lost.

The displayed objects did not provide their own narrative. They were to be textualized, and thus required written and verbal explication in the form of handbooks and visual illustrations if they were to be anything more than a mere accumulation of disoriented, albeit wondrous, objects (cf. Breckenridge 1989:205). As such, the explications offered by the

Handbook and Guide to the World in Boston appear to have been altogether insufficient. For this reason, stewards were effectively ventriloquists whose task it was to make the objects speak, or rather, to narrativize the objects (Kirshenblatt-Gimblett 1990:398).

In enkindling the visitors' interest in the exhibit and communicating the success of evangelism, the stewards gave illustrated talks on the power of the Gospel in reaching the Native American world, moving between the civility of the Chapel and the primitive wilds of the dwellings. Here the quotidian was available for contemplation, the life space of others effectively penetrated, and consequently the incongruity between Christian civilization and Native life established. The purpose of the exhibition was to subordinate the objects on display to this disparity. Accordingly, the stewards demonstrated through the eye ("Eyegate") and the ear ("Eargate") the sustained need of the American Indians for the Gospel (YPMM 1911:4).

The eye was considered far more helpful than the ear in conveying accurate impressions even when lecturers were adept at "word-painting" (LMS 1908:4). In keeping with the Orient in London, textual descriptions and lectures were taken to be unsatisfactory. The eye was understood as the broker of the soul. No sense other than sight was considered to bring so many things to the soul. Wonder could be excited through the eye, thereby remaining an easy avenue for instruction for the message of the Gospel to the masses (cf. Buck-Morss 1989:87).

Nevertheless, if the eye and the ear were effectively combined, information could be communicated easily and pleasantly, and the visitor could "see truth" (LMS 1908:4; Philips 1910:11). Since truth was something following on wonder, rather than inherent to it, "word-painting" was an attempt at controlling wonder's potential insubordination (Pels 1998:107). To this end, it was held that if the object lesson succeeded with minimum intellectual effort on the spectator's part, great truth or righteousness could be seen.

Our Native American Folklore

While the stewards acted as interlocutors, five Carlisle Indian School students in the Chapel were, in effect, cosseted showcases (Humphrey 1912:10). Though having advanced from a "primitive" to a "civilized" state, the self-representing Native Americans were precluded from enacting their pre-Christian lives or the unredeemed lives of other tribal members. Their progress could only be witnessed when set against the costumed stewards' performances and discussions of those Indians as of yet unreached by Christianity. The American Indians who came under the audience's gaze were made to appear in dress and demeanor as players in the constructed theater of power: their roles signaled by prescribed dress, their parts authored by Christians who sought to determine how American Indians were to act in the scenes they had constructed (cf. Cohn 1996:10).

In missionary discourse and exhibition, dress was relied on to tacitly acknowledge the difference between Christian Self and non-Christian Other. Clothes were important as an object lesson precisely because they were the outward representation of the state of the soul, an index of conscience. Moreover, dress was essential to the inculcation of modesty and civility (Keane 2005:14; McAllister 1998:128; Spyer 1998:154). Proper dress simultaneously declared a person's Christianity and manifested one's inner redemption. In contrast to the stewards' narrated enactments of the tribal condition, the presentation of the American Indians, clothed in Christ's deliverance, provided visible proof of the success of Christianity. In this way, dress instantiated change for both the convert and the spectator.

In the American Indians section the palpable juxtaposition between the evangelized and the primitive was intended to convey the effectiveness of the proselytizing activities of the Presbyterian Church. The movement of the Native American students was circumscribed by the Chapel, which represented the shared humanity of Christianity at the interstice between this world and the "primitive" world from which they had been saved. The student's "Sunday Best" implied a new temporal order and a new spatial orientation. The Chapel was both a space of worship on the Sabbath and a theater in which Native Americans enacted their conversion (see also Thomas 1999:18). The Native Americans, having been converted and in the process undertaken a Christian education leading to their moral improvement, were themselves object lessons in the World in Boston.

In the words of Thomas King (2003:68) "Native Americans were performers in an Aboriginal minstrel show for White North America." Native performances were a conventional modernist scene mounted for the pleasure of large White audiences, typical to the World's Fairs of the

19th and early 20th centuries. At the St. Louis World's Fair in 1904, the desirability of civilizing North American Indian peoples was an important subject. Their "dull-minded and self-centered tribal existence" had to be replaced by the "active, constructive and broad-minded life of modern humanity" (Francis 1913:529, quoted in Corbey 1993:344). The fairs, framed by way of this progressivist ideology, confirmed in Westerners a sense of their own racial and cultural superiority.

The imposition of internal colonialism and assimilation practices characterized the Fairs in the United States and appears to have resonated well with the World in Boston. However the exposition and other missionary expositions of the time went one step further in demonstrating the redeemable nature of Natives through object conversion and education. Evangelism – partnered with social progress – presumed shared humanity and potential human equality and entailed an interest in the incorporation of the other rather than the mere imagination of a savage condition which was separate, distant, and inferior (Thomas 1991:152). Salvage ethnography – the mission to preserve native cultures and their "things" believed threatened with extinction – became the rhetorical frame through which spectators were invited to regard native inhabitants as relics of a forgotten age (Griffiths 2002:79). The Indian students were living examples of those who, with such intervention, had been excised from the very savage state construed by the stewards. Though Native peoples were represented in the exhibition as being primitive, their potential, as realized through missionary intervention, was also articulated.

Under the direction of Reverend William Brewster Humphrey, the American Indians section coordinator and the Executive Secretary of the Board of Home Missions of the Presbyterian Church of America, five Indian students participated by singing the harmonized songs from the collection, *Native American Folk-lore*, in the Chapel. The songs were intended to take their audience through the life of an Indian "from the papoose board to the grave" (Humphrey 1913:7). Just as Indianness was revised in the exhibit by the White stewards, so too were the songs harmonized and rewritten by Humphrey: "To render in English the true meaning as understood in the Indian's mind considerable amplification is necessary" (1913:2).

Leaving the exhibition with a copy of the booklet from the Book Stall, visitors could sing the songs Humphrey had made discernable to the Western ear, such as the Arapho "Lullaby," the Chippewa child's song, "Why Should I be Jealous," and the Navajo song of home, "The Hogan Blessed" (Humphrey to Wissler, February 25, 1911; Humphrey 1913:10) at home or in church, and reiterate the evangelical success of the domestic missions' activities in the field. In this way the exhibition organizers achieved the purpose of such booklets "to educate and inspire the mind after the eye had seen the exhibits" (WIB 1911:92). The sheet music was a palpable and auditory object lesson that the missionaries had successfully assimilated "our foreigners at home."

Although a fragment of Native American reality, the songs were also intended, and accepted, as a means of making the unfamiliar and exotic tangibly accessible for the visitors in a Christian environment. The directness and immediacy of live performances would have confronted audiences with the fact of the Native performers' contemporaneousness and bodily presence at a time when missionary exhibitions constituted the earliest interactions that many Americans, and particularly those from the Northeastern seaboard, would have had with Native Americans. The effect of the performance would have been somewhat analogous to travel to the Christianized American frontier, with its reality insured by the presentation of Indian students. At the World in Boston, the realism of the display was intended to be a brokered substitution for the direct experience most visitors would never have had (cf. Jenkins 1994:247; Lee 1999b:37).

As Native American culture was being uprooted, missionary societies objectified it in the context of performances. At the exposition, Native American culture was represented as having undergone a transition from the disparate dwellings of the four geographical regions of the exhibit to the harmonized songs in the integrated Chapel. With the harmonized songs performed by the American Indian students, visitors were made aware that lyrics were vestiges of a Native American culture which had come to properly belong to American tradition. The songs were relegated to the past, in what Bruce Trigger (1989:295) calls "conscious archaism," and were thereby considered as underpinning contemporary sanitized expressions, or folklore. Thus, Native American folklore objectively demonstrated the assimilationist claim of Manifest Destiny. As William Brewster Humphrey wrote in the Annual Report of the American Indian League, "The nation is becoming aroused as never before to the necessity of preserving its own folklore. American Indian music today is one of the foremost topics on our lecture and concert platforms and in the papers and magazines of the country" (1913:9).

Handwork

While the showcased Native Americans had been excluded from the presentations of Indians attending to their domestic duties, space was provided in the World in Boston for the performance of their industrial activities. In the Indians of the Southwest display, the Navajo were presented as "a shepherd people especially gifted in making blankets" which were "so tightly woven that they could hold water" (WIB 1911:63). Here, the technical ability of Navajo weavers and their capacity to make a good living from the sale of their blankets was highlighted (Humphrey 1913:13).

During the exhibition, an Indian student wove a blanket on a native loom next to the reconstructed hogan, demonstrating her skill at an industry for which peoples of the Southwest were noted. The young Native American's ability to weave established her untapped potential for improvement, which could only be realized through missionary pedagogic regimes (Eves 1998:51; WIB 1911:13). Native craftsmanship and ingenuity was considered a measure of the extent to which a group could be uplifted. The Indian's weaving was an object lesson of the latent possibility of the Indians of the Southwest, and the American Indians in general, to be civilized and educated in Western habits and demeanor.

From the late 19th to the early 20th century, industry was viewed as the culmination of a progression of the "Anglo-Saxon race" from its primitive roots and a possible means of all others to social progress (Bronner 1989:224). Consequently, weaving indexed not only the state of progress reached, but the potential of the Indians of the Southwest to proceed to a higher level of civilization. Considering Native culture was doomed to be relegated to the past, missionaries saw it as their moral imperative to replace its institutions with their own (Krech 1999:11; Lee 1999b:37–38). The positive acknowledgment of craft skills spoke clearly of the missionary program of fabricated cultural change. By presenting industries at which the Indians excelled, domestic missions emphasized to White congregations that Native Americans were capable of being morally uplifted through Western education and industrial advancement, and above all, successfully assimilated as Christians.

If education was integral to the project of civilizing Native Americans, it was the ulterior motive of the Protestant churches to provide access to the Christian Bible. Mission schools were part of the institutional policies set in motion by the Dawes Act of 1887, also known as the Allotment Act, which was endorsed to impose assimilation by breaking up the great tribal mass (Dubin 2001:21, Penney and Roberts 1999:22). Reformers had intended to Americanize the Indians by destroying tribalism and its communal base and substituting individualism which marked White society. However, it was the federal government's ongoing neglect of its educational responsibilities to Indian Americans that reinforced the home missions' activities in according teachers an active role in conversion (Lee 1999b:38). The educational curriculum of the Presbyterian Church in particular included a strong component of Christian doctrine emphasizing moral uplift. In all, the legislation that had been designed to indoctrinate Indians with American civilization and reform them into citizens also led to their conversion. The Americanism that was imposed upon the Native Americans was conceived in evangelical Protestant terms.

The American Indians section of the WIB conformed to the missionary view that native industry was indexical to the potential of group improvement. However, what the Board of Home Missions had in mind in preparing the exhibit was not simply the replacement of Native industry with Christian education, but rather its maintenance and augmentation. The Board appears to have been influenced by the philanthropic movement, which since the 1880s had worked to promote Native American material culture because of a view of its value to America as a uniquely American contribution to the world.

Whereas Americans may have tended to recoil at the Native American aesthetic, by the 19th century a taste for a distinctly American art had developed. A new economic elite in North America, allied with an affluent middle class, financed expeditions of "salvage" anthropology to collect or record objects, myths, and descriptions of industries and ceremonial practices. Native Americans had been appropriated as their pre-modern ancestors, an ideological construction designed to define American identity (see Cohodas 1999:145–146; Patterson 1998:14; Wade 1985:168–176). Of additional significance to the philanthropists was a hegemonic perception of the possibility of a Native American "art," in the Western sense of the term, both as a cultural endeavor and as an economic activity (Penney and Roberts 1999:23).[6]

What the philanthropists considered art, the Board of Home Missions regarded as "handwork." Handwork consolidated the emphasis on the potential skill of Native Americans as manufacturers of ingeniously crafted objects. The Board appears to have been concerned primarily with encouraging the production of a marketable commodity congenial to Christianity that could improve the moral and economic condition of Native Americans on reservations rather than fostering "traditional" Indian art. Central to the conversion of Native Americans was their economic upliftment through participation in the market economy as producers of objects conforming to non-Native material worlds and tastes.

The Board appears to have seen objects that were made with Euro-American materials (or with overt paraphrases of Euro-American forms) as visible proof of the nascent potential of the recently Christianized. The Board displayed standard commodities American Indians were thought to excel at producing, and offered them for sale alongside goods from other mission fields at the Foreign Sales Stalls in the exhibition. Articles for purchase included dolls dressed in native costumes, embroidered waists, dresses, and shawls (WIB 1911:63, 94). These hybrid objects provided visible proof that natives were willing to incorporate non-Native materials, and more abstractly, American and Christian concepts into their lives (cf. Gardner 2000:48).

Objects of the American Indian League

Reverend William Brewster Humphrey had founded the American Indian League (AIL) with his wife, Marie E. Ives Humphrey, in 1910 "to assist in preserving native industries; establishing if need be, industrial schools and missions where the young Indians might be taught to keep up the old arts." In so doing, it was their intention "to arouse interest in the North American customs and to preserve and foster their native music and industries in every possible way" in making "a market for their handicrafts" (Humphrey 1912:7).

The Humphreys' work differed from the philanthropists who found their sole goal in preserving and conveying the unique and special characteristics of Native American Indian art. While secular philanthropists were concerned with showing the nation that this was a heritage worth saving, the Humphreys endeavored to reform the American Indians because of "a realization of what they [could] add to the country's assets" "with all the rights and responsibilities that citizenship implies" (Humphrey 1912). In the AIL Annual Report for 1912 William Humphrey writes:

> No work could be more patriotic than that which strives to ameliorate the conditions of the backward races of our land and make them self-supporting. Especially is this true when in so doing it is possible to preserve one of the greatest treasures America possesses, namely its ancient arts and industries. It is this supreme and patriotic function that the League has undertaken. (AIL 1913:3)

The Humphreys' activities were not dissimilar to the work of the Presbyterian industrial missions. The industrial missions emphasized that "working with the hands" had an equal value to "book learning." The gospel of work was preached on the colonized periphery to instill the self-discipline and self-denial that would make people good American wage earners. It taught the disciplines of punctuality, cleanliness, moral purity, self-restraint, and industriousness that were required of efficient workers and good Christians. In this way, religious improvement and character formation were seen as being closely related to disciplined work and the development of commercial activities (Chidester 2000:519; WIB 1911:51, 120).

It was the Humphreys' assumption that Native handicraft production would uplift American Indians educationally, physically, and morally in the same way that industrial education would foster not only Christianity but also legitimate commerce. The Indian goods were secured through missionaries, who apparently rarely charged anything for their services, so that the artists were fully reimbursed for their work. According to Humphrey, the League was responsible for providing a market for Native American handicraft production: "The missionaries, by helping the Indians to dispose of their baskets, beadwork, and other handicrafts through the American Indian League, are able to keep their converts about them" (1912:9).

In promoting handicraft production, the Humphreys intended to make it profitable and respectable for Native Americans as a means of livelihood that would enable them to remain on reservations. The League was rendered as the only means the Indians had of self-support, and were it not for the work of the missionaries they would have been forced to seek employment in the "railroad towns," where it was thought that corrupting influences would undo years of faithful work on the part of the missionaries. Thus, handicraft production was congenial to the mission program, and prevented "backsliding," maintaining the hearers in whose hearts they had firmly planted the Gospel of Christ (Humphrey 1912:9).

The enthusiasm for furnishing curiosity corners of rooms with Indian baskets and curios became in vogue in the Arts and Crafts Period (ca. 1880–1920). In the increasingly urbanized and industrialized America, yearnings for rapidly disappearing rural life provided for a nostalgic vision of untouched Native culture and an appetite for their crafts (Cohodas 1992:90; Lee 1999b:29; Linn 1990:128; Patterson 1998:14). Similar to other objects of indigenous manufacture – ceramics, textiles, and woodcarvings – baskets were adduced to the sympathetic constitution of indigenous aesthetics and creativity, appealing to predominantly female collectors in the metropole. During 1911, the League advertised its sale of handicrafts, though principally baskets, at its headquarters in New York (Humphrey 1912). Responding to a general trend in the consumption of Southwestern, Californian, and Northwest Coast baskets,[7] the American Indian League channeled baskets to New York and, in so doing, provided a market both congenial to and supportive of evangelism.

In the mission statement of the League, William Brewster Humphrey (1912) articulates that baskets were "unique and distinctively American full of symbolism, legendary lore, ceremonials and tribal history." The attraction of Indian basketry to American collectors rested on exactly this fortuitous blend of aesthetics, and ideological consideration:

> The Indian woman weaves into her basket objects of religious veneration: the thunder bird, the ceremonial katchina, the swastika and the Greek fret patterns she has known for centuries before the White man came to America. Prayers for rain are found in the baskets, in endless variety. Other baskets indicate a wish for good life, prosperity, good luck, plentiful harvest, high aspiration, benediction and eternal life. (Humphrey 1913:5)

Baskets were seen as being richly decorated with sacred symbolism, and like the other handicrafts, supposed a strong connection between handwork and personal fulfillment premised on a sense of American individualism (Hinsley 1992:17; Lee 1999a:273).

Baskets objectified the romantic ideals that collectors had about the vanishing Indian, and were adopted by the American Arts and Crafts Movement. As the Indian menace had long since faded, Native American imagery was mostly of a noble and romantic variety, appearing in photos, on pottery, and in baskets (Linn 1990:127; see also Thomas 2000:24). Baskets – condensed symbols of nostalgia – mediated between the metrople and the reservation, accumulated into the object world of a young America. With the more or less separation of these two societies, Indian and White, White collectors could safely admire baskets (Patterson 1998:13). In this way, the sale of baskets by the League appears to have played a part in satiating the appetite for Native American decorative art in its connection to an American "past" and in contrast to an industrializing mainstream American culture.

Burden Basket, Pomo, AMNH Catalogue # 50/773

At the WIB the stewards presented objects to an audience of listeners so as to provide object lessons of the progress of evangelism. Among these objects in the American Indians exhibit was a Pomo burden basket on loan by Clark Wissler, Curator at the American Museum of Natural History, to William Brewster Humphrey for the American Indians section (AMNH Catalogue # 50/773; Figure 5.2). In 1900 the Museum

Figure 5.2 Pomo burden basket (AMNH #50/773), California. Collected by Carl Purdy. Photo courtesy of the Division of Anthropology, American Museum of Natural History

purchased the basket along with a collection of other Pomo baskets from the collector, Carl Purdy. Having conducted ethnological research in Northern California from 1899–1904 with collecting an important objective, Roland Dixon (1902:2) published an article entitled "Basketry Designs of Northern California" on the Purdy Collection (Freed 1976:74). He described the large woven basket as being of the pack-basket and storage type and showing a repetition of the same design; ". . . the upper row, immediately, about the edge, is meshes in a fishnet, and consists of a succession of parallelograms or squares. This is succeeded, in passing toward the base, successively by zigzag, red mountains, half arrow-points, red mountains and zigzag combined, zigzag, red mountains and zigzag" (Dixon 1902:21).

What struck Dixon (1902:23–24) about this burden basket and Pomo baskets in general when compared with those of their neighbors – the Wintun, Pit Rivers, and Maidu – was the paucity of designs, and within this, the absence of animal motifs. It was Dixon's impression that while the Pomo had developed the art of feather decoration to a high degree, they were at the same time very far behind the other tribes in the number and variety of designs used. He conjectured that the energy devoted to the elaborations of feather ornament had drawn their attention away from the development of new designs. Consequently, Dixon wrote that while large Pomo burden baskets demonstrated the greatest artistic poverty, they did show manual dexterity and technical skill unrivaled by any other Californian tribe.[8]

Although both the AMNH correspondence records and the *Handbook and Guide to the World in Boston* fail to provide a rationale for the inclusion of the Pomo basket in the exhibition, it could be argued that the basket was selected for display for two reasons. First, Pomo feathered baskets had been egregiously collected since 1870s because of their aesthetic appeal. On the whole, Pomo feathered basketry had been credited as the only Native craft to be elevated to the status of an independent art (Coe 2003:95). In a discussion about Pomo baskets, Humphrey writes, ". . . at least one kind of Indian basket is appreciated at its full value, and that its makers receive just compensation for their work" (1913:13). To this end, it seems possible some of the visitors at the WIB would already have been familiar with Pomo basketry – an aesthetic that was familiarly "theirs" – and intrigued by its display in the exhibit.

Second, the basket selected was a burden basket of utilitarian character, which showed neither elaborate decoration nor profuse ornamentation.

Similar to the Handbook's description of Navajo blankets (see above), the Pomo basket was characterized by Dixon as being so finely stitched that it was "watertight" (1902:1). By the early part of the 20th century, dealers and collectors favored traditional basketry, seeking to keep the art pure in form and design. They insisted on good craftsmanship and unadulterated forms, but ironically only after Native American culture and its products had been appropriated by White consumers. Collectors vying for the finest pieces sought finely stitched baskets, and thus counting stitches became one of the principal criteria for purchasing basketry (Linn 1990:19). As a consequence, in exhibiting the burden basket at the World in Boston Pomo basketry technique would have been emphasized over its aesthetic.

Since the purpose of displaying objects at the WIB was to illustrate the success of evangelism and the possibility of the gospel of work in stimulating improvement, technical skill would again have been highlighted. A preoccupation with the technique evidenced by fine stitches over form subordinated the basket to skill and, by extension, knowledge. In this way, the basket's exhibition contributed to demonstrating the technical merit and manual dexterity of the Pomo, and, like the Navajo, their general aptitude for industrial advancement with missionary investment.

Such an approach would have revealed the object by diffusing its aesthetic value to the ideas it illustrated. In the exhibition, the basket would have metonymically suggested a larger and coherent whole – that of evangelism. The displayed basket demonstrates that an understanding of the world could be reimagined by a collection of things removed from their contexts of origin, and specific histories of production and appropriation (cf. Clifford 1988:220; Jenkins 1994:243). This was a Christian world which encompassed only the assimilated, herein the non-Christian superseded. Thus, the basket cannot be separated from the evangelist agenda of the exhibition, but rather it should be seen as being integral to it.

As Loaned by the Natural History Museum

In general, missionary exhibition practices did not specify any particular objects but usually comprised broad statements of particular types or classes of objects. Even at the Orient in London, only the most cursory explanatory labels were provided for the items on display (Coombes 1997:178; cf. Eves 1998:51). The Orient in Providence – a smaller scale missionary exposition than that of the WIB, held in September of 1911 – drew on those same objects that were displayed in the American Indians section of the World in Boston. When the stewards at the Providence exhibition were not using objects for illustrated discussions, they were kept in a glass case labeled "As Loaned by the Natural History Museum" (Humphrey to Wissler, October 11, 1911).[9] In this way, a great deal of evangelical discourse inculcated by these missionary expositions took as its focus the generic undefined object, rather than referring to an artifact's provenience.

Objects were generally situated as being the products of anonymous heathens rather than geographically located groups. In using the term "curio," additional meanings were ascribed to objects which conveyed a negative image of Native people in general. By abstracting these objects from their human uses and purposes as "curios," they were decontextualized and their primary or indigenous meanings were rendered irrelevant. The exhibit order of displaying objects was characterized by a discourse of representation based on the idea that the things displayed "stood for" something else, or in this case, the progress of Christianity (cf. Pels 1998:104). For example, stewards would have revealed the AMNH Pomo basket while the progress of evangelism in one of the four regions exhibited was being illustrated, even though the Northern California Pomo did not belong to any of the regions (Young People's Missionary Movement 1911:4). Stewards gave object lessons, recontextualizing "things" within the broader context of the missionary project of intervention and reform, and Native assimilation into the Christian totality.

Objects produced in the context of non-Western societies – Native American societies in particular – appear to have been collected, reclassified, and displayed as exemplars of the defining characteristics of the "primitive other" in order to relationally define the modern West (Cohodas 1996:7). Protestant American society constructed its self-image not only by objectifying its concept of the other distanced peoples, but also by conflating the dimension of space and time. Contemporary peoples living in distant areas were viewed as though they were vestiges of the past. Native American culture was visualized as it was being displaced. In this way, placed into an alien system of meaning, Indians existed paradoxically in the exhibition and simultaneously in the timeless past (Dubin 2001:15; Jenkins 1993:11; 1994:256; Miller

1987:124). For this reason, material culture denuded of cultural context essentialized the timeless pre-Christian state of Native Americans, thereby leaving room for missionary intervention and "tales of the wonderful power of the Gospel to advance the Kingdom of God" (Young People's Missionary Movement 1911:4).

Although the displayed curios lacked accompanying text and would have been accorded a generic status, this is not to say that attention to detail was lacking in the American Indians section. The authority lay not in the objects, but in the scientific process of collection, which inscribed, at the moment of acquisition, the character and qualities associated with the objects themselves. Ethnological objects made salient what would otherwise remain obscure. Objects were the sites of meaning and knowledge, and through exhibition they were regarded as a primary nexus where new facts about the world could be created and given order.

With a newly emergent anthropology that took as its foundation the study of material culture, ethnological specimens were not merely objects to be looked at, but were facts, or exponents of ideas (Buchli 2002:2).[10] For Tylor and other members of the British school of social anthropology, the recourse to actual objects was seen as being of inestimable use in the abstract investigation of ideas. The sight of material things among the habits of distant and outlandish peoples was to give a reality and sharpness of appreciation to their habits, social conditions, modes of government, and ideas of religions, thereby adding to the meaning of words (Tylor 1896:x).

The faith in objects as a source of knowledge lay at the center of how Americans of the late Victorian period understood the world, and also at the heart of the entire missionary discourse in dialogue with, and strengthened by, a museum-based anthropology (Conn 1998:9). The deployment of the ethnological specimens in missionary exhibitions reflected an interest in social evolutionism, as well as the Christian impulse to maintain human equivalence across racial boundaries and to claim the equal capability under an all-encompassing Christian God. According to Michael O'Hanlon (2000:5) social evolutionism, the main anthropological paradigm which preceded the functionalism of the 1920s, ascribed a central role to artifacts as facts – all the more since anthropology at that time took as its subject matter societies that lacked other material evidence of their past such as written histories.

Protestant missionaries attached importance to participation in the discourse of the new science of anthropology and its emphasis on social evolutionism. Since the latter part of the 19th century missionary societies had embarked on a policy to establish some sort of academic credibility. With the publication of the British Academy of Science's *Notes and Queries on Anthropology* (1874), missionaries based much of their anthropological writing and collecting activities on its directives, accumulating data which would be useful both to contemporary and later anthropologists. They were in touch with current ideas of anthropology and were interested in, or at least recognized, the scientific status beginning to be attached to the study of non-Western cultures (Coombes 1997:166, 173). In this way, anthropology was enlisted to validate the "seriousness" of their work.

While the object systems of missiology and anthropology had been institutionalized, they were not impermeable. Ethnological specimens were enmeshed within a visual economy that reflected wide reaching scientific and social networks overlapping these institutions. Specimens crossed the boundary between scientific and missionary knowledge. Therefore, it is important to resist the inclination to view missionary and ethnological collections as being self-sufficient, and instead see them as mutually sustaining – sharing a single object world.

While the missionaries affiliated with the Board of Home Missions had contributed costumes and objects for the World in Boston, only ethnological specimens would have provided the necessary scientific credibility for the American Indians section (Humphrey to Wissler, February 25, 1911). They were the backbone to the exhibition. It seems it was for this reason that Reverend William Brewster Humphrey borrowed objects, and the Pomo basket in particular, from the American Museum of Natural History. Of the twenty-two objects on loan from the AMNH for the American Indians section,[11] five had been published in the *Bulletin of the American Museum of Natural History*, four by Alfred Louis Kroeber, and the basket by Roland Dixon (see above) (Wissler to Humphrey, April 20, 1911).

The AMNH's objects were invested with knowledge which visibly reinforced the exhibition's exegetical aim and supported the scientific location of the civilized. Nothing could have been more validating for a missionary exhibition than the display of objects that had been sanctioned by an esteemed scientific publication and by renowned anthropologists of the day. Moreover, visited by an audience of 300,000 to 400,000 people and pronounced the most attractive section of the entire exhibition, the American Indians exhibit would have played a mutually important part in the contemporary trend of disseminating and popularizing anthropological theory (Humphrey to Wissler, May 27, 1911; Humphrey 1912:10).[12]

Conclusion

The World in Boston was an effective medium for disseminating knowledge about missionary activities at home and abroad to a cross-section of the American public, many of whom would have been unfamiliar with missionary work. The exhibition began with the American Indians, "our foreigners at home," whose missionization was requisite to Manifest Destiny. In this way, the total missionary enterprise was presented in the image of the American Indians section. Subsequent foreign missionary activities into the newly acquired American territories – Hawaii, Puerto Rico, and the Philippines – were based on those initial experiences at home, and structured as such in successive sections in the exhibition hall.

The exhibition was a spectacle of religious progress, infused with a sub-theme of shared humanity. The crude dwellings, indexical to the pre-contact lifestyles of the American Indians, provided the background to the advancement of Christianity in the material form of the Christian Indian Chapel. The costumed stewards made manifest the domestic activities of Native Americans of an earlier time, or those "Indian tribes and parts of tribes ... still unreached by the Gospel of the Lord Jesus Christ" (WIB 1911:66). With the exception of the young Indian student weaving a blanket in the space allocated for the Southwest, Native Americans in the exhibit were confined to the Chapel, singing harmonized Indian songs. Together the Indian students served as testimony to the civilizing force of Christianity and visible proof of the success of Christianity. From the vantage point of the visitor, the Indian students, extricated from heathenism, were encased in a new Christian life.

From blankets to baskets, the objects demonstrated the technical adeptness of the North American Indians, and consequently their inclusion in the Presbyterian Church's industrial and educational home missions. These objects were abstracted from their indigenous uses, and assimilated into a Christianity that insisted on the 19th-century paradigm of social progress which underpinned the emergent discipline of anthropology. In the case of the Pomo basket, which was loaned by the AMNH for the duration of the exhibition, aesthetic form was subordinate to technical skill, and by extension knowledge. In its display at the WIB, the basket – along with the other specimens from the AMNH – would have given the exhibit an air of scientific authority. Similar to the Orient in London, anthropology was enlisted in the exhibition to validate the seriousness of missionary work, which in turn popularized the newly emergent science.

The American Indians section of the World in Boston provided visible proof of Christian expansion, proselytism, and ultimately the assimilation of America's Other into a distinctly Christian American identity. Beginning with the American Indians, the exhibition established a positional superiority in relation to the pre-Christian makers of those objects and the environments from which they originated. The exposition was an act of representational knowing in that it claimed to offer an adequate image of the world having extricated the objects and peoples from the originating environs (cf. Hinsley 1992:15). Christianity was presented as having full control over the material world. In this way, the exhibition was a claim of possession, and itself the object of possession embodied and encased by an evangelical Christianity driven by the Word. The World in Boston was more than a mere show; it was a mighty object lesson on the assimilatory success of American Christianity, itself impelled by Manifest Destiny.

Acknowledgments

I thank Jonah Friedman, Judith Hasinoff, Webb Keane, Bruce MacKay, Lynn Meskell, Fred Myers, Robert Preucel, Nan Rothschild, Matt Weiner and the participants of the SAR Materiality seminar for their helpful comments on earlier drafts. I also thank Kristen Mable for her assistance in the Archives and Barry Landau in the Digital Imaging Office, Division of Anthropology, American Museum of Natural History.

Notes

1 From its founding in 1905, the object of the Movement was to aid affiliated Baptist, Congregational, Methodist, Episcopal, Methodist-Episcopal, Presbyterian, Reformed, and Universalist Church missionary societies in "flooding the churches with the spirit and knowledge of missions, through existing agencies, and to make each follower of Christ faithful in extending his kingdom throughout the world" (WIB 1911:127).

2 The missionary societies affiliated with the YPMM were each given the responsibility of preparing a section of the WIB so as to publicize their individual successes in the field (WIB 1911:109).
3 The hogan, teepee, and lodge were taken to exemplify the Indians of the Southwest, Indians of the Plains and Indians who live in the woods. An "Alaskan hut" was placed on display in the Models and Diagrams section of the exhibition.
4 The structure of the section seems to have mirrored the North American Indian exhibit at the World's Columbian Exposition in Chicago in 1893. There, fairgoers would also begin their tour with the "prehistoric cliff-dwellers, who faded from history's pages when the earth was yet young" proceeding to those "races" not yet disposed, "Indians of every kind" (A Week at the Fair 1893:106 quoted in Jenkins 1994:258).
5 Correspondence between Clark Wissler (AMNH) and William Brewster Humphrey (AIL, BHM, Presbyterian Church of America) (Correspondence Box 12, Folder 32), the Division of Anthropology Archives, American Museum of Natural History.
6 In stimulating the production of an "authentic" art, philanthropists discouraged the souvenir atrocities produced for sale to tourists and hobbyists. For example, in 1903 Grace Nicholson, a philanthropist and professional dealer at the time, encouraged the Pomo artists Mary and William Benson to produce baskets using natural materials, and traditional techniques and designs to make their creations as fine as possible (Linn 1990:130).
7 Native women, often elderly, with strong ties to the home and family, produced baskets in their backyards and kitchens. Basketry making was deemed consonant with Victorian notions of the domicile (see Chidester 2000:520; Lee 1999a:275; Mullin 1992:402).
8 An interesting rationale that might have been behind Dixon's (1913) emphasis on technical skill was the strong reaction that archaeology was having at that time to the non-scientific collection of objects based on aesthetic appeal without a "scientific agenda." Along with Wissler (1917:100), Dixon was at the forefront of the debate, and one result was his enthusiasm for collecting "non-spectacular data" (artifacts) over "curios and expensive objects" to emphasize the necessity for a certain systematic rigor in the data collection process.
9 The content, arrangement, and location of the displayed objects was left out of the *Handbook* and newspaper descriptions of the exhibition. Any attempt at reconstruction can only come from the AMNH correspondence records, comparison with other sections of the exhibit (see *Missionary Expositions: Notes for Stewards in the Hawaiian Court*), and other missionary exhibitions such as the Orient in Providence.
10 Franz Boas ended his career as a museum anthropologist at the AMNH, recognizing the bias of the object-based approach, its social-evolutionary underpinning, and its monopoly over museum anthropology. He argued that objects, decontextualized in museum cases, were inadequate to portray cultural realities: "The psychological as well as the historical relations of cultures, which are the

only objects of anthropological inquiry, can not be expressed by an arrangement based on so small a portion of the manifestation of ethnic life as is presented by specimens" (Boas 1907:928).
11 In addition to the Pomo basket, the objects on loan from AMNH included: parfleches, tomahawks, bows and arrows, war clubs, and pipes and stems (Wissler to Humphrey, April 20, 1911).
12 The display of the AMNH Pomo basket at the WIB appears to have resonated well with the AMNH, Smithsonian Bureau of Ethnology, and the Field Columbian Museum's general trend of exhibiting baskets at regional and national fairs, attracting visitors and educating the public on North American ethnology (Smith-Ferri 1998:16–17).

References

American Museum of Natural History 1911 Correspondence Box 12, Folder 32. New York: Division of Anthropology Archives, AMNH.
Altick, R. D. 1978 The Shows of London. Cambridge: Belknap Press.
A Week at the Fair 1893 Rand McNally and Company.
Boas, F. 1907 Some Principles of Museum Administration. Science 25:921–933.
Breckenridge, C. A. 1989 The Aesthetics and Politics of Colonial Collecting: India at World Fairs. Society for the Comparative Study of Society and History 31:195–216.
Bronner, S. J. 1989 Object Lessons: The Work of Ethnological Museums and Collections. *In* Consuming Visions: Accumulation and Display of Goods in America, 1880–1920. S. J. Bronner, ed. Pp. 217–254. New York: W.W. Norton and Company.
Buchli, V. 2002 Introduction. *In* The Material Culture Reader. V. Buchli, ed. Pp. 1–22. New York: Berg.
Buck-Morss, S. 1989 The Dialectics of Seeing: Walter Benjamin and the Arcades Project. Cambridge: The MIT Press.
Cannizzo, J. 1998 Gathering Souls and Objects: Missionary Collections. *In* Colonialism and the Object: Empire, Material Culture and the Museum. T. Barringer and T. Flynn, eds. Pp. 153–164. New York: Routledge.
Chidester, D. 2000 Christianity: A Global Perspective. Middlesex: Allen Lane Penguin Press.
Clifford, J. 1988 The Predicament of Culture: Twentieth-Century Ethnography, Literature, and Art. Cambridge: Harvard University Press.
Coe, R. T. 2003 The Responsive Eye: Ralph T. Coe and the Collecting of American Indian Art. New York: The Metropolitan Museum of Art.
Cohodas, M. 1992 Louisa Keyser and the Cohns: Mythmaking and Basket Making in the American West. *In* The Early Years of Native American Art History: The Politics of Scholarship and Collecting. J. Berlo, ed. Pp. 88–133. Seattle: University of Washington Press.

—— 1996 Authenticity Paradigm: As Evidenced in the Marketing and Recontextualizing of the Hickox Baskets. Unpublished manuscript.

—— 1999 Elizabeth Hickox and Karuk Basketry: A Case Study in Debates on Innovation and Paradigms of Authenticity. *In* Unpacking Culture: Art and Commodity in Colonial and Postcolonial Worlds. R. Phillips and C. Steiner, eds. Pp. 143–161. Berkeley: University of California Press.

Cohn, B. S. 1996 Colonialism and its Forms of Knowledge: The British in India. Princeton: Princeton University Press.

Conn, S. 1998 Museums and American Intellectual Life, 1876–1926. Chicago: University of Chicago Press.

Coombes, A. E. 1997 Reinventing Africa: Museums, Material Culture and Popular Imagination. 2nd edition. New Haven: Yale University Press.

Corbey, R. 1993 Ethnographic Showcases, 1870–1930. Cultural Anthropology 8:338–369.

—— 2000 Tribal Art Traffic: A Chronicle of Taste, Trade and Desire in Colonial and Post Colonial Times. Amsterdam: Royal Tropical Institute.

Deloria, P. J. 1998 Playing Indian. New Haven: Yale University Press.

Dixon, R. B. 1902 Basketry Designs of the Indians of Northern California. Bulletin of the American Museum of Natural History XVII:1–32, Plates I–XXXVII.

—— 1913 Some Aspects of North American Archaeology. American Anthropologist 15:549–577.

Dubin, M. 2001 Native America Collected: The Culture of an Art World. Albuquerque: University of New Mexico.

Eves, R. 1998 Commentary: Missionary or Collector? The Case of George Brown. Museum Anthropology 22:49–60.

Fine-Dare, K. S. 2002 Grave Injustice: The American Indian Repatriation Movement and NAGPRA. Lincoln: The University of Nebraska Press.

Francis, D. R. 1913 The Universal Exposition of 1904. St. Louis: Louisiana Purchase Exposition.

Freed, S. A. 1976 The American Museum of Natural History Department of Anthropology. American Indian Art 5:68–75.

Gardner, Helen 2000 Gathering for God: George Brown and the Christian Economy in the Collection of Artefacts. *In* Hunting the Gatherers: Ethnographic Collectors, Agents and Agency in Melanesia, 1870s–1930s. Pp. 35–54. New York: Berghahn Books.

Graves-Brown, P. M. 2000 Introduction. *In* Matter, Materiality and Modern Culture. Pp. 1–9. New York: Routledge.

Griffiths, A. 2002 Wondrous Difference: Cinema, Anthropology and Turn of the Century Visual Culture. New York: Columbia University Press.

Hinsley, C. 1992 Collecting Cultures and Cultures of Collecting: The Lure of the American Southwest, 1880–1915. Museum Anthropology 16(1):12–20.

Humphrey, W. B. 1911 North American Indian Folk-lore Music. New York: American Indian League.

—— 1912 Annual Report of the American Indian League. New Haven: American Indian League.
—— 1913 Annual Report of the American Indian League. New Haven: American Indian League.
Jacknis, I. 1985 Franz Boas and Exhibits: On the Limitation of the Museum Method and Anthropology. *In* Objects and Others: Essays on Museums and Material Culture. G. W. Stocking, ed. Pp. 75–111. Madison: The University of Wisconsin Press.
Jenkins, D. 1993 The Visual Domination of the American Indian: Photography, Anthropology and Popular Culture in the Late Nineteenth Century. Museum Anthropology 17(1):9–21.
—— 1994 Object Lessons and Ethnographic Displays: Museum Exhibition and the Making of American Anthropology. Society for the Comparative Study of Society and History 36(2):242–270.
Jonaitis, A. 1992 Franz Boas, John Swanton and the New Haida Sculpture at the American Museum of Natural History. *In* The Early Years of Native American Art History: The Politics of Scholarship and Collecting. J. C. Berlo, ed. Pp. 22–61. Seattle: University of Washington Press.
Keane, W. 1996 Materialism, Missionaries, and Modern Subjects in Colonial Indonesia. *In* Conversion to Modernities: The Globalization of Christianity. P. Van der Veer, ed. Pp. 137–170. New York: Routledge.
—— 2002 Sincerity, "Modernity", and Protestants. Cultural Anthropology 17:65–92.
—— 2005 Signs are Not the Garb of Meaning. *In* Materiality: Positivism and its Epistemological Others (Politics, History, and Culture). D. Miller and G. Steinmetz, eds. Durham: Duke University Press.
King, T. 2003 The Truth About Stories: A Native Narrative. Toronto: House of Anansi Press Inc.
Kirshenblatt-Gimblett, B. 1990 Objects of Ethnography. *In* The poetics and politics of museum display. I. Karp and S. Lavine, eds. Pp. 386–443. Washington: Smithsonian Institution Press.
Krech III, S. 1999 Introduction. *In* Collecting Native America. S. Krech III and B. Hail, eds. Pp. 386–443. Washington D.C.: Smithsonian Institution Press.
Lee, M. 1999a Tourism and Taste Cultures: Collecting Native Art in Alaska at the Turn of the Twentieth Century. *In* Unpacking Culture: Art and Commodity in Colonial and Postcolonial Worlds. R. Philips and C. Steiner, eds. Pp. 267–281. Berkeley: University of California Press.
—— 1999b Zest or Zeal? Sheldon Jackson and the Commodification of Alaska Native Art. *In* Collecting Native America, 1870–1960. S. Krech and B. Hail, eds. Pp. 25–42. Washington, D.C.: Smithsonian Institution Press.
Linn, N. F. 1990 In Search of the Natural: American Indian Basketry and the Arts and Crafts Movement. Antiques and Fine Art 8:126–131.
London Missionary Society 1908 The Orient in London. London: London Missionary Society.

McAllister, S. F. 1998 Cross-Cultural Dress in British Missionary Narratives: Dressing for Eternity. *In* Historicizing Christian Encounter with the Other. J. C. Hawley, ed. Pp. 1–16. London: Macmillan Press Ltd.

Meyer, B. 1997 Christian Mind and Worldly Matters: Religion and Materiality in Nineteenth-Century Gold Coast. Journals of Material Culture 2(3):311–337.

Miller, D. 1987 Material Culture and Mass Consumption. New York: Basil Blackwell.

Missionary Education Movement in the United States and Canada 1911 Notes for Steward in the Hawaiian Scene. New York.

Mullin, M. H. 1992 The Patronage of Difference: Making Indian Art "Art," not Ethnology. Cultural Anthropology 7:393–424.

New York Times 1911 Ten Thousand People to Portray Missionary Life, Great Exhibition in Boston Will Give Vivid Reproductions of How Natives Live in Foreign Lands where Church Work is Carried On. January 22, 1911, SM 14.

O'Hanlon, M. 2000 Introduction. *In* Hunting the Gatherers: Ethnographic Collectors, Agents and Agency in Melanesia, 1870s–1930s. M. O'Hanlon and R. Welsch, eds. Pp. 1–34. London: Berghahn Books.

Patterson, V. 1998 Change and Continuity: Transformations of Pomo Life. Expedition 40:3–13.

Pels, P. 1998 Spirits of Matter: On Fetish, Rarity, Fact and Fancy. *In* Border Fetishisms: Material Objects in Unstable Places. P. Spyer ed. Pp. 91–121. New York: Routledge.

—— 2003 Spirits of Modernity: Alfred Wallace, Edward Tylor, and the Visual Politics of Fact. *In* Magic and Modernity: Interfaces of Revelation and Concealment. B. Meyer and P. Pels, eds. Pp. 241–271. Stanford: Stanford University Press.

Penney, D., and L. Roberts 1999 America's Pueblo Artists: Encounters on the Borderlands. *In* Native American Art in the Twentieth Century. W. J. Rushing III, ed. Pp. 21–38. New York: Routledge.

Philips, A. L. 1910 An Appreciation. *In* A Book of Object Lessons with Magical and Mechanical Effects. C. H. Woolston, ed. Pp. 10–11. Philadelphia: The Praise Publishing Company.

Phillips, R. 2001 Performing the Native Woman: Primitivism and Mimicry in Early 20th Century Visual Culture. *In* Antimodernism and Artistic Experience: Policing the Boundaries of Modernity. Lynda Jessup ed. Pp. 26–49. Toronto: University of Toronto Press.

Rydell, R. 1984 All the Word's a Fair: Visions of Empire at American International Expositions, 1876–1916. Chicago: University of Chicago Press.

Smith-Ferri, S. 1998 The Development of the Commercial Market for Pomo Indian Baskets. Expedition 40:15–22.

Spyer, P. 1998 The Tooth of Time, or Taking a Look at the "Look" of Clothing in Late Nineteenth-Century Aru. *In* Border Fetishisms: Material Objects in Unstable Places. P. Spyer, ed. Pp. 150–182. New York: Routledge.

The World in Boston 1911 Handbook and Guide to the World in Boston. Boston.

Thomas, N. 1991 Entangled Objects: Exchange, Material Culture and Colonialism. Cambridge: Harvard University Press.

—— 1999 The Case of the Misplaced Ponchos: Speculations Concerning the History of Cloth in Polynesia. Journal of Material Culture 4:5–20.
—— 2000 Skull Wars: Kennewick Man, Archaeology, and the Battle for American Identity. New York: Basic Books.
Trigger, B. 1989 A History of Archaeological Thought. Cambridge: Cambridge University Press.
Tylor, E. B. 1896 Introduction. *In* The History of Mankind. F. Ratzel, ed. Pp. v–xi. London: Macmillan and Co., Ltd.
Wade, E. 1985 The Ethnic Art Market in the American Southwest, 1880–1980. *In* Objects and Others: Essays on Museums and Material Culture. G. W. Stocking, ed. Pp. 167–191. Madison: The University of Wisconsin Press.
Wissler, C. 1917 The New Archaeology, American Museum Journal 17:100–101.
Woolston, C. H. 1910 Seeing Truth: A Book of Object Lessons with Magical and Mechanical Effects. Philadelphia: The Praise Publishing Company.
Young People's Missionary Movement 1911 Missionary Expositions: Notes for Stewards in the Hawaiian Court. New York: Young People's Missionary Movement.

6

The Texture of Things: Objects, People, and Landscape in Northwest Argentina (First Millennium A.D.)

Marisa Lazzari

> Every useful thing is a whole composed of many properties; it can therefore be useful in various ways. The discovery of these ways and hence of the manifold uses of things is the work of history.
>
> Marx, *Capital*, p. 125

The ambiguous powers of material objects to organize and/or subvert social life have attracted numerous scholars since early days. Halbwachs' statement that "man is an animal that thinks with its fingers" inspired Mauss (1950:365; 1968:162) to explore bodily engagement in the world asserting the importance of objects in social life as well as the dual character of matter, simultaneously animate and inanimate. Mauss's work thus predates by several decades the more recent rejection of the notion of materiality as a passive domain, only accessible to human knowledge by means of its measurable properties (Gell 1998; Hodder 1986; Latour 1993; Miller 1987; Myers 2001; Pels 1998; Shanks and Tilley 1987; Taussig 1993; J. Thomas 1991; 1996; N. Thomas 1991; 1997; Warnier 1999). Bodily practices, with or without the aid of objects, disclose that subjects make themselves while making others who make them in return.[1]

Or as Marx put it: "renewing themselves even as they renew the world of wealth they create" (1993:712).

Dealing with the materiality of social life implies accepting that objects and social relationships act as conditions for each other's existence (J. Thomas 1998). Materiality is thus a recursive relationship between people and things; a spiraling series of continual reflection, opposition, affirmation, similarity, and difference between the way people make things and the ways things make people. But what does this mutuality really mean? At least since Marx's definition of commodity fetishism, the problem of the phenomenal presence of the thing and its "hidden" conditions of existence (social relations) has been dominant in social sciences. This problem has often been met with anxiety, fearing that giving objects a primary role would overlook social relations. More importantly, it was feared it could lead scholars to disregard the capacity of objects to evoke and create the imaginary, thus regressing analysis into empiricist accounts of social life (Battaglia 1994:639, 643 n. 13). Clearly the relation between presence and representation is one full of tension, and several scholars have felt that it was safer to turn the balance against material things. However, by seeing objects mainly as the material representations of invisible meanings and relations, the Cartesian division of mind and matter has been perpetuated at the expense of things and their evocative powers (Stallybrass 1998:207).

Material objects render palpable infinite kinds of relations, sensations, thoughts, and actions, most of which do not occur before our eyes, as archaeologists know so well. But this sort of paradox of presence through absence that things foreground can be compared to bodily symptoms: they are not the superficial expression of some inner, essential state, but they are the state of affairs itself. The object, like the human body "expresses total existence, not because it is an external accompaniment to that existence, but because existence realizes itself in the body, this incarnate significance is the central phenomenon of which body and mind, sign and significance, are abstract moments" (Merleau-Ponty 1962:190). According to this, the invisible (the idea) cannot be separated from its material existence, as the latter gives the former its depth, its dimensions, while the idea gives to the sensible "its lining and its depth" (Merleau-Ponty 1973:149).

Unlike Descartes, who sought to detach the mind from all sensory experience in order to produce unbiased knowledge, or Hegel, who considered sensory knowledge as of a lesser kind that ought to be transcended in gaining "absolute knowledge," Merleau-Ponty calls our attention to the fact that certain ideas can only be grasped through our bodies and the sensory experience of matter.

This observation has been productively followed up by social studies concerned with the lived human body as non-reducible to either the mechanical-physical body or its representations (Connerton 1989; Csordas 1994; Grosz 1994; Meskell 1999; Meskell and Joyce 2003). Landscape studies have also addressed this point to different degrees, trying to emphasize dwelling and practice rather than seeing the landscape as either a pre-given natural surface or as a system of signs to be decoded (Ashmore and Knapp 1999; Barret 1994; Edmonds 2000; Gell 1995; Gow 1995; Ingold 2000; Küchler 1993; J. Thomas 2001). Yet the body has often been seen in archaeology as a site of inscription, a vehicle for representation, and even an artifact in the crudest sense (Meskell 2000:16; Meskell and Joyce 2003:10). It has also often been taken as the stable ground for interpretation (e.g., Tilley 1994:74), which contradicts the phenomenological orientation of such studies by overlooking the principle that every perceiving body is always in relation to the world and to others, and thus historically situated (Merleau-Ponty 1962:66–67, 120–121). A changed relation to the body creates a new understanding of the world, its time, its spatiality, and its objects (Jensen 2000:59).

Embodiment has thus been predominantly conceptualized in archaeology as a social process of inscribing mental images, ideas, or notions in the physical body, which then becomes the locus for "reading" and "decoding" cultural norms and signs. In like manner, objects and material constructions have been usually treated as the effects of social inscription, the "materialization" of ideas and norms in a substantive medium (e.g., DeMarrais et al. 1996). Following the path opened by phenomenological studies of the body and the landscape, I argue that materiality is a process of embodiment in the sense of incorporation rather than inscription, in which artifacts, like houses and landscapes, incorporate in their bodily form the rhythms of the practices that gave rise to them (Ingold 2000:193–194, 347).

This line of thinking might help us understand the social efficacy of things that circulate between people and places creating large-scale social spaces; a long-standing interest in the social sciences. While most recent studies focus on the circulation of commodities and capital in modern global spaces of interaction (e.g., Harvey 1996), archaeology has shown that human societies have always stretched beyond their boundaries with the aid of various kinds of objects (e.g., Ericson and Earle 1982; Renfrew 1969; Renfrew and Shennan 1982; Sabloff and Lamberg Karlovsky 1978). Yet, it is in this tradition of inquiry where things have been persistently taken as passive conveyors of social and individual messages (but see Gamble 1998).

It is useful to address this gap by extending to all material objects what Bakhtin (1994:177–179) observed about works of art. Things have a bodily, temporal existence, a presence whose particular properties induce distinct ways of seeing and acting in the world. Objects are indeed different from the model of the arbitrary linguistic sign, as their materiality and durability are conditions of possibility for their movement across social and semiotic domains (Keane 2001:73; Saunders 2001). For instance, materials such as lithics and ceramics can be seen as different genres. They have different substance, durability, and they involve diverse techniques of the body and spatial practices. Like genres, lithics and ceramics may foster different ways of conceptualizing reality and performing in everyday life.

But beyond genre differences, circulating objects make a nice example of things that embody a mode of social existence. Rather than showing ethnic identity, gender, or rank, and beyond indicating distant places, exchange partners, or rivals, the materiality of circulating things is in itself a particular state of the interconnection and relatedness that characterizes social existence. Looking at northwest Argentina (NWA) during the first millennium A.D. (Formative period)[2] reveals how these objects delineated the horizon of interconnected practices, places, and meanings that both reproduced and challenged the lifeworld in the transition toward a basically sedentary social formation.

Landscapes of Living Things: The Social Efficacy of Objects in Motion

The experience of time and space as either compressing or stretching between subjects and places has been studied as a trait of modernity, largely as the outcome of new communication and transportation technologies (e.g., Giddens 1979; Kern 1983; Stein 2001). Yet, there is plenty of archaeological and ethnographic evidence that indicates that similar effects are created in non-market economies through medium and long-distance exchanges (Bradley and Edmonds 1993; Descola 1996; Gamble 1995; Humphrey and Hugh-Jones 1992; Munn 1986; Weiner 1992). This raises the question of the significance of distant worlds beyond daily interaction for the constitution of both individual and collective identities; a question that demands exploring the common ground between past and present without conflating them. Importantly, these studies agree on the idea that space is an active dimension of social life, both conditioning and conditioned by social practice. Exploring how different social formations require large-scale spaces beyond those of face-to-face interaction for their reproduction, they assert that the relevant limits of the lifeworld are, more often than not, far beyond the scope of daily movements and tasks.

In prehistory the concept of landscape understood as simultaneously cultural and natural can help us investigate these issues. The landscape is inseparable from the movements of people and things between places, what has been named the *taskscape* (Ingold 2000:195). As an array of related features, the landscape is created and reproduced through the taskscapes (an array of related activities) generated by lived bodies through their dwelling. Thus the temporality of social life (i.e. the rhythms and sequences of tasks and exchanges) acquires depth, density, and volume.

As a perfect "chronotope" (a rhetorical figure that synthesizes time and space, Bakhtin 1981:84–85) the landscape redefines the traditional archaeological region as a lived, active dimension of social life. It gives flesh to what has been called "regionality," the experience of the world beyond the local by means of ceremonies, exchanges, and the spread of information through complex networks of alliances and rivalries (Munn 1990:2). Likewise, artifacts can perform similar roles to these events, enabling the experience of the region as a shared social space. Specifically, objects and materials that circulate through long distances participate in several transactions and contexts of use. Non-local items used in everyday activities link distant people and places, rendering material previous transactions, users, and routes (Weiner 1994).

In the Andes, barter transactions have been described as "an electrical wire that connects traders to each other" (Mayer 2002:144). This connection involves ecological as well as meaning zones, as the geography of the land is also a cosmic geography. Contemporary caravan trade illustrates the intertwining of the physical, symbolic, and lived dimensions of the landscape, built through a specific array of tasks and places. As a "total social fact," the trek is an economic journey, a social event, a political opportunity, a time travel, and a rite of initiation (Lecoq 1987; compare Nielsen 2001a). Linking all these aspects, the movement across environmental zones is also a movement in time in which different areas and their products have polisemic character and multi-faceted value. The tasks undertaken by the caravan members (human and non-human) occur simultaneously in the present, lived space, and in a ritual space where the past waits ahead (Lecoq 1987:29). Weaving the ordinary, quotidian space with the extra-ordinary, cosmologic space, the caravan offers to youngsters the opportunity to become adult members of the social body, and to adults, the chance to encounter their roots and fortify their alliances.

Thus circulating people and things also have the capacity to expand and/or compress "inter-subjective space-time," the experience of space and time that is both constitutive of and constituted by social relations. Traveling objects link people to places thereby building a landscape that is a dynamic, tense, collective creation, and thus, a large-scale social space. Circulating things and people refer to places and people that are not immediately present in everyday life, thus concretizing in material form the presence of other people and places. They render visible in daily life what is invisible to face-to-face interaction. Circulation thus reveals the entangled nature of social life, the "infinite reciprocity" between spheres of social practice (Simmel 1990:56). Through circulation and exchange, the landscape is woven as a dense object itself, which cannot be alienated from the bodies – humans, animals, plants, things – that dwell in it. As a dynamic collective creation, the landscape is a component of the lifeworld in perpetual exchange with other components. We see once more how Mauss's (1925:10, 43) observations, this time on the active role of objects in social networks, are still relevant today.

Obsidian for instance, as a geographically restricted resource, certainly had the phenomenal capacity to link people to distant places, concretizing in perceptible form the powers of people to act (see Munn 1986:6–11). This material traveled long distances, as the sources located in the *Puna* area, a high-altitude desert shared by Argentina, Chile, and Bolivia, supplied sites widely spread across NWA. Obsidian from one of the largest and finest sources (Ona, 320 kilometers northwest from the Aconquija sites as the bird flies) connected sites in different microenvironments that were otherwise unconnected. Figure 6.1 (see later in the chapter) shows the available information from obsidian provenience studies, revealing the complexity of these connections. The postulated dispersion area might change after the results of ongoing sourcing studies,[3] and it does not represent homogeneous cultural areas. For instance, although Campo del Pucará, Ambato, Abaucán, Antofagasta de la Sierra, and the Aconquija share stylistic features with Hualfín, the material assemblages of these sites (house shapes, site layout, predominant ceramic styles, stonework, etc.) present remarkable differences. Yet some of those areas with few ceramics styles or other things in common did participate in the use of Ona obsidian (e.g., Antofagasta de la Sierra and Aconquija). Furthermore, in some regions such as Quebrada del Toro or the Lerma valley, sites combine Ona raw material with obsidian coming from northern sources which apparently did not supply the NWA southern sites (Yacobaccio et al. 2003; Figure 6.1).

Thus obsidian and ceramics made diverse distant places and spaces in-between relevant for everyday life in the Aconquija. The selective references performed by various classes of material objects are not merely observable today. Rather, they structured a meaningful "field of understandings and expectations" (N. Thomas 2001) in the past as well. In order to better explain the role of artifacts in the constitution of such a field, it might be useful to discuss first some of the relevant literature about material culture and everyday life before moving on to NWA Formative period things.

Difficult Matters: The Tangible and the Unspoken in Everyday Life

The obscure zone where social bonds are woven with substances and objects is now the focus of several researchers seeking to counterbalance the role of discourse in social analysis (Gosden 1994; Graves-Brown 2000; Ingold 2000; Miller 2001; Warnier 1999; 2001). Worlds are built through human practice and discourse, but it is because "the social cannot be constructed with the social that it needs keys and holes" (Latour 2000:19). In spite of its internal diversity (compare Lemonnier 1992; 2003; Meskell 2004; Tilley 1993; 1999), this attempt to fully re-insert the tangible into social theory stands apart from evolutionary and behavioral approaches, where social meanings are epiphenomenal, and the power that organizes value regimes is seen as an external force that operates in a comparable way to natural selective pressures (Skibo and Schiffer 2001; see also Wilk 2001:117).

Earlier efforts initiated research traditions that focus on the social character and potency of technical processes (Dietler and Hembrich 1998; Dobres 2000; Gosselain 1992; 1998; Hosler 1995; Lechtman 1979), the capacity of commodities and spatial arrangements to modify consciousness, build ideologies, and discipline practices (Funari and Zarankin 2003; Leone 1984; McGuire and Paynter 1991), and on the productive yet controversial metaphor of "material culture as text" (Beaudry et al. 1991; Yentsch and Beaudry 2001; Hodder 1982b; 1986; 1989; Joyce 1993; Shanks and Tilley 1987; compare Buchli 1995:183; Thomas 1996:53, 236).

Many supporters of the text metaphor have repeatedly argued that although material culture might share some aspects with language, it cannot be conflated with language (Hodder 1989:256–257; Hodder and Preucel 1996:300; Tilley 1991:180). Yet the question of how social significance works outside representation remains unanswered. It is because things have capacities beyond their role in effecting cultural codes, rules, and messages that they work in social strategies. Social significance implies more than the use of conventional systems of symbols, and meaning is apprehended in action and through use (Graves-Brown 1995:91).

This level of significance goes beyond the function of a thing (whether economic or symbolic) and implies that social practice is much more than instrumental action. However, functionalist and evolutionary approaches in archaeology assume the preeminence of matter and the environment over social relations, while many social archaeologists assume that the latter precedes the former, and that the main function of material culture is to convey meanings in ways that are at times complementary to, at times subversive of linguistic communication. Poststructuralist archaeology tried to overcome the construction of material culture as the "other" of the discursive, often dissolving both as different manifestations of the overarching phenomenon of textuality (Bapty and Yates 1990:28).

Yet things have been mainly seen as animated by the social strategies of the people involved. The performance of objects as social mediators has been constrained to their signifying capacities in a system of rules and differences, rather than as full social members of a collective of people, things, and other beings (Latour 1993). Acknowledging the capacity of objects to create, modify, and even distort practices and meanings implies focusing on objects while refusing both constructionism and materialist causal determinism. As Gell (1998:96) argued, things can be considered social beings because through their phenomenal presence (which involves their history, material, technological, and representational traits) they have body-like performance capacities that make them both the source and target of social action. Thus even artifacts with seemingly representational traits may not have been considered as representing (i.e., as standing for another person, being, or idea) their makers, but as full social members with distinctive performing capacities.

Speaking of materiality implies therefore a different way of conceiving the tangible, beyond function and technicality, but including the capacities of the physical properties of things to modify human perception and action. Artifacts help us enter beyond the physical into the realm of the imaginary, but we never advance into this other territory without those properties. Dealing with materiality means going beyond the instrumental aspect of things, even if we are considering "social functions," like the communication of ideology, class, or identity. Although these might prevail at specific moments in history, and under particular conditions of social struggle (Wilkie 2001:229–231), communicative function is not what essentially defines the intervention of artifacts in the social world. Before assuming the communicative or representational aspect of things and the semiotic ideologies making sense of these aspects, the presence of things as social bodies has to be explored (Keane 2003).

The long lineage of the idea that people make themselves while making a world that shapes them in return gives credit to this point. From Vico and Marx to Lukács, Simmel, Lefebvre, and Merleau-Ponty among many others, philosophers have been inquiring about the mutual constitution of social and material worlds for a long time (see Meskell 2004:ch. 1). With different emphases, writers in this tradition have tried to overcome Western notions of the ontological division between mind and matter. The social – relations, institutions, conflict – is woven by lived human bodies in everyday practice and in conjunction with other non-human bodies (organic, inorganic, and imaginary). Rather than a text to be read or decoded, the world is a "texture" to sense and to use; a lived fabric of rhythms and relationships understood through praxis (Lefebvre 1991a[1974]:222). If anything, this highlights that speaking about matter and attending to its full experiential aspects is as difficult as speaking about our bodies, which do not exist as objects for us, but become so after specific reflective and ideological processes (Csordas 1994:7).

Matter has a primary role in everyday life, as it can either stabilize or disrupt habits, routines, understandings, and expectations in silent, pre-discursive ways. According to Schutz and Luckmann (1973:4–6), the lifeworld encompasses that province of reality experienced intersubjectively; what is assumed, what goes unsaid and is taken for granted in everyday life until disrupted by the unexpected. Simultaneously natural and social world, the lifeworld is the arena of reciprocal action. People, animals, and things offer to our actions a resistance which we must either subdue or to which we must yield. The lifeworld is the "source of a thick concept of self/other relations," and "the surrounding sense that anyone has who has any sense of the institutions, customs, and know-how into which we are all born" (O'Neill 1994:7).[4]

It is a premise of social phenomenology, and of anthropology in general, that to understand how subjects are constituted we must look at how the world is constituted; we must follow the threads holding people's existence. This existence, which is not immediately transparent and conscious for people, is by no means unquestioned or unreflective (O'Neill 1994; Thompson 1978). Contrary to Habermas's (1984:113–152) communicative reading of the concept, in the lifeworld the potential for change is present before conscious reflection and discourse, that is, in the sensuous engagement with the material world (Schutz and Luckman 1973:6; 1989:1, 105).

Praxis involves creative, emotive, and imaginative practices as well as the repetitive transformation of the world through instrumental action (Gardiner 2000:80; Lefebvre 1991b:96, 132). Therefore everyday life is contradictory, both the locus of routine and the fertile ground for change. As Merleau-Ponty argued (1962:199), human bodily existence is indeterminate, irreducible to any of its components (economics, sexuality, politics) although these may alternatively prevail in certain historical contingencies. This means that no matter how repetitive everyday life may be or how deeply rules are incorporated, human bodies are ultimately uncontrollable. Contrary to some opinions (e.g., Gardiner 2000; but see O'Neill 1994), this aspect is fully incorporated in Schutz and Luckmann's work. The concept of the lifeworld thus provides tools to define those materials, beings, and places whose knowledge and presence is necessary to perform in everyday life, while at the same time avoiding a romantic, "pastoral" view of the past. The lifeworld allows us to understand how social existence is woven through the pre-discursive or pre-reflective daily experiences in which objects, those quiet performers, dominate. The mundane has a *poesis* (O'Neill 1994:94–95) that gives everyday life both transcendence and transgressing potential, but is also paved with the minute cruelties of social sanction, routine, and repression. Nowhere else is this better seen than in the study of how objects and people come into being in mutual yet non-deterministic ways, both at the individual and collective level (Warnier 1999:135).

In the lifeworld objects, people, animals, atmospheric conditions, and immaterial things have similar ontological status: tools, dwellings, preys, pets, insects, rain, dust, dreams, ancestors, and storytelling coexist and affect each other's continual existence. As archaeologists, we may attempt to trace this mutual constitution by focusing on how past social worlds interwove themselves with both human and non-human beings, creating complex worlds of represented and non-represented experiences (Ingold 2000:348). Different materials are usually part of different spatio-temporal practices that often generate and reproduce different meanings and values (Munn 1986:chs. 5, 6). Thus, we could ask which relations are mediated by specific kinds of artifacts, such as those that seem to "represent" aspects of the world, and those without representational traits, such as tools.

For instance, ceramics and lithics usually involve diverse places, rhythms, and sequences that made these objects part of different social practices and regimes of value. Studies have amply shown that objects with representational traits create different experiences than those without them, from effecting silent yet ironic comments on rulers (e.g., Meskell 2004: 156–163) to apotropaic performances that grant objects the capacity to intervene as social beings (Boric 2002; Nakamura 2004; Scattolin In press). Likewise, non-local materials create different experiences than local items for the people who use them (Helms 1988; McBryde 1984; Taçon 1991). The interplay between the represented and the non-represented, and the local and non-local, opens interstices for interpreting past social life. The landscape provides the gate to understand the emergence and constitution of a particular form of social life, a lifeworld filled with contradicting forces, during the first millennium A.D.

Dwelling and Circulating: The Aconquija Mountains, Past and Present

In NWA, the hunter-gatherer lifestyle experienced changes around 5000 B.P. leading to the domestication of plants and camelids. Around 3600–2900 B.P., the first evidence of ceramic production and a sedentary way of life started to appear in the dry highlands or *Puna* (Aschero 2000a). It is generally believed that by the beginnings of the first millennium A.D., sedentary life was well established, often combining agriculture and pastoralism as well as hunting and gathering.

Unlike other areas in the Andes, Formative period societies in the region were small-scale communities with loosely structured internal hierarchies. Despite their size, these communities established connections across large areas, acquiring objects and resources from different south-central Andes microenvironments, often including the Pacific coast. In fact, long-distance circulation of goods existed from the Archaic Period throughout the whole prehistory of the area. However, it is in the first millennium A.D. when we find communities that combined lifestyles in more diverse ways. Highland llama caravans were apparently the main form of connection across the diverse south-central Andean microenvironments, bringing goods to settled valley communities in exchange for their products (Dillehay and Núñez 1988). Although it is unlikely that only one modality can account for the circulation of things throughout the whole prehistory of NWA, caravans have left a substantial material record constituted by paths, roads, temporary settlements, and rock art in different periods (Aschero 2000b; Korstanje 1998; Nielsen 2001a; Pérez Gollán and Gordillo 1993; Sinclaire 1994). The record of connections indicates that places were not the stable and isolated grounds for local identity archaeologists often imagine, but dynamic nodes in a network of threads holding people's existence.

The major shift in lifestyle enabled a different engagement with materiality, representations, and the landscape. In this context, artifacts with and without representational capabilities circulated across long distances, rendering material both previous and future transactions, users, and places in different ways. Most Andean studies of circulation of things interpreted these artifacts as passive material signs of the invisible social values of solidarity, reciprocity, status, or rank. Contrary to this, I argue circulating things had full status as mediators (in the sense of Latour 2000), as they were active agents in the constitution of a lived landscape that was a large-scale social space.

The Aconquija chain is a high mountain fringe (5600 m.a.s.l.) that spreads north–south creating a stark contrast between the humid eastern areas and the dry western lands. Daily life in Formative times was mainly organized around tasks related to agriculture, llama herding, hunting of wild animals such as guanaco, vicuña, taruca (small deer) and smaller game (Izeta 2004), and the procurement of both food and non-food resources. There is evidence of trails that connected both sides of the chain spanning from pre-Formative to modern times (Scattolin and Korstanje 1994). Ceramics, architectonic features, seeds, and lithics indicate the possibility of connections with places in diverse directions, such as Tafí (east), Campo del Pucará (southeast), Hualfín (southwest), Cajón Valley (northwest) and Laguna Blanca (west), among others (Figure 6.1). Given the distances of some of these places, and the lack of evidence of political centralization, it is safe to assume that Aconquija dwellers did not establish colonies to acquire products or goods in these regions. However, the mostly sedentary nature of the settlements (Scattolin and Albeck 1994) does not preclude the possibility of periodic trips to other regions to obtain resources whenever there was a relative reduction in local crop-related activities. Most likely, several modalities for the acquisition of objects and raw materials coexisted according to the rhythms and the circuits of tasks, both in the Aconquija and beyond (see Mayer 2002:143–171 for a rich ethnographic description of possibilities).

Two of the sites, Antigal de Tesoro and Ingenio Arenal (respectively located at the northern and southern extremes of the chain) are in direct communication with areas considered to be of key importance for the origins of regional social complexity (Tafí and Campo del Pucará). All the sites on the Aconquija offer striking views of the western desert lands immediately at the feet of the mountain, as well as the entrances to the western dry valleys of Cajón, Hualfín, and Santa María. On clear days it is even possible to see some of the accesses to the highlands (Puna) located as far as 50–60 kilometers away. The sites are thus places with a long history of multiple connections and interactions. In fact, current local middle-age and older residents remember seeing caravans from the Puna (mostly with donkeys rather than the traditional llamas) coming to trade highland products to the Aconquija and the nearby valley of Santa María in their youth, while some youngsters acknowledge having heard abut these encounters.

Until a few years ago these roads and herding posts at different altitude levels on both sides were still in use (Scattolin 1994). More recently, this circuit has been restricted to the western side by the creation of a provincial national park to preserve the remains of a famous high-altitude Inca shrine that overlooks the eastern side. Despite these restrictions, the rhythms and recurrences of everyday tasks reproduce

Objects, People, and Landscape in Northwest Argentina

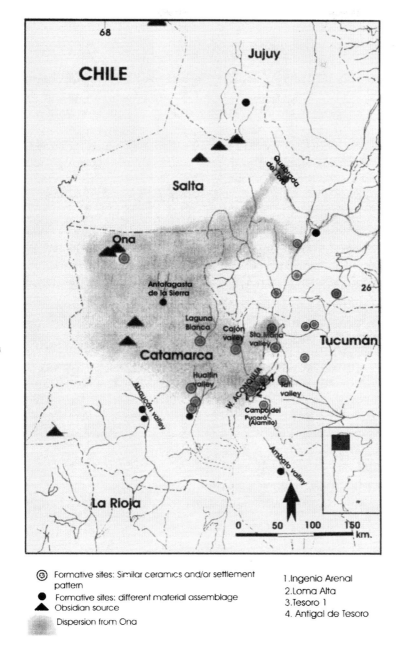

Figure 6.1 Map of northwest Argentina, with dispersion area of obsidian from the Ona source

old paths and open new ones. Today, people come and go between places constantly, mostly walking or by horse. They circulate vertically, taking their cattle to grazing pastures, looking for wood or game. The vertical movement of people, animals, and tools complements frequent horizontal circuits. The members of the few families that are dispersed along the 20 kilometers of the chain, – some owners of their land but most of them employees and/or tenants in large land properties owned by city dwellers – are constantly in contact through grazing arrangements, relations of friendship, kinship, and any combination stemming from the obligations imposed by work, religious festivities, or annual events such as the rodeo and branding of cattle. Some of these dwellers also own houses in the nearby town of San José (10–15 kilometers north) where they send their children to school, and almost all of them pay frequent visits to the city of Santa María, the economic and political centre of the region (around 20 kilometers north). In conversations they made clear that the real-and-imagined place (Soja 1996) for them is the city and its urban life, rather than the distant highlands or the eastern rainforest.

It is likely that everyday life in the past was also organized both in a vertical and horizontal way, however, the experience of the landscape and the perception of real-and-imagined places was oriented differently. Considering the paths and tracks between sites, posts, and shelters connecting both sides of the mountain we could safely argue that both land and lifestyle were carved in a recursive way in the past. In this carving people used artifacts that connected them to either neighboring or distant areas, by means of their raw material, their technique of manufacture, their shape, and/or their iconography. How these materials stretched local boundaries and generated a meaningful inter-subjective space-time can be grasped by looking at the interactions between different classes of artifacts, their circulation roads, and the spaces for their consumption.

Lithics and Ceramics: Dissolving Boundaries

The practices associated with ceramic and lithics are often quite different. This should not foster the imposition of a hierarchy of substances over archaeological materials: equally entangled in social life, their joint study can offer more nuanced approaches to the past. Andean archaeology has been reluctant to cross these apparent boundaries between materials (but see Burger et al. 2000; Gero 1989), resulting for instance in the predominance of ceramic evidence in the study of social interaction. In Formative NWA, the long-standing debate about cultural areas and spheres of interaction has been largely based on iconographic (ceramic and metalwork mostly) and organic (drugs, seeds) evidence, with less emphasis on tools and other non-decorated objects (compare Escola 1996; González 1979a; Tartusi and Núñez Regueiro 1993). This has often resulted in modeling rather rigid spheres of interaction. However, lately this has been contradicted by the spatial evidence of obsidian distribution. As mentioned before, obsidian from the Ona source has been found in sites with very different material culture assemblages, at least judging from their stylistic repertoire and settlement pattern.

The conceptualization of ceramics as indicative of well-defined social boundaries has also been challenged. Recent studies have documented the occurrence in the same sites of ceramic types usually attributed to seemingly mutually exclusive spheres of interaction. Likewise, attributes normally classified as part of different "types" and thus not expected to appear in the same vessel have been frequently observed in single potsherds (Scattolin and Lazzari 1998). Technological analysis has also shown that the assemblages are highly diverse and non-standardized in spite of the existence of identifiable general types (Scattolin and Bugliani In press).

The tangible world of daily objects thus indicates a complex, diverse, and possibly a contradictory networked sociality in the Formative period. This confirms Hodder's (1982a) ethnoarchaeological observations that social boundaries often do not correspond with the spatial distribution of stylistic patterns. But beyond indicating the existence of such a world to us, I argue these artifacts created this particular lifeworld. As two different material genres, ceramics and lithics were complex social beings that embodied different versions of the tension between representation and presence.

Seemingly representational objects have always played a major role in the interpretation of past societies. The motifs represented in NWA Formative ceramics range from geometric designs to highly diverse combinations of anthropomorphic and zoomorphic features (e.g., González 1979b; 1998; Scattolin 2003 In press). Stone was also employed in image-making practices in the form of masks, monoliths, and statuary showing combinations of anthropomorphic and zoomorphic motifs (García Azcárate 2000; Pérez Gollán 1994). Given these features, both mobile and non-mobile artifacts with figurative traits have dominated the inquiry of prehistoric social life in NWA, ranging from the analysis of structural relations between signs to the interpretation of meanings and practices.

Yet there is another dimension that remains overlooked and becomes evident when considering ordinary, non-decorated tools and artifacts, particularly those that circulated between people and places. As discussed previously, the biography of all materials, substances, and objects becomes meaningful when transiting different locations and uses. What is left aside by overlooking more "mundane" artifacts is the "presence" of these objects, charged with the invisible places and people from where they come and to where they might go. One could say that there is an immanence of the larger social world embodied in these objects. As Schutz and Luckmann (1989:104) put it "no experience of the world is self-contained."

This can be better understood by exploring the peculiarities of both ceramic and stone tool use and technology. While both are deeply rooted in what Mauss (1950:368, 371) described as habitual techniques of the body (Dobres 2000; Gosselain 1992), their plasticity is quite different and they foster different practices and understandings. Clay is a medium that allows various shapes and images through modeling and other decoration techniques that do not affect the containing functions of the vessel. Formative ceramics enabled the visual consumption of images and motifs throughout daily practices of the consumption of food and beverages, and possibly drugs as well. On the contrary, stone artifacts with figurative traits such as statues and masks, were usually more removed from daily practices, although in Tafí decorated monoliths are associated with corrals and thus with everyday tasks (García Azcárate 1996). In spite of these examples stone intervened in Formative daily life basically in the form of tools, flakes, grinding stones, and walls.

Although clay is the plastic medium par excellence, stone tools are basically fluid objects, always in the process of becoming something else through various forms of modification and/or use (Andrefsky 1998:30–39; Dobres 2000:149). Their capacity for becoming another tool, a flake, or waste is more immediate, more at hand than with other materials. Ceramics can certainly have very complex use lives, even after breakage. But unlike ceramics, the use of lithic tools usually implies some degree of transformation. Furthermore, both the locations of the different stages of lithic operative chains and the tasks in which they participate are usually widely scattered across the landscape. Ceramics can also circulate long distances, but their use is often more circumscribed to houses and settlements. Lithics thus offer a good perception of how ancient taskscapes must have looked like, and experientially speaking, they have a high capacity to embody transitivity and change. A closer look at the evidence from archaeological contexts from four sites on the western slope of the Aconquija chain will hopefully provide more substance to this interpretation.

The Rhythms of Lithics and Ceramics in the Aconquija

The consumption and deposition of lithics and ceramic are quite different in the Aconquija. While ceramics are largely present in domestic areas and burials, lithics mostly appear in domestic areas, with only a few cases of grinding stones in burials (Lazzari 1997). This largely domestic pattern of lithic use and deposition contrasts with other Formative sites in NWA, where for instance obsidian projectile points are found in graves (e.g., Raffino 1977) or obsidian flakes are deposited in what appear to be domestic caches (Gero and Scattolin 1995). Unlike these cases, obsidian in most Formative sites including those on the Aconquija was not removed from circulation.

Formative lithic assemblages in the Aconquija show a majority of expediently manufactured (flake tools, end-scrapers, scrapers, drills, burins) and poorly formalized (projectile points and preforms) tools made with locally available raw materials, most of them of lower quality than obsidian (varieties of andesite, quartz, quartzite, schist, etc.). There are a few raw materials of better quality 18–25 kilometers distant, depending on the site, such as basic andesite and some basalt (González Bonorino 1954). They usually constitute smaller proportions of the assemblages (17–25 percent). Unlike coarser local raw materials, the initial steps of the reduction sequence of these raw materials started mainly outside the sites, but there is evidence of most reduction stages in each of them. Obsidian was the only non-local lithic raw material, coming from at least three different sources (two remain unidentified), among which the most important was Ona (Lazzari 1999, Figure 1; Yacobaccio et al. 2002).

The geographically-limited occurrence of obsidian in NWA is probably responsible for the low frequencies of this material in Aconquija lithic assemblages (3–9 percent). However, the scarcity of this high-quality raw material did not foster its reservation for either special practical purposes or ritual activities. Unlike in other areas of the world such as Mesoamerica, the "technologies of enchantment" in NWA during Formative times were not related to the enchantment of obsidian technology (compare Gell 1996; Saunders 2001). Technological analysis has shown the relative simplicity of obsidian technology, at least compared to hunter-gatherer sites. In spite of the low percentages, obsidian is generally treated slightly less expediently than local materials. Apart from minimal differences, such as artifact size and a more advanced stage of usage when discarded, obsidian shows neither special investment in production, nor differential contexts of consumption and deposition. Although it cannot be said that obsidian was not preferred over other raw materials, people used a variety of lithic resources for precision artifacts such as projectile points, including those of much lower knapping qualities (e.g., andesite, quartz). The proficient manipulation of alternative resources indicates that although obsidian was probably appreciated, it was not particularly emphasized as a key resource. Although obsidian is far more efficient at tasks such as invading animal flesh, most stone types provide lethal weapon tips as well, without the risk of excessive breakage and the consequent lower reliability of the weapon and the maintenance and/or production time (Ellis 1997:50, 60–63).

The reduction sequence of obsidian started outside the Aconquija. When entering the area, obsidian had already been reduced from nodules[5] and re-worked in many ways. Once the blanks reached the sites they were used for making projectile points and expediently manufactured scrapers, drills, and burins. The percentage of obsidian instruments is still very low. There is some indication that it circulated among the Aconquija sites. There are variations in frequency and flake sizes that suggest that Ingenio Arenal-Faldas del Cerro (at the southern end of the chain) had a more fluent or frequent access. But in spite of the small sizes and low frequencies, very few obsidian artifacts show re-sharpening and/or re-utilization.[6] The overall technical quality of the artifacts does not differ substantially from others made of varieties of basalt and andesite. If there was a "need" (Wilk 2001) for obsidian, it was not only based on its superior knapping qualities.

These observations partially contradict some of the usual expectations regarding obsidian use according to the increasing distance from the source (Renfrew 1969). Indeed, it is unclear the degree to which obsidian was maximized, as studies often argue. Although this coincides with the expected low energy investment in lithic technology for sedentary societies (Torrence 1989), we must consider in this context that obsidian might have been the by-product of transactions involving the exchange of local goods for more appreciated highland products.[7] Andrefsky (1994:29) has observed that when a non-local raw material becomes abundant through social networks stone tools tend to be less formalized. Obsidian was far from being "abundant" in this area yet it is possible that its circulation was embedded in the movement of other things and people, without this implying direct access. After all, it is a well-documented ethnographic fact that small gifts often open barter transactions (Göbel 1998:879; Mayer 2002:156), while small things are normally swapped for what caravan members might need along their journey (Nielsen 2001a). What matters most is that the structure of the lithic assemblage reveals a technological style (Lechtman 1979:33) which is the embodiment of a field of understandings and practices that characterized the Formative period's lifestyle as partially unstructured and contingent.

If obsidian was not treated with any specific regard, neither in economic terms nor as part of symbolic/political strategies, we have to look elsewhere to understand the power of its presence. Although all things have a use, not every value system is based on utility (symbolic or otherwise). The material configuration of the lifeworld in the first millennium might give us a hint on this matter. As mentioned earlier, ceramics made visually explicit connections with certain areas in particular. However, obsidian of the same source appears in several sites, most of which do not share the same styles in ceramics. On a regional scale obsidian seems to have united places otherwise unconnected; a silent network of non-explicit connections still indicated and possibly experienced indirectly by the very use of this material in everyday activities. As part of different networks, the interplay between these materials generated a peculiar landscape of references that were explicit in diverse ways. Obsidian seemed to work as an index of the world beyond, and the world it referred to was more fluid and flexible than the one indicated by ceramics.

Ceramics in the Aconquija are mostly locally manufactured (see note 3) displaying nevertheless a repertoire of widespread Formative attributes and techniques. The stylistic repertoire of the period shows a consistent interest in the fluidity of form and image, often involving half-states between human and non-human beings (Figure 6.2). It is possible to see Formative ceramics as embodying the fluidity of social relations and

Figure 6.2 Fragment of Formative period ceramics from Antigal de Tesoro (western slope of the Aconquija Mountains)

networks in a fixed form. It is as if the qualisign (Munn 1986:16–18, 74)[8] of fluidity sedimented temporarily in objects whose shape, once designed for a purpose, did not vary according to usage (as lithics do). In spite of their fixed nature as material forms, ceramics were not immobile objects. For instance, it is believed that some fine wares traveled associated with the circulation of hallucinogenic drugs such as cebil (*Anadenanthera colubrina var. cebil*, González and Baldini 1989; Tartusi and Núñez Regueiro 2001). Truly the effect of a network, these ceramics illustrate the point made by Ingold (2000:345) that artifacts do not express an idea first conceived in the mind, but rather they "grow" out of a field of relations and practices.

Decorated ceramics show us the tension between representation and presence in Formative times. The visual references they made to other places and beings coexisted with their capacity to materialize this contingent state of social relations, to actually be complex social beings. Their potential to embody shared views and images, to be part of a representational project oscillating between doxa (in the sense of Bourdieu 1977) and the challenging and re-interpretation of established norms and rules cannot be discarded. Thoroughly discussed by Scattolin (2003; In press), both ceramic and stone Formative period objects with figurative features demarcated places and bodily habits significant for the constitution of subjects and for the reproduction of a sexed order of the world, which had founding effects for the development of vectors of difference and inequality in NWA later societies.

In the case of obsidian, the qualisign of fluidity had a different tone. Obsidian both expressed and created a different understanding of the world, one that was not based on conveying a meaning though the creation of images but in transformation while moving, in practice. In a non-representational way, obsidian made it impossible to ignore the world beyond the local. I say this precisely because there is a whole array of material culture, namely ceramics, which makes explicit, visually figurative and non-figurative references to other places in ways that stress fluidity and flexibility. In such a context, the indexical nature and the creative powers of obsidian were probably not indifferent. Likewise, the qualisign of fluidity as embodied in ceramics becomes more poignantly relevant because of the presence of obsidian. In this particular historical and social formation, these interconnections among different material forms could be part of a semiotic ideology, a dominant way of understanding meanings (Keane 2003:419).

But beyond the existence of a dominant way of understanding things, signs, people, and places, there is the power of presence these materials embody. Both obsidian and ceramics made unavoidable the existence of distant people and places in everyday local routines. They embodied this quasi-presence of the far and beyond in importantly different ways. Ceramics solidified social relations in mobile images and designs, thereby shaping the form, direction, and meaning of specific regional connections. Through the spatial and technological practices associated with its use, obsidian rendered the experience of these connections mutable and more importantly, non-exclusive. These objects were ultimately both silent reminders as well as active creators of distance as simultaneously important (as a constitutive element of the networks themselves) and meaningless (as a cost to overcome).

This interplay of selective references and practices shows us that through the lenses of regionality and the landscape, the local/foreign distinction becomes questionable. The ambivalent interplay between presence and representation in ceramics, and the intersection between ceramics and obsidian, were both the effects and the creators of a world that oscillated between the sedimentation of practices in places and circulation; a world in which people combined settling with traveling in various ways. Lifestyle and technological styles go hand in hand, creating each other in the sphere of practice (see Rival 1996).

In historical terms this implies that Aconquija dwellers had to face the demands – in labor time, gifts, hospitality – of multiple, possibly contradictory social connections and alliances. This is certainly a major point in small communities such as these, where "internal" economics and political life are not highly differentiated (Saitta 1997). In this setting the image-making effort displayed in ceramics is meaningful because it bears the elements of a crystallized way of understanding and representing the world, a way of imposing practical and semantic order upon the more contingent nature of daily life. As different material genres, the representational, more explicit project of ceramics encounters the silence of obsidian, which renders connections visible only after noticing its spatial movement. But in the same way that silence is not contrary to language, obsidian and ceramics are not mutually negating, opposed forces. They are two sides of the same thing; they are for each other the invisible of the visible.

I chose to dissolve the traditionally rigid separation between lithics and ceramics to explore how each element's significance was affected by the other and shaped a particular field of expectations and understandings within the Formative period lifeworld. The story would probably differ, were lithics studied together with rock art, or ceramic with fauna, or any other possible combination of archaeological materials. But this labyrinth of endless connections has, after all, grounding. As Bakhtin said "the conceptualization of reality develops and generates in the process of ideological social intercourse" (1981:180). The analysis of genres (here of material forms) has to be primed to their contingencies in space and time.

In this case, the different spatial practices around obsidian and ceramics hint the existence of multi-layered connections, alliances, and demands. The concretization of this contradicting situation carried the force of historical change, for never before had the region seen such a proliferation of objects, material images, and socio-spatial relations, and it never saw this proliferation again. Indeed, in later times the representational canon and the spatial practices of people became more restricted, in spite of the increasing caravan activity, and coincident with major sociopolitical changes toward centralization and inequality (Aschero 2000b; Pérez Gollán 2000; Tarragó 2000; Nielsen 2001b, 2004 for different areas of NWA). In the first millennium A.D., ancient, highly mobile social networks were reconfigured around the new settled life. The tensions between image-making and spatial practices, representation and presence, were changing alongside the changes in lifestyle.

The Lining of Mundane Things

As embodied forms of social practice, technologies imply the temporal and spatial relation between people, materials, and places (Ihde 1990). The elements involved in these connections vary according to both social projects and materials. In a world of explicit and selective social references and practices (which ceramics sought to portray as durable), obsidian performed the reality of a larger, more complex and possibly more contingent social world. But the same people used these ceramics and lithics, dwelling in the same places and circulating along the same paths, even if they did so when involved in different practices. The tensions between presence and representation in any lifeworld cannot be understood through artificially segregating spheres of practice, such as circulation and production, or materials, such as lithics and ceramics. Colloredo-Mansfeld has recently pointed that although "lives and values become materialized in durable ways, the capacity to act often lies in flows of substances. Some things we need to liquefy, not objectify" (2003:248).

In this case it seems that obsidian liquefied apparent borders that ceramics struggle to solidify, albeit in ambivalent manner. The materiality of obsidian, a sharp, dark, brittle, and scarce stone from somewhere else, was a condition of possibility for its movement across social domains. Compared to ceramics in the same period, its capacity to subvert crystallized understandings of the world becomes more relevant. As different material genres, obsidian and ceramics enabled different bodily gestures, routines and, ultimately, understandings of the world that were complementary, but which had the potential to develop into competing social tactics and strategies. But more importantly, what created this potential was that both materials, through their presence, rendered palpable a complex world of social and spatial connections. Both ceramic and obsidian introduced the realm of the imaginary into the everyday. They enabled the experience of real-and-imagined places; those places (sources, other villages) to which the Aconquija settlements became connected by means of these artifacts. These objects wove together worlds of represented and non-represented experiences. As active social bodies, obsidian and ceramics were particular forms of the interconnected existence that characterized the first millennium A.D.

This chapter certainly illustrates the difficulty of grasping the recursive relationship between people and objects. Things are stubborn participants in society, refusing to fully yield to (while instigating as well) the human imagination. Do things exist because of social relations or do social relations come into being because of objects? Conventional theoretical terms seem inadequate to convey how subjects and objects come to being hand in hand because they miss that this process is made real in practice (Lefebvre 1991a[1974]:159).

Marx (1993[1973]:807) sustained that to understand a social fact it had to be followed in its motion, in its constant becoming into something else. This analytical principle has a more general application. Inseparable from other spheres of social life, the circulation of objects illuminates the highly diverse ways of making things, people, and spaces. Through circulation, the texture of things becomes a dense concentration of relations that extend beyond their actual physical and spatial dimensions. The "essence" of things is in fact a texture: they are interdependent, and they show in concrete instances our basic relation to the world (Simmel 1990:118, 129). Archaeology has a privileged role in this quest, as archaeological knowledge is produced, for better or worse, through the sensuous engagement with the world, the handling and carving of the land, the "things themselves." We cannot escape the tangible, but our practice also reveals that the concrete is made of the imaginary and that everyday life makes and unmakes worlds in both discursive and unspoken ways.

We undoubtedly notice the social efficacy of things in motion in the past because of the peculiarities of today's spatial practices and discursive formations, which emphasize movement and fluidity (Friedman 2000). The current global configuration of social life highlights the role of things as quasi-presences of distant places and people. We live and circulate through the double bind of commodities, half way between agents of alienation and emancipating creativity. While our own existence and historical contingencies open us to these aspects in the past, this opening is not made at the expense of past social worlds but toward and with them. I hope that in this chapter NWA Formative things have, as they present themselves today, drawn us into their own texture and beyond my personal fascination with them.

Acknowledgments

I would like to thank Lynn Meskell and all the participants in the "Materiality in Archaeology" workshop for the opportunity to discuss my work in the context of such a uniquely rich assemblage of cases and perspectives. María Cristina Scattolin shared her information, insights, and work in progress openly. I am as always indebted to her generosity. Andrés Izeta kindly allowed me to quote information from his unpublished Ph.D. dissertation, as well as observations stemming from his current research. Lucas Pereyra Domingorena provided the photograph. Tim Ingold, Alejandra Korstanje, Lynn Meskell, Axel Nielsen, Matt Palus, and Nan Rothschild read different drafts. I am deeply grateful to all of them for their helpful suggestions, incisive comments, and kind support. Needless to say, all mistakes and confusing points are entirely my responsibility.

Notes

1 See Warnier (1999; 2001) for a direct use of "techniques of the body" in the study of materiality.
2 The first millennium A.D. falls within NWA Formative period (600 B.C.–A.D. 900, Núñez Regueiro 1972). In macro-regional terms, NWA Formative period coincides partially with the Formative, the Early Intermediate period and the Middle Horizon of the south-central Andes.
3 Obsidian sources have been traced through INAA (Lazzari 1997; 1999; Yacobaccio et al. 2002). More INAA results for obsidian and ceramics are expected in 2005.
4 While the lifeworld is not the same as "culture" (see Sommer 2001), it is close to Bourdieu's (1977) *habitus*. Yet unlike the latter the lifeworld emphasizes the continuous stream of human consciousness, i.e. the inseparability of real and imagined, subjective and objective aspects of human existence (Jackson 1996:21).
5 Both core and cortex indexes (Ericson 1982) are very low.
6 The percentage of instruments with complementary edges is less than 2 percent in most sites, and no obsidian artifact was transformed into another typological category through successive re-sharpening.
7 Camelid herding and hunting were well-established activities in the Aconquija during the Formative, therefore people did not depend on highlanders for meat,

hides, and wool. Yet recent research suggested the likelihood that vicuña parts circulated long distances (for hides and wool, email from Izeta to author 2004). Salt could possibly be a desired good from the Puna (Lazzari 1997), while the rich copper mines of the Aconquija could have been an incentive for the visit of caravans (see Nielsen 2001a), apart from the agricultural products.

8 Peirce's qualisign, as Keane (2003:414) explains: "refers to certain sensuous qualities of objects that have privileged role within a larger system of value. The idea of qualisign . . . is that significance is borne by certain qualities beyond their particular manifestations . . . lightness; for instance, can pertain to canoes, garden plots, decorations, bodies, and so forth."

References

Andrefsky, W. 1994 Raw Material Availability and the Organization of Technology. American Antiquity 59:21–35.

—— 1998 Lithics. Macroscopic Approaches to Analysis. Cambridge: Cambridge University Press.

Aschero, C. 2000a El poblamiento del territorio. In Nueva Historia Argentina, vol. 1. Los Pueblos Originarios y la Conquista. M. Tarragó, ed. Pp. 7–60. Buenos Aires: Editorial Sudamericana.

—— 2000b Figuras humanas, camélidos y espacios en la interacción circumpuneña. In Arte en las Rocas. Arte Rupestre, Menhires y Piedras de Colores en Argentina. M. Podestá and M. de Hoyos, eds. Pp. 15–44. Buenos Aires: Sociedad Argentina de Antropología.

Ashmore, W., and B. Knapp, eds. 1999 Archaeologies of Landscape: Contemporary Perspectives. Malden, MA: Blackwell.

Bakhtin, M. 1981 The Dialogic Imagination: Four Essays. Austin: University of Texas Press.

—— 1994 The Bakhtin Reader: Selected Writings of Bakhtin, Medvedev, and Voloshinov. P. Morris, ed. London and New York: E. Arnold.

Bapty, I., and T. Yates 1990 Introduction: Archaeology and Poststructuralism. In Archaeology after Structuralism: Post-Structuralism and the Practice of Archaeology. I. Bapty and T. Yates (eds.). Pp. 1–32. London: Routledge.

Barret, J. 1994 Fragments from Antiquity. An Archaeology of Social Life in Britain, 2900–1200 B.C. Cambridge, MA: Blackwell.

Battaglia, D. 1994 Retaining Reality: Some Practical Problems with Objects as Property. Man, New Series 29:631–644.

Beaudry, M., L. Cook, and S. Mrozowski 1991 Artifacts as Active Voices: Material Culture as Social Discourse. In The Archaeology of Inequality. R. McGuire and R. Paynter, eds. Pp. 150–191. Oxford: Blackwell.

Boric, D. 2002 "Deep Time" Metaphor. Memory and Apotropaic Practices at Lepenski Vir. Journal of Social Archaeology 3(1):46–74.

Bourdieu, P. 1977 Outline of a Theory of Practice. Cambridge: Cambridge University Press.
Bradley, R., and M. Edmonds 1993 Interpreting the Axe Trade: Production and Exchange in Neolithic Britain. Cambridge: Cambridge University Press.
Buchli, V. 1995 Interpreting Material Culture: The Trouble with text. *In* Interpreting Archaeology. Finding Meaning in the Past. I. Hodder, M. Shanks, A. Alexandri, V. Buchli, J. Carman, J. Last, and G. Lucas, eds. Pp. 181–193. London and New York: Routledge.
Burger, R., K. Mohr Chávez, and S. Chávez 2000 Through the Glass Darkly: Prehispanic Obsidian Procurement and Exchange in Southern Peru and Northern Bolivia. Journal of World Prehistory 14(3):267–362.
Colloredo-Mansfeld, R. 2003 Introduction. Matter Unbound. *In* Fleeting Objects. Journal of Material Culture 8(3):245–254.
Connerton, P. 1989 How Societies Remember. Cambridge: Cambridge University Press.
Csordas, T. J. 1994 Introduction: The Body as Representation and Being-in-the-World. *In* Embodiment and Experience. The Existential Ground of Culture and Self. T. Csordas, ed. Pp. 1–21. Cambridge: Cambridge University Press.
DeMarrais, E., L. Castillo, and T. Earle 1996 Ideology, Materialization, and Power Strategies. *In* Agency, Ideology, and Power in Archaeological Theory. Current Anthropology 36:15–31.
Descola, P. 1996 The Spears of Twilight. Life and Death in the Amazone Jungle. New York: The New Press.
Dietler, M., and I. Hembrich 1998 Habitus, Techniques, Style: An Integrated Approach to the Social Understanding of Material Culture. *In* The Archaeology of Social Boundaries. M. Stark, ed. Pp. 232–263. Washington D.C.: Smithsonian Institution Press.
Dillehay, T., and L. Núñez A. 1988 Camelids, Caravans, and Complex Societies in South-Central Andes. *In* Recent Studies in Pre-Columbian Archaeology. N. Saunders, and O. de Montmollin, eds. Pp. 603–634. Oxford: BAR International Series 421(ii).
Dobres, M. A. 2000 Technology and Social Agency. Oxford: Blackwell.
Edmonds, M. 2000 Ancestral Geographies of the Neolithic. Landscape, Monuments and Memory. London: Routledge.
Ellis, C. 1997 Factors Influencing the Use of Stone Projectile Tips. An Ethnographic Perspective. *In* Projectile Technology. H. Knecht, ed. Pp. 37–74. New York: Plenum Press.
Ericson, J. 1982 Production for Obsidian Exchange in California. *In* Contexts for Prehistoric Exchange. J. Ericson and T. Earle, eds. Pp. 129–148. New York: Academic Press.
Ericson, J., and T. Earle, eds. 1982 Contexts for Prehistoric Exchange. New York: Academic Press.
Escola, P. 1996 Riesgo e incertidumbre en economías agro-pastoriles: consideraciones teórico-metodológicas. Arqueología 6:9–24. Buenos Aires.

Friedman, J. 2000 Americans Again, or the New Age of Imperial Reason? Global Elite Formation, its Identity and Ideological Discourses. Theory, Culture and Society 17(1):139–146.

Funari, P., and A. Zarankin 2003 Social Archaeology of Housing from a Latin American Perspective. Journal of Social Archaeology 3(1):23–45.

Gamble, C. 1995 Making Tracks, Hominid Networks and the Evolution of the Social Landscape. *In* The Archaeology of Human Ancestry. Power, Sex and Tradition. J. Steele and S. Shennan, eds. Pp. 253–276. London: Routledge.

—— 1998 Paleolithic Society and the Release from Proximity: A Network Approach to Intimate Relations. World Archaeology 29(3):426–449.

García Azcárate, J. 1996 Monolitos-huancas: un intento de explicación de las piedras de Tafí (Rep. Argentina). Chungará 28:159–174. Chile.

—— 2000 Símbolos, piedras y espacios: una experiencia semiológica. *In* Arte en las Rocas. Arte Rupestre, Menhires y Piedras de Colores en Argentina. M. Podestá and M. de Hoyos, eds. Pp. 73–81. Buenos Aires: Sociedad Argentina de Antropología.

Gardiner, M. 2000 Critiques of Everyday Life. London: Routledge.

Gell, A. 1995 The Language of the Forest: Landscape and Phonological Iconism in Umeda. *In* The Anthropology of Landscape. Perspectives on Place and Space. E. Hirsch and M. O'Hanlon, eds. Pp. 232–254. New York: Oxford University Press.

—— 1996 Vogel's Net: Traps as Artworks and Artworks as Traps. Journal of Material Culture 1(1):15–38.

—— 1998 Art and Agency. An Anthropological Theory. Oxford: Clarendon Press.

Gero, J. 1989 Assessing Social Information in Material Objects: How Well Do Lithics Measure Up? *In* Time, Energy and Stone Tools. R. Torrence, ed. Pp. 92–105. Cambridge: Cambridge University Press.

Gero, J., and M. C. Scattolin 1995 Household Production as Glue: Insights from the Early Formative of Northwest Argentina. Paper presented at the symposium "Re-examining Theoretical and Methodological approaches to production and specialization: where do we go from here?" Society for American Archaeology 60th Annual Meeting, Minneapolis, Minnesota.

Giddens, A. 1979 Central Problems in Social Theory. Action, Structure and Contradiction in Social Analysis. Macmillan Press: London.

Göbel, B. 1998 "Salir de Viaje." Producción pastoril e intercambio económico en el noroeste Argentino. *In* 50 Años de Estudios Americanistas en la Universidad de Bonn. Nuevas Contribuciones a la Arqueología, Etnolingüística y Etnografía de la Américas. Bonner Amerikanistische Studien 30. S. Dedenbach Salazar-Saenz, C. Arellano Hoffman, E. König, and H. Prüners, eds. Pp. 867–891. Markt Schwaben, Germany: A. Saurwein.

González, A. R. 1979a Dinámica cultural del N.O. Argentino. Evolución e historia en las culturas del N.O. Argentino. Antiquitas 28–29:1–15. Buenos Aires.

—— 1979b Arte, Estructura y Erqueología. Lima: Universidad Nacional Mayor de San Marcos.

—— 1998 Arte Precolombino. Cultura La Aguada. Arqueología y Diseños. Buenos Aires: Filmediciones Valero.

González, A., and M. Baldini 1989 Vaquerías: la más antigua alfarería polícroma del noroeste Argentino. Más Allá del Objeto, Artinf Edición 78–79(14):8–12. Buenos Aires.

González Bonorino, F. 1951 Descripción Geológica de la Hoja 12e "Aconquija", Catamarca, Tucumán. Boletín N° 75. Ministerio de Industria y Comercio. Buenos Aires: Dirección Nacional de Minería.

Gosden, C. 1994 Social Being and Time. Oxford: Blackwell.

Gosselain, O. 1992 Technology and Style: Potters and Pottery among Bafia of Cameroon. Man, New Series 27(3):559–586.

—— 1998 Social and Technical Identity in a Clay Crystal Ball. In The Archaeology of Social Boundaries. M. Stark, ed. Pp. 78–106. Washington: Smithsonian Institution Press.

Gow, P. 1995 Land, People and Paper in Western Amazonia. In The Anthropology of Landscape: Perspectives on Place and Space. E. Hirsch and M. O'Hanlon, eds. Pp. 43–62. New York: Oxford University Press.

Graves-Brown, P. 1995 Fearful Symmetry. World Archaeology 27(1):88–99.

—— 2000 Matter, Materiality, and Modern Culture. New York: Routledge.

Grosz, E. 1994 Volatile Bodies: Toward a Corporeal Feminism. St. Leonards, NSW, Australia: Allen and Unwin.

Habermas, J. 1984 The Theory of Communicative Action, vol. 2. Lifeworld and System: A Critique of Functionalist Reason. Boston: Beacon Press.

Harvey, D. 1996 Justice, Nature, and the Geography of Difference. Cambridge, MA: Blackwell.

Helms, M. 1988 Ulysses' Sail. An Ethnographic Odyssey of Power, Knowledge and Geographical Distance. New Jersey: Princeton University Press.

Hodder, I. 1982a Symbols in Action. Cambridge: Cambridge University Press.

—— ed. 1982b Symbolic and Structural Archaeology. Cambridge: Cambridge University Press.

—— 1986 Reading the Past. Current Approaches to Interpretation in Archaeology. Cambridge: Cambridge University Press.

—— 1989 This is Not an Article About Material Culture as Text. Journal of Anthropological Archaeology 8:250–269.

Hodder, I., and R. Preucel 1996 Contemporary Archaeology in Theory. Oxford: Blackwell.

Hosler, D. 1995 Sound, Color and Meaning in the Metallurgy of Ancient West Mexico. In Symbolic Aspects of Early Technologies. World Archaeology 27(1):100–115.

Humphrey, C., and S. Hugh-Jones, eds. 1992 Barter, Exchange and Value. An Anthropological Approach. Cambridge: Cambridge University Press.

Ihde, D. 1990 Technology and the Lifeworld: From Garden to Earth. Bloomington: Indiana University Press.

Ingold, T. 2000 The Perception of the Environment: Essays on Livelihood, Dwelling and Skill. London: Routledge.

Izeta, A. 2004 Zooarqueología del Sur de los Valles Calchaquíes. Estudio de Conjuntos Faunísticos del Período Formativo. Ph.D. Dissertation, Facultad de Ciencias Naturales y Museo, Universidad Nacional de La Plata, Argentina.

Jackson, M. 1996 Introduction. Phenomenology, Radical Empiricism and Anthropological Critique. *In* Things as they Are. New Directions in Phenomenological Anthropology. M. Jackson, ed. Pp. 1–50. Bloomington: Indiana University Press.

Jensen, O. 2000 Between Body and Artefacts. Merleau-Ponty and Archaeology. *In* Philosophy and Archaeological Practice: Perspectives for the 21st Century. C. Holtorf and H. Karlsson, eds. Pp. 53–67. Göteborg: Bricoleur Press.

Joyce, R. 1993 Women's Work: Images of Production and Reproduction in Pre-Hispanic Central America. Current Anthropology 34(3):255–274.

Keane, W. 2001 Money is No Object. Materiality, Desire, and Modernity in an Indonesian Society. *In* The Empire of Things. Regimes of Value and Material Culture. F. Myers, ed. Pp. 65–90. Santa Fe, NM: School of American Research Press.

—— 2003 Semiotics and the Social Analysis of Material Things. Language and Communication 23:409–425.

Kern, S. 1983 The Culture of Time and Space: 1880–1918. Cambridge, MA: Harvard University Press.

Korstanje, M. A. 1998 El Médano, es un sitio caravanero? Apuntes sobre contextos de tráfico y territorialidad para el Formativo. *In* Los Desarrollos Locales y sus Territories. M. B. Cremonte, ed. Pp. 33–64. Facultad de Humanidades y Ciencias Sociales, UNJU, Argentina.

Küchler, S. 1993 Landscape as Memory: The Mapping of Process and its Representation in a Melanesian Society. *In* Landscape. Politics and perspectives. B. Bender, ed. Pp. 85–106. Oxford: Berg.

Latour, B. 1993 We Have Never Been Modern. New York and London: Harvester Wheatsheaf.

—— 2000 The Berlin Key or How to Do Words with Things. *In* Matter, Materiality, and Modern Culture. Paul Graves-Brown, ed. Pp. 10–22. New York Routledge.

Lazzari, M. 1997 La economía más allá de la subsistencia: intercambio y producción lítica en el aconquija. Arqueología 7:9–50. Buenos Aires.

—— 1999 Nuevos datos sobre la procedencia de obsidianas en el Aconquija y áreas aledañas. Cuadernos del Instituto Nacional de Antropología y Pensamiento Latinoamericano (INAPL) 18:243–256. Buenos Aires.

Lechtman, H. 1979 Issues in Andean Metallurgy. *In* Pre-Columbian Metallurgy of South America. E. Benson, ed. Pp. 1–41. Washington: Dumbarton Oaks.

Lecoq, P. 1987 Caravanes de lamas, sel et echanges dans une communauté de Potosí en Bolivie. Bulletin de l'Institut Francais d'Etudes Andines 16(3–4):1–38.

Lefebvre, H. 1991a[1974] The Production of Space. Oxford: Blackwell.

—— 1991b[1958] Critique of Everyday Life. London: Verso.

Lemonnier, P. 1992 Elements for an Anthropology of Technology. Ann Arbor, MI: Museum of Anthropology, University of Michigan.

—— ed. 2003 Technological Choices. Transformations in Material Cultures since the Neolithic. London: Routledge.
Leone, M. 1984 Interpreting Ideology in Historical Archaeology: Using the Rules of Perspective in the William Paca Garden in Annapolis, Maryland. *In* Ideology, Representation and Power in Prehistory. C. Tilley and D. Miller, eds. Pp. 25–35. Cambridge: Cambridge University Press.
MacBryde, I. 1984 Kulin Greenstone Quarries: The Social Contexts of Production and Distribution for the Mt. William Site. *In* Mines and Quarries. World Archaeology 16(2):267–285.
McGuire, R., and R. Paynter, eds. 1991 The Archaeology of Inequality. Oxford: Blackwell.
Marx, K. 1993[1973] Grundrisse. Foundations of the Critique of Political Economy. Trans. and Foreword by M. Nicolaus. London: Penguin.
Mauss, M. 1925 The Gift. The Form and Reason for Exchange in Archaic Societies. London: Routledge.
—— 1950 Les techniques du corps. *In* Sociologie et Anthropologie. C. Levi-Strauss, ed. Pp. 365–386. Paris: Quadrige/PUF.
—— 1968 Conceptions qui ont précedé la notion de matiére (Conference, 1939). *In* OEuvres II. V. Karady, pres. Pp. 161–166. Paris: Editions de Minuit.
Mayer, E. 2002 The Articulated Peasant. Household Economies in the Andes. Westview Press.
Merleau-Ponty, M. 1962 Phenomenology of Perception. London: Routledge.
—— 1973[1964] The Visible and the Invisible. Evanston: North Western University Press.
Meskell, L. 1999 Archaeologies of Social Life: Age, Sex, Class Etcetera in Ancient Egypt. Oxford: Blackwell.
—— 2000 Writing the Body in Archaeology. *In* Reading the Body: Representations and Remains in the Archaeological Record. A. Rautman, ed. Pp. 13–21. Philadelphia: University of Pennsylvania Press.
—— 2004 Object Worlds in Ancient Egypt: Material Biographies Past and Present. Oxford: Berg.
Meskell, L., and R. Joyce 2003 Embodied Lives: Figuring Ancient Maya and Egyptian Experience. London and New York: Routledge.
Miller, D. 1987 Material Culture and Mass Consumption. Oxford: Blackwell.
—— 2001 The Dialectics of Shopping. Chicago: University of Chicago Press.
Munn, N. 1986 The Fame of Gawa. A Symbolic Study of Value Transformation in a Massim (Papua New Guinea) Society. Durham and London: Duke University Press.
—— 1990 Constructing Regional Worlds in Experience: Kula Exchange, Witchcraft and Gawan Local Events. Man, New Series 25:1–17.
Myers, F. ed. 2001 The Empire of Things. Regimes of Value and Material Culture. Santa Fe, NM: School of American Research Press.
Nakamura, C. 2004 Dedicating Magic: Neo-Assyrian Apotropaic Figurines and the Protection of Assur. World Archaeology 36(1):11–25.

Nielsen, A. 2001a Ethnoarchaeological Perspectives on Caravan Trade in the South-Central Andes. *In* Ethnoarchaeology of Andean South America: Contributions to Archaeological Method and Theory. L. Kuznar, ed. Pp. 163–201. Ann Arbor: International Monographs in Prehistory.

—— 2001b Evolución social en Quebrada de Humahuaca (A.D. 700–1536). *In* Historia Argentina Prehispánica, vol 1. E. Berberián and A. Nielsen, eds. Pp. 171–264. Córdoba, Argentina: Editorial Brujas.

—— 2004 Warfare and Social History in the South Andes A.D. 1200–1450. Paper presented at the symposium "Warfare in Cultural Context: Practice Theory and the Archaeology of Violence," 69th Annual Meeting of the Society for American Archaeology, Montreal, March 31–April 4.

O'Neill, J. 1994 The Poverty of Postmodernism. London: Routledge.

Núñez Regueiro, V. 1974 Conceptos instrumentales y marco teórico en relación al análisis del desarrollo cultural del Noroeste Argentino. Revista del Instituto de Antropología V:169–190. Córdoba, Argentina.

Pels, P. 1998 The Spirit of Matter: On Fetish, Rarity, Fact and Fancy. *In* Border Fetishisms: Material Objects in Unstable Spaces. P. Spyer, ed. Pp. 91–121. New York: Routledge.

Pérez Gollán, J. A. 1994 Los Sueños del Jaguar. Viaje a la Región de la Sabiduría y los Señores Iluminados. Museo Chileno de Arte Precolombino.

—— 2000 El jaguar en llamas (La religión en el noroeste Argentino). *In* Nueva Historia Argentina, vol 1. Los Pueblos Originarios y la Conquista. M. Tarragó, ed. Pp. 229–256. Buenos Aires: Editorial Sudamericana.

Pérez Gollán, J. A., and I. Gordillo 1993 Alucinógenos y sociedades indígenas del Noroeste Argentino. Anales de Antropología 30:299–350. México.

Raffino, R. 1977 Las aldeas del Formativo Inferior de la Quebrada del Toro (Provincia de Salta, Argentina). Obra Homenaje al Centenario del Museo de La Plata, Sección Antropología, Tomo II. Pp. 253–299. La Plata.

Renfrew, C. 1969 Trade and Culture Process in European Prehistory. Current Anthropology 10(2–3):151–169.

Renfrew, C., and S. Shennan, eds. 1982 Ranking, Resource and Exchange. Cambridge: Cambridge University Press.

Rival, L. 1996 Blowpipes and Spears. The Social Significance of Huaroni Technological Choices. *In* Nature and Society: Anthropological Perspectives. P. Descola and G. Pálsson, eds. Pp. 145–163. London: Routledge.

Sabloff, J., and C. C. Lamberg-Karlovski, eds. 1978 Ancient Civilization and Trade. Albuquerque: University of New Mexico Press.

Saitta, D. 1997 Power, Labor and the Dynamics of Change in Chacoan Political Economy. American Antiquity 62(1):7–26.

Saunders, N. 2001 A Dark Light: Reflections on Obsidian in Mesoamerica. World Archaeology 33(2):220–236.

Scattolin, M. C. 1994 Un circuito ganadero en el Aconquija. Revista de la Escuela de Antropología 2:99–109. Rosario, Argentina.

—— 2003 Representaciones sexuadas y jerarquías sociales en el noroeste Argentino prehispánico. Acta Americana 11(1):30–48. Uppsala University. Sweden.

—— In press Contornos y Confines del Universo Iconográfico Precalchaquí del Valle de Santa María. Estudios Atacameños. Chile.

Scattolin, M. C., and M. E. Albeck 1994 El asentamiento humano en la falda occidental del Aconquija (Catamarca, Argentina). Shincal 4:35–65. Catamarca, Argentina.

Scattolin, M. C., and F. Bugliani In press Un repertorio surtido. Las vasijas del osis de Laguna Blanca, Puna Argentina. Revista Española de Antropología Americana.

Scattolin, M. C., and M. A. Korstanje 1994 Tránsito y Frontera en los Nevados del Aconquija. Arqueología 4:165–197. Buenos Aires.

Scattolin, M. C., and M. Lazzari 1998 Tramando redes: obsidianas al oste del Aconquija. Estudios Atacameños 14:189–209.

Schutz, A., and T. Luckmann 1973 The Structures of the Life-World, vol. 1. Evanston: Northwestern University Press.

—— 1989 The Structures of the Life-World, vol. 2. Evanston: Northwestern University Press.

Shanks, M., and C. Tilley 1987 Re-Constructing Archaeology: Theory and Practice. London: Routledge.

Simmel, G. 1990 The Philosophy of Money. London: Routledge.

Sinclaire, C. 1994 Los sitios de "muros y cajas" del río loa y su relación con el tráfico de caravanas. In Taller "De Costa a Selva." Producción e Intercambio entre los Pueblos Agroalfareros de los Andes Centro Sur. M. T. Albeck, ed. Pp. 51–76. Instituto Interdisciplinario Tilcara: Universidad de Buenos Aires.

Skibo, J., and M. Schiffer 2001 Understanding Artifact Variability and Change: A Behavioral Framework. In Anthropological Perspectives on Technology. M. Schiffer, ed. Pp. 139–149. Albuquerque: University of New Mexico Press.

Soja, E. 1996 Thirdspace. Journeys to Los Angeles and Other Real-and-Imagined Places. Oxford: Blackwell.

Sommer, U. 2001 "Hear the instruction of my father, and forsake not the law of thy mother." Change and Persistence in the European Early Neolithic. Journal of Social Archaeology 1(2):244–270.

Stallybrass, P. 1998 Marx's Coat. In Border Fetishism. Material Culture in Unstable Spaces. P. Spyer, ed. Pp. 183–207. New York and London: Routledge.

Stein, J. 2001 Reflections on Time, Time-Space Compression and Technology in the Nineteenth Century. In Timespace. Geographies of Temporality. J. May and N. Thrift, eds. Pp. 106–119. London: Routledge.

Taçon, P. 1991 The Power of Stone: Symbolic Aspects of Stone Use and Tool Development in Western Arnhem Land, Australia. Antiquity 65:192–207.

Tarragó, M. 2000 Chakras y pukara. Desarrollos sociales tardíos. In Nueva Historia Argentina, vol. 1. Los Pueblos Originarios y la Conquista. N. Tarragó, ed. Pp. 257–300. Buenos Aires: Editorial Sudamericana.

Tartusi, M., and V. Núñez Regueiro 1993 Los centros ceremoniales del N.O.A. Publicaciones 5: 1–49. Tucumán, Argentina.

—— 2001 Fenómenos cúlticos tempranos en la subregión valliserrana. *In* Nueva Historia Argentina Prehispánica. E. Berberián and A. Nielsen, eds. Pp. 127–170. Córdoba, Argentina: Editorial Brujas.

Taussig, M. 1993 Mimesis and Alterity. A Particular History of the Senses. New York: Routledge.

Thomas, J. 1991 Rethinking the Neolithic. London: Routledge.

—— 1996 Time, Culture and Identity. London: Routledge.

—— 1998 Reconfiguring the Social, Reconfiguring the Material. Paper presented at the I Reuniao Teoria Arqueologica na America do Sul, Vitoria, Brasil, April 1–4.

—— 2001 Archaeologies of Place and Landscape. *In* Archaeological Theory Today. I. Hodder (ed.). Pp. 186–75. Cambridge: Polity Press.

Thomas, N. 1991 Entangled Objects: Exchange, Material Culture, and Colonialism in the Pacific. Cambridge, MA: Harvard University Press.

—— 1997 In Oceania: Visions, Artifacts, Histories. Durham: Duke University Press.

—— 2001 Introduction. *In* Beyond Aesthetics. N. Thomas and C. Pinney, eds. Pp. 1–12. Oxford: Berg.

Thompson, E. P. 1978 The Poverty of Theory and Other Essays. London: Merlin.

Tilley, C. 1991 Material Culture as Text. The Art of Ambiguity. London and New York: Routledge.

—— 1993 Interpretive Archaeology. Oxford: Berg.

—— 1994 A Phenomenology of Landscape. Places, Paths and Monuments. Oxford: Berg.

—— 1999 Metaphor and Material Culture. Oxford: Blackwell.

Torrence, R. 1989 Tools as Optimal Solutions. *In* Time, Energy and Stone Tools. R. Torrence, ed. Pp. 1–6. Cambridge: Cambridge University Press.

Warnier, J.-P. 1999 Conclusion: le sujet comme "roue d'engrenage". *In* Approches de la Culture Matérielle. Corps á Corps avec l'Object. M.-P. Julien and J.-P. Warnier, eds. Pp. 135–142. Paris Montréal: L'Harmattan.

—— 2001 A Praxeological Approach to Subjectivation in a Material World. Journal of Material Culture 6(1):5–24.

Weiner, A. 1992 Inalienable Possessions. The Paradox of Keeping-While-Giving. Berkeley: University of California Press.

—— 1994 Cultural Difference and the Density of Objects. American Ethnologist 21(2):391–403.

Wilk, R. 2001 Towards an Archaeology of Needs. *In* Anthropological Perspectives on Technology. M. Schiffer, ed. Pp. 107–122. Albuquerque: University of New Mexico Press.

Wilkie, L. 2001 Communicative Bridges Linking Actors Through Time. Archaeology and the Construction of Emancipatory Narratives at a Bahamian Plantation. Journal of Social Archaeology 1(2):225–243.

Yacobaccio, H., P. Escola, M. Lazzari, and F. Pereyra 2002 Long Distance Obsidian Traffic in Northwestern Argentina. *In* Geochemical Evidence for Long Distance Exchange. M. Glasscock, ed. Pp. 167–203. Westport, CT: Greenwood Press.

Yentsch, A., and M. Beaudry 2001 American Material Culture in Mind, Thought and Deed. *In* Archaeological Theory Today. I. Hodder, ed. Pp. 214–240. Cambridge: Polity Press.

7
Building an Architecture of Power: Electricity in Annapolis, Maryland in the 19th and 20th Centuries

Matthew M. Palus

> The human body is a reservoir of force constantly escaping, constantly being renewed from the one center of force – the sun. A perfectly healthy man has a large amount of nerve-force in reserve, and this reserve is not often exhausted... The neurasthenic is a dam with a small reservoir behind it, that often runs dry or nearly so through the torrent of the sluiceway... a battery with small cells and little potential force... an electric light attached to a small dynamo and feeble storage apparatus, that often flickers and speedily weakens when the dynamo ceases to move.
> George Beard, *Sexual Neurasthenia (Nervous Exhaustion)*
> (1972[1898]:58–61)

Introduction: The Current Approach

During the later half of the 19th century, electricity was willfully materialized to allow telecommunications, via the telegraph and telephone, and later to provide illumination at a municipal scale, first outdoors on city streets, then inside stores and businesses, government offices, and finally homes. The functioning of these apparatuses can illuminate the project of this volume, in that they make material what we would otherwise consider to be categorically immaterial, things such as light, warmth, magnetism, and vital forces that seem to motivate machines as well as animal life, effectively blurring the borderline between these two conditions, matter made tangible, and unformed, invisible, immaterial things. The archaeology of electricity begs to become the archaeology of the immaterial and its place in modern life, and yet electricity is difficult to locate outside of these various materializations. Even the parapsychological effects connected to electricity, such as mesmerism, derive from power that is supremely material, believed to originate from the vital force and personal, animal magnetism of people's bodies, and bearing a close relationship to their will and being (de la Peña 2003:4, 92–98; Simon 2004:171–175). From the mid-18th century experimenters with electricity conceived of its relationship to the organic energies that imbued animal life, and this perception formed the basis for the medicinal application of electricity into the present day (Schiffer 2003:133–160). Galvanism linked electricity to biological life. "The galvanic and electric fluids were not regarded as being different in themselves but were treated separately because they were produced through the use of different items of apparatus." Animation of frog's legs gave way to the animation of "the heads of oxen and on several occasions the bodies of executed criminals" (Morus 1998:126–127). What then might be immaterial about electricity, a force that seemed common if not constitutive to many different phenomena? So long as each apparatus functioned tolerably, electricity was very much materialized.

Perhaps then, electricity fails to be materialized as the apparatus fails: fails to function according to the desires of its operators, or fails to fulfill the promise that legitimated its initial and ongoing construction. Errant arcs, tics, shorts, spasms, shocks, and outages betray this failure. The strange etheric substance again becomes what is only imperfectly grasped – really fetishized – by engineers, philosophers, and experimental scientists, and every single consumer of electrical products, major and minor. What seems to be applied systematically becomes confounded, irregular, unpredictable, and *nervous* in every sense of the word (Taussig 1992). So is it nervous, or is it a system, and why do we say that it is one or the other?

To put faith into electricity, and perhaps much 19th-century technology, seems to require that one forget this nervousness and see it as a rationally applied and governed system. Wolfgang Schivelbusch addresses this possibility concerning early railroad transportation. One could not enjoy train travel unless one continually forgot the possibility of disaster from derailment or collision. He quotes a 1940 letter from Theodor Adorno to Walter Benjamin: "All reification is forgetting: objects become mere things at the moment they are fixed without being actually present in all their parts – the moment when some part of them has been forgotten" (Schivelbusch 1986:163). Another member of the Frankfurt School, Herbert Marcuse, articulated a critical theory of technology premised on a new form of fetish developing in modern, authoritarian states at the end of the 19th century, in which the fetishization of *technique* or *efficiency* replaced commodity fetishism (Arato and Gebhardt 1982:138). Marcuse refers to this new ideological form as *technological rationality* (Marcuse 1982). This specific form of thought, also considered carefully by Horkheimer and Adorno in *Dialectic of Enlightenment* (2000[1972]) is not necessarily the result of living with technology, making use of it daily or purchasing mass-manufactured goods, rather it is the emergent ideology through which that materiality was produced, in which machinery and mass manufacturing predominate in the material conditions of life. The fetishism of technique lends a morality to efficiency; "machine truths" widen and solidify at the expense of other values and other truths.

In this chapter I wish to explore these tensions, including the tension drawn between electricity's materiality and its nervousness in application, drawing on the installation of electric lights in Annapolis, Maryland during the late 19th century. In July of 1889 the small southern community of Annapolis first experienced light that was produced with electricity on a citywide scale. As such, Annapolis, then as now the capital of Maryland, seat of the State Legislature and home to the United States Naval Academy, began the transition from gas to electric light in step with similarly-sized cities in Maryland, not far behind the initial conception of central supply electricity in the United States. While individual arc lights powered by single generators had been in use since the mid-19th century, central supply was an American innovation that involved wiring a series of lights together in a circuit, creating a mass of light, subdivided almost endlessly in Edison's phraseology and powered by a central plant (Jonnes 2003:58). The Brush Arc Lighting Company based in Cleveland, Ohio installed 23 arc lights in New York City in 1880 at its own expense, in order to demonstrate their effectiveness.

Electricity in Annapolis, Maryland

Thomas Edison conducted the first demonstration of his direct current electrical generation and transmission systems in 1879, and completed his first permanent central power station in New York in 1882 (see Hughes 1983; Nye 1997; Schivelbusch 1988). These systems spread throughout North America rapidly, and by the later 1880s many small towns were adopting electricity to light their streets. The Annapolis Electric Light Company was incorporated in 1888, "for the generation and transmission of Electricity over or through wires for lighting or for motive power" (Anne Arundel County Circuit Court 1888). While the utility was owned and developed privately, with an apparatus purchased on a new and growing national market in such machines, the decision to use electricity to light city streets was made by the Mayor and Aldermen for the community, who since 1859 had contracted with a local company to light the streets with gas produced from coal. It took a matter of weeks for a combination of arc and incandescent lights to be mounted on poles throughout the city, and the first contract to light the streets with electricity commenced in July of 1889. Until 1912 electricity continued to be generated in Annapolis and its use was adopted in homes and businesses, though not universally and never in any industrial applications. One means of lighting replaced another, in all of these contexts, but the city would always be the single biggest consumer of local electricity. As such this was "administered light," the product of a political apparatus as much as a technological one (Asendorf 1993:162). One premise of this chapter is that the two are indivisible. Technological and political apparatuses retrace one another in Annapolis, creating a historical geography of power.

A few months before the lights were turned on in Annapolis, in May of 1889, the newly-incorporated electrical utility ran an advertisement in the local newspaper, informing readers that

> An opportunity is now offered to our people, in the way of lighting, not only their places of business, but their private dwellings, places of worship, public halls, &c., at a wonderful low cost, besides being entirely free from a very serious objection – heat – as also from danger as has been charged. While they say danger attends the Electric Light without explanation, they lose sight of thousands who have been sacrificed by the improvident use of gas, kerosene and other oils. Satisfactory reasons will be given why the Electric Light is even less dangerous than any other light heretofore known, upon application at the office. (*Evening Capital* (EC) 1889h)

The concern with heat stems from a phenomenon that accompanies gaslight, and which electrical lights do not produce in appreciable amounts. The number of gas burners required to light a large space not only produced enormous amounts of heat, they consumed oxygen such that conduits had to be installed in some large auditoriums that fed the combustion of gas with air from outside the building, in order to prevent the depletion of oxygen within the enclosure that could cause dizziness, headaches, and fainting (Schivelbusch 1988:45–47). What is still curious is the avoidance of actually calling electricity *safe*. Electric light is "even less dangerous" than any other source of illumination; "Satisfactory" reasons can be provided why electricity should be considered so, upon inquiry with the agent of the electrical utility. A survey of Annapolis' major newspaper from 1889 to 1891 shows that no death or injury resulted from the introduction of electricity in Annapolis, at least not for several years after electricity began to be produced locally. Still, this reticence seems to *contrast* with the materialization or constitution of electricity as a public utility, safely domesticated and pressed into the service of Annapolis residents.

Machine Truths and The Body

In a recent history of 19th-century electricity and its anxieties, Linda Simon observed that while the American public was slow to accept electrification into their homes for domestic heating, lighting, and power, the application of electricity in medicine as "electrization," "galvanization," "faradization," or even "Franklinization" was commonplace. Americans entered the Electric Age with bodies that – for all intents and purposes – already ran on electricity (Simon 2004). In spite of this fact, the consumer market for electricity grew very slowly. Nineteenth-century inventor-entrepreneurs like Edison and Brush courted the top echelon of urban industrialists with electricity in order to secure support for their workshops and manufactories during the 1870s, in the years before electric light was at all marketable (Davis 2003; Jonnes 2003). Historian David Nye reports that by 1910 just one in every ten American homes had been electrified, some thirty years after municipal lighting systems using electricity became competitive with gas. Private utility companies, many conglomerated from small local electric utilities established during the 19th century, marketed their products and services aggressively throughout the early the 20th century. In part, the task was to domesticate electricity that was produced *artificially*, and make it appear safe in proximity to people's bodies (de la Peña 2003). In 1920 many urban homes and apartments had been electrified, but many more areas waited for the large rural electrification projects of the 1930s (Nye 1997:239).

Certainly the distribution of electric light and home service broke down geographically and within cities upon lines of race and class, reinforcing these by selective development, investment, and disinvestment. But Simon proposes that the apparent contradiction between the general/popular acceptance of therapeutic electricity or electrotherapy, which to a degree transcended one's social class, and resistance to its more utilitarian application stems from the widespread belief in the oneness of artificial electricity and nervous animal energy. "Vitalism, which held that electricity was the source of life itself, justified the conviction that applying electricity to the human body could strengthen and energize" and simultaneously implied a threat from surrounding our bodies with apparatuses of artificial electricity, perhaps subsuming ourselves to the newer, larger apparatus for the production and distribution of power (Simon 2004:7). Vitalism preceded notions of electricity-as-utility, and "urged people, even those who had never used a telegraph, to examine their beliefs about the relationship between artificial and animal electricity; it aroused superstitions" (2004:46).

Electrotherapy was not parascience or superstition, nor did it resemble the convulsive electroshock treatments of modern psychiatry, or least of all the lethal application of electricity in capital punishment (Davis 2003:264–267; Essig 2003; Jonnes 2003). Since the mid-18th century physicians and experimental scientists had applied gentle currents and "baths" of electricity seldom attaining sufficient strength to "shock" the recipient, initially to treat headaches, paralysis, muscular spasms, and persistent pain (Morus 1998; Schiffer 2003). Later in the 19th century, neurologist George Beard described a new disease particular to white Americans called *neurasthenia*. "American nervousness" was literally a weakness in the nerves, and writing with colleague A. D. Rockwell he promoted the use of various forms of electricity – for instance static, faradic, galvanic, alternating or direct – in different strengths to rejuvenate depleted nerves and bring patients back from their nervousness. "Neurasthenia is a chronic, functional disease of the nervous system, the basis of which is impoverishment of nervous force; deficiency of reserve, with liability to quick exhaustion, and a necessity for frequent supplies of force... 'Nervousness' is really nervelessness" (Beard 1972[1898]:36). As a catch-all for symptoms ranging from depression to constipation, dyspepsia, stomach and mouth ulcers, lack of appetite, back pain, hysteria, and trouble with the reproductive organs in both men and women, including poor sexual performance and impotence in men, neurasthenia captured the attention of the medical community, finding supporters among neurologists, gynecologists and other physicians, not to mention their patients (Beard 1972[1898]; de la Peña 1999; 2001; 2003; Schivelbusch 1988:70–73).

Electrical energy and magnetism was for the vitalist or the electro-therapist in the 19th century what psychotherapy was for Freud in the 20th century (Gosling 1987). The most powerful materializations of Freud's theory lie in the experience of uncanniness; in contrast, the basis for the treatment of neurasthenics and a virtual diagram of the disease was being erected in towns and cities across the United States and Europe, seeming in fact *to follow the disease*. There was a "popular conflation of artificial and animal electricity," such that telegraphs were likened to nerves transmitting electrical impulses, and the enervation of the muscles and the brain, personal magnetism and energy, and the current flowing through wires to power electric lights and machinery shared a basic sameness (Simon 2004:46–47). The immensity of this technological feat threatened to sublimate individual bodies of feeble spark, mere conductors or conduits for energies vastly more powerful.

> The wickerwork of nerves finds its counterpart in the transmission cables threatening to connect to the subject from all sites and annihilate him. The invisible electrical currents are the metaphor of the life of the nerves: the body becomes a force field, a contingent intersection of events determined elsewhere... electro-hysteria unfolds before the background of the quickly changing anonymous social relationships in the big city, in which objects, things as well as people, are experienced as nothing more than nerve stimuli. (Asendorf 1993:177)

Electric power and the growing electrical infrastructure was not merely a metaphor for the vital animal forces described and experimented on by physicians and philosophers. It represented a competing materiality; like artificial electricity, animal electricity or magnetism was also material. This fact expresses the inseparability of subject and object, animation that is sometimes artifice and automatic. Beard's theory of neurasthenia had a place within contemporary, scientific debates between materialist and spiritualist notions of the soul, arguably an interrogation of the place of mind between subject and object states. Was it a chemical entity activated within the brain, or was it spiritual activation of the nervous tissues from outside? Beard's theory was purposefully a compromise between these two positions (Simon 2004:188). He proposed that neurasthenia, the "impoverishment of nervous force" (Beard 1972[1898]:36), resulted from "specific features of the young American society – in particular the telegraph, the railroads, the periodical press, the sciences, and the atmosphere of political and religious liberty – [which] had increased mental demands on Americans, especially on the urban professionals who labored with their heads rather than their hands" (Gosling 1987:11). In other words, American nervousness was a secondary consequence of these new technologies and the nerve-draining pressures that they created, not simply the presence of these new materialities. It was also exclusive to the sensitive bodies of those who were white and native born; just at Nietzsche wrote that black-skinned people did not feel pain to the same degree as whites (1989:68), Beard used Native Americans to exemplify the limitless reservoir of energy in the prehistoric condition.

Nervousness produced an uncanny correspondence between the sufferer and the system, as though the sufferer became a conduit or transmitter of signals. Medicine was dominated by a somatic theory of illness during the later 19th century, in that all disease was believed to be caused by lesion or irritation that was localized. In other words, every disease had a local cause. In contrast, neurasthenia had no visible cause and rather resembled a suite of related symptoms, and as a diagnosis it enclosed and made respectable numerous individuals who suffered from no legitimate malady and were consequently dismissed as hysterics, hypochondriacs, or malingerers. In part it gave way to psychotherapy – though it did prepare the ground for it – because no specific organic cause for neurasthenia was ever discovered (Gosling 1987:17–18). Beard suggested first, that neurasthenia did have a discrete cause but that no method for detecting it had been developed, and second that irritation was transmitted freely inside the body of a neurasthenic, as the depleted nerves had little resistance and allowed the stimuli to move from one part of the body to another. The irritations causing neurasthenia "may arise from any part of the body and may be transmitted to any other part" via the sympathetic nerves, and this impeded the discovery of a local cause for the disease (Beard 1972[1898]:36).

Of this very phenomenon, Christopher Asendorf writes, "The nervous body is noncorporeal, immaterial, arbitrarily subject to being charged with tensions. Nervous conditions assume ... the form of an electrohysteria: objects transform themselves into electrified machines that render the subject a victim of currents" (Asendorf 1993:176). Just as irritations can be transmitted from any point in the body to any other, displacing the irritation and concealing its origins, so goes the city networked sublimely into numerous circuits and subsystems. And yet, in the body perfect intercommunication, conductivity, and ease of transmission was a disease state. The neurasthenic body becomes a transmitter; it embodies the transmission system above the streets. Every irritation is perforce shared throughout the body because the nerves are so highly attuned and excitable, and resistance so low that communication of unnecessary signals is irresistible. This capacity of the body was only understood once the metaphor of electrocommunications was available. It is possible that Beard reversed the facts of the matter. Nervousness was brought about by these improvements. They compelled the body to transmit and be more conductive, to be less resistant, to conjure currents and set them moving. In this way people's bodies came to resemble the regnant apparatus and conform to what Herbert Marcuse called "machine truths" (1982).

The Shape of Electricity in Annapolis from 1889–1912

Writing about the 19th-century modernization of Annapolis, Christopher Matthews (2002) argues that railroad connections to the industrial and commercial centers of Baltimore and Washington, D.C. that reached the city in 1840 allowed it to be perceived as part of the technologically and politically modern state. However, Annapolis was completely overshadowed economically by Baltimore during the early 19th century and seemed to exhibit nervousness regarding its own commercial development. Wrote one editor for the *Evening Capital,*

> Shake off your sleepiness, and go to work! ... Welcome a wide-awake, progressive man whenever one comes along. Don't be eternally discussing why your town is so slow. Better take off your coat and do a little something towards making it otherwise ... If you are a man of means and

influence, take the lead. If you can help your town, remember you are helping yourself. (EC 1889b)

In some ways the U.S. Naval Academy at Annapolis, patterned after the military academy at West Point, was an alternative to industry. Towards the end of the 19th century Annapolis produced two things: oysters, and officers. Maintaining Annapolis as a suitable home for the Naval Academy and the state government provided the city with an impetus to develop a modern infrastructure, sufficient to sustain these institutions and their facilities. In December of 1888, the *Evening Capital* ran a local item stating that

> A bill is pending before the House naval committee providing for lightning [sic] the grounds surrounding the Naval Academy, at Annapolis, with electricity. To carry out the provisions of the bill an electric plant will have to be established at the Academy. An electric light company has been established in Annapolis, and it is proposed to have the bill amended so that the company may . . . supply the electric light for the Academy grounds. (EC 1888b)

The city entertained bids to install a network of electric street lights several years earlier, and after receiving bids from a gas light company in Pennsylvania, and reviewing conditions for receiving a franchise from Edison's incandescent light company, the city offered its contract for street lighting to a local group that had recently incorporated. Articles of incorporation for the Annapolis Electric Light Company of Anne Arundel County were delivered to the Anne Arundel County Court clerk in March of 1888.

Since 1859 the city had been lit by gas, provided by the generating plant of the Annapolis Gas Light Company. In the late 1880s the city paid approximately $2,000 annually out of a $20,000 to $25,000 budget to have its streets lighted with gas, maintaining its own reflector lamps as needed. Maryland towns of comparable size were changing over to electrical lights, which were found preferable or wanting depending on the source consulted. Elihu S. Riley, who served as the clerk for the corporation of aldermen who led the town and later as their legal counselor, was also a founding partner in the new electrical utility as well as the chief editor of the *Evening Capital*. He incorporated news items strategically, or at least it seems that way:

> Frederick City and Hagerstown are at this time agitating the question of lighting their cities with electric light. Many towns and cities in this and adjoining States have already adopted the system and wherever introduced it has been found a paying investment. The enterprising town of Easton, just across the bay, has adopted the electric light, and find [sic] it superior to the old system of lighting the town. It gives to the place a business like cosmopolitan air, and shows enterprise on the part of its citizens ... (EC 1888a)

Poles of chestnut were erected and prepared for wires and lamps in May; an agent for the company named William Watts solicited customers for electric light beginning on May 15, two months before the wires carried a current. However, one staff writer for the newspaper noted in May of 1889 that "Many persons are waiting to see their neighbors use electric lights before they take hold themselves" (EC 1889a; EC 1889h). "Business has taken a rest and will not be revived until the electric current is turned on," was the editorial one day (EC 1889a). In another column it was printed, in a single line and without embellishment or substantiation, "Electric lights will give Annapolis a boom" (EC 1889a).

Much anticipated, the generation of power was mentioned almost daily in the *Evening Capital* in the weeks preceding the first night that was lighted with electricity. Then, on July 1, 1889, The Annapolis Electric Light Company initiated a two-year contract to light the city streets, and the contract formerly held by the gas light company was terminated. Wrote an anonymous staff writer for the *Evening Capital*, "For the first time in the history of our city, it was lighted last night by Electric lights. ... It was another step in the city's progress in the march of improvement, and shows that Annapolis is keeping pace with her sister cities in all the improvements of the times ..." (EC 1889f). The newly constructed plant (Figure 7.1), which had been completed in the previous Spring, was supervised for the first month by a representative from Westinghouse, who trained the first crew of electricians in Annapolis and the first plant superintendent (EC 1889c). The rationale for adopting electricity is clear from these passages; more than mere boosterism, these notes reflect the anticipation that progress will follow behind electricity, with the re-vitalization of an economically depressed community.

The electric lights initially installed were a combination of arc lights and incandescent ones, hung on 35- to 40-foot poles along the streets

Figure 7.1 View of the Annapolis Gas and Electric Light Company Plant, ca. 1895 (Maryland State Archives SC182-02-0809)

of Annapolis. These lights are based on different conductive materials and each offers a different quality of light. The arc lighting system initially installed in Annapolis was purchased from a local franchise of the Brush Electric Light Company in Baltimore. One newspaper article indicates that workmen erecting poles and installing the system had come from Baltimore to do the work, as well as train local workmen to maintain the system. Arc lights give off a harsh light that nearly matches daylight in glare and brightness. Further, people tended to stare directly into arc lights when first introduced to a city, and those marketing electric lights worked to educate the public against such unsafe practices (Simon 2004:75). Arc light is generated by combustion of a pair of conductive carbon rods that allow a spark to arc across a narrow gap between the rods, the reaction consuming the carbon and producing an extremely bright and penetrating light. The intensity of arc light is measured in thousands of candle-powers, while gaslight can be estimated in a few dozens. Additionally, arc light cannot be modulated, but shines at full brightness while the current is applied; the light it gives off is utterly, strikingly *steady*, in contrast with the softness of wavering gaslight. In cases of failure, due to atmospheric conditions or other difficulties, arc lights produce dazzling affects, lowering and raising their light suddenly if not explosively. In the more familiar incandescent bulb light is produced by a heated filament, and much more resembles light produced by gas lamps, only the filament replaces the gas-jet. Incandescent light is softer, but like arc lighting the filament is consumed and lamps themselves must be replaced. The successful incandescent lamps that Edison developed used a carbon filament prepared from a bamboo fiber. A variety of metal filaments were introduced in the 1890s, but the practical tungsten-filament lamp was not introduced until before the First World War (Schivelbusch 1988:55–64).

The relatively early introduction of electricity in Annapolis, "keeping pace with her sister cities" so to speak, seems to address Simon's thesis that there was popular resistance to electrification rooted in anxiety about the relationship between artificial electricity and the enervation of people's bodies. What seems to be the case is that electricity was cultivated and fostered in Annapolis by the city government, and only later did a market develop. In fact, the local electrical utility in Annapolis actually failed by 1912 and was absorbed into a larger electrical conglomerate, and eventually became an extension of the enormous Baltimore gas and electric utility (King 1950). There are several sources available that allow us to draw out specific information regarding the demand (need? desire?) for electricity, and the growth of the network in Annapolis. First, the mayor of Annapolis published a report on the state of the city's finances and other projects annually, and as such we can define what part the city played in the development of electricity from its introduction.[1] The city was the first large consumer of electric power when this utility was established, and though there were hopes that the local utility would receive a government contract to provide lighting to the United States Naval Academy, this was never the case. In fact, there was never a large consumption of electric power in Annapolis for manufacturing, no high-voltage consumers supported this utility in same way as they did in other American cities. Beyond this, what the mayor's reports show is that the city as a consumer of electrical power did not expand its consumption to a great degree while power was produced locally (see Table 7.1 below).

Table 7.1 City expenditures on selected public utilities, 1884–1914[a]

Year	Fiscal year	Total city spending for period[b] (in $)	City expenditures for public utilities (in $)			
			Annapolis Gas Light Co.	Annapolis Water Co.	Annapolis Gas and Electric Light Co.	Annapolis Public Utilities Co.
1884	Jan 1 to Dec 31	20,789.15	2,565.12	600.00	—	—
1885	Jan 1 to Dec 31	28,865.28	2,133.92	700.00	—	—
1886	Jan 1 to Dec 31	24,371.42	2,548.52	700.00	—	—
1887	Jan 1 to Dec 31	27,761.22	1,961.73	1,031.28	—	—
1888	Jan 1 to Dec 31	25,764.10	2,134.64	1,316.68	—	—
1889	Jan 1 to Dec 31	28,917.89	2,264.65[c]	584.37	—	—
1890	Jan 1 to Dec 31	28,703.87	—	812.47	—	—
1891	Jan 1 to Dec 31	36,216.81	174.00	1,016.68	3,493.69[d]	—
1892	Jan 1 to Dec 31	34,480.31	—	1,115.47	4,525.30	—
1893	Jan 1 to Dec 31	29,569.91	—	765.47	4,785.87	—
1894	Jan 1 to Dec 31	30,236.61	—	1,450.47	4,996.34	—
1895	Jan 1 to Dec 31	42,818.60	—	655.00	3,519.35	—
1896	Jan 1 to Dec 31	37,408.58	—	1,794.34	4,337.09	—
1897	Jan 1 to Dec 31	35,402.46	—	1,322.48	4,702.52	—
1898	Jan 1 to Dec 31	72,951.14	—	1,322.48	5,668.58	—
1899	Jan 1 to Dec 31	44,886.04	—	991.86	4,446.15	—
1900	Jan 1 to Dec 31	73,881.65	—	1,572.48	5,209.75	—

Table 7.1 (continued)

Year	Fiscal year	Total city spending for period[b] (in $)	City expenditures for public utilities (in $)			
			Annapolis Gas Light Co.	Annapolis Water Co.	Annapolis Gas and Electric Light Co.	Annapolis Public Utilities Co.
1902–03	July 1 to June 30	51,917.49	–	973.75	4,873.67	–
1904	Aug 1 to Dec 31	29,445.77	–	482.50	3,479.60	–
1905–06	Aug 15 to June 30	53,794.40	–	682.50	7,071.99	–
1906–07	July 1 to June 30	49,519.74	–	850.00	5,795.49	–
1909–10	June 30 to June 30	57,101.52	–	600.00	6,287.58	–
1910–11	July 1 to June 30	59,927.66	–	750.00	5,795.49	–
1911–12	July 1 to June 30	61,687.73	–	600.00[e]	5,790.17	–
1913–14	July 1 to June 30	77,675.37	–	600.00	–	5,434.70

Notes:

[a] Taken from Mayors Reports to the City Council of Annapolis, printed between 1885 and 1914, inclusive. Marylandia Collection, University of Maryland Libraries Special Collections, College Park, Maryland.

[b] Figures refer to simple expenditures and do not take into consideration debts, bonds, dividends, sinking fund, etc.

[c] The city terminates its contract with the Annapolis Gas Co., and initiates a two-year contract with the Annapolis Electric Light Co. on July 1, 1889. In 1890 these companies merge forming the Annapolis Gas and Electric Light Co, which appears to receive the first payments from the city.

[d] It is worth noting that this sum does not seem to include expenditures by the city for infrastructure, indicating that the newly formed corporation owned the physical plant, poles, wires, and other equipment.

[e] In 1911 the City of Annapolis issued $100,000.00 in bonds to purchase all stock held by the State of Maryland and private stockholders in the Annapolis Water Company, becoming owner of its own water supply and making water a public utility.

Comparison of city expenditures on public utilities also shows the municipality to be fairly conservative in terms of growth, and this is reflected by a relatively flat trajectory for total spending and little increase in spending on municipal lighting in the later 19th and early 20th century. From 1884 to 1889, payments to the Annapolis Gas Light Company comprised approximately 8.9 percent of the annual spending for the city, on average. However, between 1891 and 1911, payments made to the Electric Light Company average 11.1 percent of city spending, in some years rising above 16 percent of the total expenditures of the city (in 1893 and 1894). Geographically, the city does not increase in size over this period, but rather is ringed with small communities that are administered within surrounding Anne Arundel County. Consequently there is little demand for additional lights once the infrastructure was more-or-less established. City expenditures on electricity to light the streets and some public buildings, including city hall, some fire houses and the market space at the waterfront are relatively flat during the period from 1891 to 1912, averaging around $5,000 annually and exceeding this amount by less than a thousand dollars most years. The lowest expenditure during this time is just $3,400 in 1904. Meanwhile, overall city spending was doubled during this period, from $29,000 in 1889 to $61,000 in 1912, probably reflecting the increasing services that the city supported.

Another valuable source of data regarding the local electrical utility in Annapolis are reports made to the Maryland Public Service Commission[2] organized by an act of the General Assembly of Maryland to regulate public service industries in the state (King 1950:181). The Maryland Public Service Commission had the authority to set rates for utilities across the state, and as such it collected information in the form of standardized reports completed by every company in operation, starting in 1910. These reports document the end of electrical production in Annapolis, and suggest the shape of the utility at the turn of the century. Concerning the city's consumption, again the evidence suggests a lack of expansion. From 1911 through 1913 the city was charged – by the lamp – for 47 arc lights and 79 incandescents; surrounding Anne Arundel County paid the utility to maintain 24 arc lights outside of the city, probably lighting incipient suburbs that grew up around Annapolis but fell outside of its corporate boundaries. By 1920 the city had added 20 additional arc lights and reduced the number of incandescents by ten, which probably reflects simple maintenance with some reorganization and additional illumination. Reports to the Public

Service Commission also include revenue from commercial lighting, which is approximately double the revenue from street lighting. The local utility reported a meager 290 consumers for electricity in Annapolis in 1911, including commercial and residential service, and a total of 320 meters in operation throughout its range in Annapolis and its fringes. There were no consumers for commercial power in the city or in adjacent areas, and locally-produced electricity found no real manufacturing applications until the market was expanded to adjacent towns in later years.

Electricity in Annapolis did not draw industry to the town as might have been expected, if this can be argued from the fact that there were no significant consumers of electricity for these purposes while electricity was being produced in Annapolis. It did not contribute toward industrialization and commercial growth as many had hoped or promised, however it did allow working hours to be extended. This was seen almost immediately:

> Painting by Electric Light – One of the great advantages of electric light[,] its glare is almost equal to that of the noon day's sun and turns night almost into day wherever its rays fall. Last night a gentleman was observed on East street [sic] painting his house by the rays of the electric light which fell with such effulgence on his residence as to enable him to apply his vocation with as much perfectness as in the day time. On another street, where the light was favorably situated, a lady was observed sewing at her window. Persons have been seen frequently reading their evening paper by the rays of the electric light. (EC 1889g)

This tour of a lighted Annapolis creates the impression of a neurotic attempt to make work, simply because light was available. Further, electric light played a role in promoting nightlife and especially shopping in Annapolis, as it did in many American cities. By 1891 some businesses were making use of electrical light, as indicated by one report of a blackout caused by a burst pipe at the plant: "The drug stores and a few other places of business, such as the confectionary and cigar stores, which use the current, were left in a provoking and embarrassing situation" (EC 1891). I take blackouts as a pivotal matter, between the organization and disorganization of electricity, nay *materiality* in Annapolis, a rich point through which to define these technics along their limits and boundaries.

"Some Disarrangement in the Machinery Which was Soon Remedied"

If work is required to enact materializations and maintain a technological system – in any context – I position the immaterial here not necessarily as raw unformed material, which is perceived as what Heidegger might call "standing stock" or otherwise enveloped by a technics (Heidegger 1977), but as something without form that literally defies technics. Especially in an industrializing society, technics seem to be about eliminating the immaterial, disciplining forms in nature, harnessing energies and, following Foucault, controlling bodies. But emergent materiality implies puddle immateriality, wherein processes constitutive of human material life are seen as only partially or temporarily effective. The immaterial is lifeless to a materializing society; alternately, it is precociously alive where societies work to fix substances as a regular aspect of technologized experience. In its failure to take form, the immaterial fails to signify. It cannot be accounted for on the planner's page; it is indeterminate to accounting and escapes enclosure. It is intractable. It is *soft*; it is like culture (de Certeau 1997). For all this, what is immaterial is not uninterpretable. On the contrary, programs of interpretation must at some point include it, not as a priori to materiality but as part of the dialectic that produces and sustains materiality, and as such the empirical experiences, desires, and memories of subjects.

The frequent occurrence of black-outs suggests a clear symptom of immateriality and the nervousness of Annapolis' electrical utility. As the city was deciding to grant its contract for street lighting to the new electric utility, a fairly negative report was published from nearby Hagerstown, Maryland. "The electric lights go suddenly out and leave parts of the city in darkness for the greater part of the night. Whether this is from bad management or imperfect machinery, we are not informed" (EC 1888c). While few if any deaths resulted from unintended contact with electricity in Annapolis in the years following its adoption – likely, few had reason to come into contact with it aside from engineers, workmen, and business owners – blackouts were frequent and rarely explained (or even, it might be argued, understood):

> About half past seven o'clock the current was turned on, and the light came up in its usual brilliancy, but for some reason it soon went out. . . . This open and shut light business continued for some time until it was finally

shut off altogether. Everybody was asking the question: "What is the matter with the electric light to-night?" but none could answer. (EC 1889c)

Last night between six and seven o'clock the incandescent lights went out on the merchants and businessmen who have introduced this light to their places of business. Fortunately the darkness was only temporary, as they soon came up again in all their effulgence – but for the time being it put many to inconvenience and they had to resort to the coal oil or tallow dip. We were not able to learn the exact cause, but presume it was from some disarrangement in the machinery which was soon remedied. (EC 1889d)

A portion of the city was left in Egyptian darkness last night, and those who were out on the street had to feel their way as best they could. . . . Several of the lamps were made to come up after a severe kicking of the poles. (EC 1889c)

The citizens of Eastport would like to know why it is that the electric lights in their thriving village are out half of the time and the village left in darkness. (EC 1890)

The system was "nervous," in that it sometimes played at being a system or at being more systematic than it actually was: "first nervous, then a system; first system, then nervous – nerve-center and hierarchy of control, escalating to the topmost echelon, the very nerve-center we might say . . . Even while it inspires confidence . . . and as such bespeaks *control, hierarchy, intelligence* – it is also (and this is the damnedest thing) somewhat unsettling to be centered on something so fragile, so determinedly other, so nervous" (Taussig 1992:1–2). This represents the failure of practice to correspond to well-established truths, even machine truths, as evidenced in the always-present failures and ruptures in an otherwise seamless construction, a perfectly organized apparatus (Figure 7.2). Reality could not match the elegant plans and diagrams meant to model it, such that the neatly diagrammed systems for the distribution of electricity became a frail and sagging mass of poles and wires.

What is On the Line? Power and Marcuse's Critical Theory of Technology

What is at stake, regarding the markets for electricity that failed to materialize, and the apparent nervousness in the system that mirrored

ELECTRICITY IN ANNAPOLIS, MARYLAND

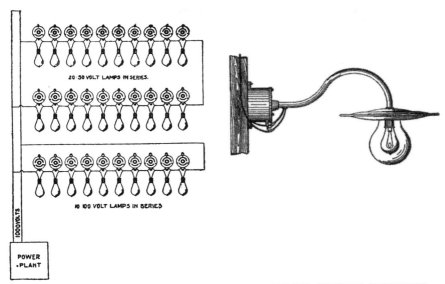

FIG. 337c.—WESTINGHOUSE INCANDESCENT SERIES STREET LIGHTING SYSTEM.

Figure 7.2 The neatly diagrammed system: multiple-series circuits for municipal lighting, from George D. Shepardson's Electrical Catechism (1901)

the nervousness in Americans confronted with a suite of social and cultural changes owing to electrification? In *The Question of Technology* Martin Heidegger (1977) concludes that the essence of modern technology is not its utility, which is merely a sliver of its fuller significance. Rather, technology has become a way of knowing in the modern world, an epistemology that produces representations amenable to various plans and projects. This notion corresponds to what Herbert Marcuse called "machine truths," specific rationalities that developed around technics and in fact fetishized technology and came to color social expressions like an irresistible ideology. While Heidegger's analysis originates in phenomenology, Marcuse embraced Marxism and found support among the critical theorists of the Frankfurt School.

Marcuse, who like Hannah Arendt split with Heidegger as he expressed greater and greater political and cultural conservatism, retained many of the concepts core to Heidegger's philosophy such as *Dasein* (being-in-the-world) and a sensitivity toward technology that gravely affected his early and late work (Held 1980:224–228; Jay 1996:28, 72). The basis for Marcuse's departure from Heidegger's phenomenology is instructive here because Heidegger has been so influential in recent social theory around technology (for instance, see Conley 1993; Dobres 2000; Dobres and Hoffman 1999; Pfaffenberger 1992). First and foremost, Marcuse found phenomenology unsatisfying in its inability to incorporate history rather than historicity as an abstraction, pursuing natural facts and truths about being, conditions that exist as a part of historicity but are not themselves contingent upon histories and historical conditions per se (Jay 1996:71). Marcuse wrote in 1928 that "... 'a phenomenology of human existence falls short of the necessary clarity and completeness' as it 'bypasses the material condition of historical existence'" (quoted in Held 1980:224). In contrast, a materialist dialectics freed analysis from one-sided (or one-dimensional) philosophical approaches by introducing lived experiences and something grounded and historical, actual events and actual conditions. This dialectics is about understanding the materiality and history that is a part of the phenomenon; materiality is tantamount to history in this formulation (Held 1980:228).

According to Martin Jay, in *Being and Time* Heidegger's philosophy arrived at the relationship between being-in-the-world, historicity, and praxis. What was dissatisfying to Marcuse and others was the failure to recognize class and its concreteness. Marcuse wanted to approach not just praxis, but a radical praxis and the possibility for radical action. "Only because of its key role in the production process does the proletariat have the potential to perform radical acts" (Jay 1996:72). At the same time, Marcuse ejected the determinism characteristic of vulgar Marxism, introducing the possibility for a more nuanced relationship between the material conditions of life and the social forms that were premised in them, including thought and ideology. Jay (1996:76) writes that at the Frankfurt School Marcuse "ceased to use Marxism as a positive philosophy answering Heidegger's question about 'authentic being' and began employing it more as a critical, dialectical methodology useful in explaining history, not historicity." This departure from Heideggerian philosophy and phenomenology is also a departure from existential philosophy, the "state of affairs that through its very existence and presence is *exempt* from all justification... an 'existential,' 'ontological' state of affairs – justification by mere existence'" (Jay 1996:122–123). The opposition of Marxism to existentialism originates in a denial of transhistorical existence, and the failure of existentialism to imagine a different future, radical praxis, and revolution.

Marcuse derived a critical approach to technology from these philosophies, presented briefly in an essay entitled "Some Social Implications of Modern Technology" (1982) and expanded in his book *One-Dimensional Man* (1991). None of the Frankfurt School philosophers supposed that technology led inexorably toward domination, however they described new forms of domination arising from within narrowly-defined rationalities. Such was Marcuse's formulation of "technological rationality." Technological rationality is the erosion of critical rationality through compliance with principles of efficiency, acceptance of a radical coordination of efforts and in various other ways accommodating the apparatus that is established as the regime of production. The example that Marcuse draws out is the journey in an automobile, which appears to cultivate compliance and an accommodation of technological truths:

> A man who travels by automobile to a distant place chooses his route from the highway maps. Towns, lakes and mountains appear as obstacles to be bypassed. The countryside is shaped and organized by the highway. ... Others have done the thinking for him, and perhaps for the better. Convenient parking spaces have been constructed where the broadest and most surprising view is open. Gigantic advertisements tell him when to stop and find the pause that refreshes. And all this is indeed for his benefit, safety and comfort; he receives what he wants. Business, technics, human needs and nature are welded together into one rational expedient mechanism. He will fare best who follows its directions [and] this attitude – which dissolves all actions into a sequence of semi-spontaneous reactions to prescribed mechanical norms – is not only perfectly rational but perfectly reasonable. ... It is a rational apparatus, combining utmost expediency with utmost convenience, saving time and energy, removing waste, adapting all means to the end, anticipating consequences, sustaining calculability and security. (Marcuse 1982:143)

Just as the iron rails or track are as much a part of the railroad as the engine and the train, the degree to which automobile transportation is arranged by an anonymous agency separate from the driver and passengers renders the landscape into one apparatus providing for efficient transportation. The extension of this idea would be that people become a part of the apparatus, a familiar argument. However, Marcuse models the relationship between the phenomenon and the kind of consciousness it manifests: compliant acceptance of these technologies and the acceptance of a role within them:

The idea of compliant efficiency perfectly illustrates the structure of technological rationality. Rationality is being transformed from a critical force into one of adjustment and compliance. Autonomy of reason loses its meaning in the same measure as the thoughts, feelings and actions of men are shaped by the technical requirements of the apparatus which they have themselves created...." (1982:147)

Further, this form of thought achieves a kind of transcendence, being placed beyond question similarly to ideology. "As the laws and mechanisms of technological rationality spread over the whole society, they develop a set of truth values of their own which hold good for the functioning of the apparatus – and for that alone" (Marcuse 1982:147). Widely adopted, technological systems become a shared frame of reference or fluency in much the same way that newspapers do for Benedict Anderson's imagined community (Anderson 1983:26–46). The political form defined by a specifically technological rationality is a *technocracy*, a word familiar from de Certeau (1984) and defined by Marcuse as a regime in which technical considerations of efficiency and rationality supercede welfare concerns, resulting in continued oppression and scarcity despite society proceeding along lines that capture and conserve greater energies than had previously been possible. And yet, all rational action perpetuates existing relationships and materialities. Like *habitus*, this regime is self-sustaining.

Initially the city was the sole consumer of electricity in Annapolis, as stated above, and by the early 1900s the city still comprised around 20 percent of the revenue generated by the utility. This interrupted the relationship between the utility as a producer and the residents of Annapolis as consumers: lighting of public ways was paid for by the corporation of the city, with tax dollars as a part of the legitimate administration of the municipality, that legitimacy being derived from providing such services in a fair and rational manner. So on the one hand, electricity was produced and sold as a commodity in an exchange between the utility and individual consumers, who paid to be connected to the network and to maintain that connection; on the other, electricity materialized as light was brought to bear on the city within the rational execution of governance in which the municipality provided this service as part of its legitimate operation.

Considering again Marcuse's characterization of the spread of technological rationality and the development of subjecthood that is premised in technology, we see here a relationship between what the municipal government provides for the city and what individuals in the city provide for themselves, their homes and businesses, their private affairs:

> Today the apparatus to which the individual must adjust and adopt himself is so rational that individual protest and liberation appear not only as hopeless but as utterly irrational. The system of life created by modern industry is one of the highest expediency, convenience and efficiency. Reason, once defined in these terms, becomes equivalent to an activity which perpetuates this world (Marcuse 1982:145)

i.e. the reproduction of existing relations and materialities and the resignation to get along within them.

Conclusion: The Context for "Modern" Utilities in Archaeology

With few exceptions and perhaps because of its closeness, contemporary technology seems to be transparent to contemporary archaeologists (Schiffer is an important exception, see his publications from 1991, 1993, 1996, 2000, as well as others mentioned in this text). Archaeological approaches to 19th-century modernization are rare, and perspectives on electricity are virtually non-existent, perhaps because archaeologically *electricity* is non-existent. It is at best difficult to trace using contemporary methodologies employed by archaeologists. However, electricity complements the current volume because it has no a priori materiality, but rather one that derives from specific productive applications and practices, enacted daily in ordinary uses and misuses.

A series of buildings illuminated by electric light occur along a circuit. What would truly be the architectural form in such a case, the buildings or the larger network into which they are wired? Such networks undermine perceptions of the city as a series of disconnected structures, each bearing an autonomous existence. Form comes to be less a matter of bricks and mortar and must begin with larger-scale constructions that resemble a diagram or a plan, though they need not be abstracted as such. The circuit is planned before the actual network is drawn out in space, but plans are subject to all sorts of appropriations and misreadings. When did planning end and execution begin? What was left unplanned, to be solved by the practical logic of engineers and workmen who carried out the actual electrification of the city? We can go further to consider this new "form" as less the circuitry materially extant, the poles, the wires, and so on, and consider instead the actual current that these constructions convey, understanding electricity metaphorically as engineers do, as a substance that flows or as a crowd of particles moving along its conduit in one direction or the other. At such point, the form described is not fixed but rather "at any given moment is a function of those who are operating within it. . . . This raises the question of whether a place is defined by a floor, roof, walls or by the point at which one enters the electrocommunication system . . ." (Bertomen 1991:4–5). One holds a place along a circuit, accessing current in varying amounts and from time to time along rhythms that are organic in some ways, mechanistic in others. Demand is a question of how the crowd behaves, and would to an extent determine "form." The mechanical workings of modern life, the utilities of our industrialized present, take on a palimpsest-like quality as the route is retraced and improved technologically and organizationally, leaving a relict network alongside the existing live one.

The fetishization of commodities extends from the truths that predominate in other areas. Thus, the best of metaphors for modern technology and modern life presents itself: not the myriad commodities, which are deceptive in their unitary existence, their individuality, interchangeability, and their invisible process of distribution, but rather, the light switch, the water tap, the gas jet that leads back to a source. One might argue that, even more than the system of objects, the network of services provided in modern life is particularly available as a graphic illustration of the connectedness implicit in technology. The connections that have existed in the past, as likely as not, persist in a form apprehendable to archaeology.

Notes

1 Mayors Reports to the City Council of Annapolis are available in the Marylandia Collection, University of Maryland Libraries Special Collections, College Park, Maryland.
2 Annual reports made by to the Maryland Public Service Commission starting in 1910 are held at the Maryland State Archives and were reviewed by the author in January of 2002.

References

Anderson, Benedict 1983 Imagined Communities: Reflections on the Origin and Spread of Nationalism. London: Verso.

Anne Arundel County Circuit Court 1888 Charter Record, Annapolis Electric Light Company of Anne Arundel County. In Anne Arundel County Circuit Court. Pp. 245–247. Annapolis.

Arato, Andrew, and Eike Gebhardt, eds. 1982 The Essential Frankfurt School Reader. New York: Continuum.

Asendorf, Christoph 1993 Batteries of Life: On the History of Things and Their Perception in Modernity. D. Reneau, trans. Berkeley: University of California Press.

Beard, George M., 1972[1898] Sexual Neurasthenia (Nervous Exhaustion): Its Hygiene, Causes, Symptoms and Treatment, With a Chapter on Diet for the Nervous. New York: Arno Press & The New York Times.

Bertomen, Michele 1991 Transmission Towers on the Long Island Expressway: A Study of the Language of Form. Princeton: Princeton Architectural Press.

Conley, Verena Andermatt 1993 Preface. In Rethinking Technologies. V. A. Conley, ed. Pp. ix–xiv. Minneapolis: University of Minnesota Press.

Davis, L. J. 2003 Fleet Fire: Thomas Edison and the Pioneers of the Electrical Revolution. New York: Arcade Publishing.

de Certeau, Michel 1984 The Practice of Everyday Life. Berkeley: University of California Press.

—— 1997 Culture in the Plural. Minneapolis: University of Minnesota Press.

de la Peña, Carolyn Thomas 1999 Recharging at the Fordyce: Confronting the Machine and Nature in the Modern Bath. Technology and Culture 40(4):746–769.

—— 2001 Designing the Electric Body: Sexuality, Masculinity and the Electric Belt in America, 1880–1920. Journal of Design History 14(4):275–289.

—— 2003 The Body Electric: How Strange Machines Built the Modern America. New York: New York University Press.

Dobres, Marcia-Anne, 2000 Technology and Social Agency. Oxford: Blackwell.

Dobres, Marcia-Anne, and Christopher R. Hoffman, eds. 1999 The Social Dynamics of Technology: Practice, Politics, and World Views. Washington D.C.: Smithsonian Institution Press.

Essig, Mark 2003 Edison & The Electric Chair: A Story of Light and Death. New York: Walker & Company.

Evening Capital 1888a Agitating Electric Light. In Evening Capital, January 3: 3. Annapolis.

—— 1888b Electric Light for the Naval Academy. In Evening Capital, December 20: 3. Annapolis.

—— 1888c Electric Lights. In Evening Capital, October 17: 3. Annapolis.

—— 1889a "Capital" Jottings. In Evening Capital, May 15: 3. Annapolis.

—— 1889b How a Town is Made to Progress. *In* Evening Capital, July 11: 3. Annapolis.
—— 1889c Left in Darkness. *In* Evening Capital, September 2: 3. Annapolis.
—— 1889d Left in Darkness. *In* Evening Capital, October 14: 3. Annapolis.
—— 1889e Left in Temporary Darkness. *In* Evening Capital, August 3: 3. Annapolis.
—— 1889f Our Electric Light. *In* Evening Capital, July 2: 3. Annapolis.
—— 1889g Painting by Electric Light. *In* Evening Capital, July 6: 3. Annapolis.
—— 1889h Solicitor for the Electric Light Co. *In* Evening Capital, May 17: 3. Annapolis.
—— 1890 "Capital" Jottings. *In* Evening Capital, December 16: 3. Annapolis.
—— 1891 A City in Darkness. *In* Evening Capital, January 2: 3. Annapolis.
Gosling, Francis G. 1987 Before Freud: Neurasthenia and the American Medical Community, 1870–1910. Urbana: University of Illinois Press.
Heidegger, Martin 1977 The Question Concerning Technology. *In* Basic Writings. D. F. Krell, ed. Pp. 284–317. New York: Harper and Row.
Held, David 1980 Introduction to Critical Theory: Horkheimer to Habermas. Berkeley: University of California Press.
Horkheimer, M., and T. W. Adorno 2000[1972] Dialectic of Enlightenment. New York: Continuum Publishing Company.
Hughes, Thomas P. 1983 Networks of Power: Electrification in Western Society, 1880–1930. Baltimore: Johns Hopkins University Press.
Jay, Martin 1996 The Dialectical Imagination: A History of the Frankfurt School and the Institute of Social Research, 1923–1950. Berkeley: University of California Press.
Jonnes, Jill 2003 Empires of Light: Edison, Tesla, Westinghouse, and the Race to Electrify the World. New York: Random House.
King, Thomas 1950 Consolidated of Baltimore, 1816–1950: A History of Consolidated Gas and Electric Light and Power Company of Baltimore. Baltimore: Consolidated Gas Electric Light and Power Company.
Marcuse, Herbert 1982 Some Social Implications of Modern Technology. *In* The Essential Frankfurt School Reader. A. Arato and E. Gebhardt, eds. Pp. 138–162. New York: Continuum.
—— 1991 One-Dimensional Man: Studies in the Ideology of Advanced Industrial Societies. Boston: Beacon Press.
Matthews, Christopher N. 2002 An Archaeology of History and Tradition: Moments of Danger in the Annapolis Landscape. New York: Kluwer Academic/Plenum Publishers.
Morus, Iwan Rhys 1998 Frankenstein's Children: Electricity, Exhibition, and Experiment in Early-Nineteenth-Century London. Princeton: Princeton University Press.
Nietzsche, Friedrich 1989 On The Genealogy of Morals: Ecce Homo. Walter Kaufmann and R. J. Hollingdale, trans. New York: Vintage Books.
Nye, David E. 1997 Electrifying America: Social Meanings of a New Technology. Cambridge: The MIT Press.

Pfaffenberger, Bryan 1992 Social Anthropology of Technology. Annual Review of Anthropology 21:491–516.

Schiffer, Michael B. 1991 The Portable Radio in American Life. Tucson: University of Arizona Press.

―― 1993 Cultural Imperatives and Product Development: The Case of the Shirt-Pocket Radio. Culture and Technology 34(1):98–113.

―― 1996 Pathways to the Present: In Search of Shirt-Pocket Radios with Subminiature Tubes. *In* Learning from Things: Method and Theory in Material Culture Studies. W. D. Kingery, ed. Pp. 81–88. Washington, D.C.: Smithsonian Institution Press.

―― 2000 Indigenous Theories, Scientific Theories and Product Histories. *In* Matter, Materiality and Modern Culture. P. Graves-Brown, ed. Pp. 72–96. London: Routledge.

―― 2003 Draw the Lightening Down: Benjamin Franklin and Electrical Technology in the Age of Enlightenment. Berkeley: University of California Press.

Schivelbusch, Wolfgang 1986 The Railway Journey: The Industrialization of Time and Space in the Nineteenth Century. Berkeley: University of California Press.

―― 1988 Disenchanted Night: The Industrialization of Light in the Nineteenth Century. Berkeley: University of California Press.

Shepardson, George D. 1901 Electrical Catechism: An Introductory Treatise on Electricity and its Uses. New York: McGraw-Hill Gook Company.

Simon, Linda 2004 Dark Light: Electricity and Anxiety from the Telegraph to the X-Ray. Orlando: Harcourt, Inc.

Taussig, Michael 1992 The Nervous System. New York: Routledge.

8

The Voices of Stones: Unthinkable Materiality in the Volcanic Context of Western Panamá

Karen Holmberg

Materiality is central to the study of culture, past or present, yet archaeologists frequently constitute the "material" versus "immaterial" in ways that are exclusive of important information regarding past lives. This is the case in the Chiriquí province of western Panamá, where Western academic examination of petroglyphs has focused on design interpretation or been neglected altogether. Rock art was designated as non-data in a number of prior analyses due to the inability to date it or authoritatively translate its symbols. The Chiriquí petroglyphs are one-dimensional until examined in the context of their larger landscape setting and pregnant ethnographic lives. Upon such examination, the Volcán Barú and the primacy of its perception are inescapable.

The volcano in general has been viewed as archaeologically immaterial outside of its catastrophic or cost-benefit analysis role, despite rich ethnographic and ethnohistoric evidence that as a "natural" entity, the volcano is heavily imbricated in "cultural" life. As a thing, the auratic volcano is intimately linked to the placement of rock art in the study area. Both rock art and the volcano can be best seen as hybrid forms that resist the assignment of strict Cartesian definition. Particularly in a study area that is bemoaned to suffer from ephemeral architectural remains and intensive long-term looting, we cannot afford to neglect the materiality of the items that do exist at our disposal for investigation.

Unthinkable Materiality in the Volcanic Context

The original material culture of many archaeological contexts can be comprised of 90–95 percent organic or perishable materials (Drooker 2001), and these items are poorly preserved in acidic volcanic soils in high rainfall areas such as Chiriquí. It is logical, therefore, to derive as much information as is possible from durable items that do exist. In essence, it is time to "think" both rock art and the volcano in prehistoric Panamá.

Relating Stones to Bodies: The Caldera Petroglyphs

Massive and covered in enigmatic designs, the Caldera petroglyph boulder in Chiriquí is visited sporadically by the adventure tourists and backpackers who flock to the nearby mountain town of Boquete. To get to the Caldera petroglyphs, you must park at a cantina; by the early afternoon horses will be tied outside while their riders drink a beer inside. You must walk around the side of the bar, through a livestock gate, and pick one's way carefully through a large cattle pasture with no protection from either the relentless sun or the potential whims of the herd.

The boulder is on private property, and the owner periodically chooses to cut back the overgrowth surrounding it and mark the dozens of anthropomorphic and abstract designs with chalk. Local youths who visit often leave superficially scratched marks with their names or initials, though these generally fade quickly and again leave only the deeper, prehistoric marks on the stone. The only understandable marker for modern visitors is a metal sign that states "80" which is planted nearby in the field; this signifies that the spot is 80 kilometers from the Pacific Ocean along the course of an oil pipeline that serves as an alternate fuel route to the Panama Canal. Lacking any contextual information regarding the age or significance of the petroglyphs, tourists generally do not stay any longer than is required to snap a few pictures in front of the rock art.

The designs on the boulder consist primarily of pecked and chiseled spirals, circles with crosses or lines within them, and assemblages that resemble faces and lizards. The boulder itself is roughly two meters high and eleven meters long, and marked on its east, west, and top faces. The boulder varies between a dark gray and an olive black color. One can hear the sound of a nearby stream that runs past the boulder during the wet season. When the sun is not burning down, storms swoop in dramatically from the Caribbean side of the isthmus and swallow the volcano that rises above the very flat field in clouds. These are the elements that

Figure 8.1 The western face of the Caldera petroglyph boulder and (inset) the split boulder that forms a "passageway"

the casual visitor will register before returning through the cattle pasture. Web logs from tourists frequently mention frustration with the site and its lack of interpretation or an ability to understand its purpose.

The first known written description and sketch of the Caldera petroglyph boulder was made by Berthold Seemann in 1853, and this work was cited and replicated in a number of subsequent 19th-century publications (see MacCurdy 1911:43). The imagery of the boulder is black and white and one-dimensional in these accounts. Like the modern tourists who visit the site, Seemann and his successors focused solely on the form of the designs. The petroglyphs, however, and their intended significance, have been permanently removed from their original social context, hence the frustration of trying to recapture their original purpose or meaning.

The Caldera site begins to take on life and form only when one looks at its larger three-dimensional context. The rock art boulder is the largest rock in the midst of a field of volcanic boulders (Figure 8.1, main picture). Most of the other rocks have been naturally sorted and are roughly coeval in size, hence the petroglyph boulder stands out as incrementally larger than the others. If you stand at the northern tip (or "front") of

UNTHINKABLE MATERIALITY IN THE VOLCANIC CONTEXT

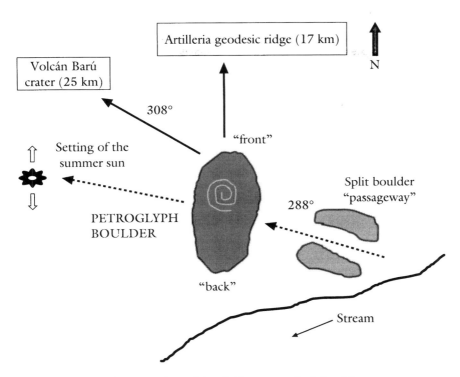

Figure 8.2 The larger setting of the Caldera petroglyph boulder

the Caldera boulder or sit on top of it, the distinctive elements of the landscape are the domed shape of the Artilleria geodesic point, directly to the north, and the volcano, at an angle of 308°.

The second largest stone in the field is a massive, split boulder that is situated between the seasonal stream and the petroglyph boulder. Split boulders can occur naturally through tree growth along softer mineral inclusions or can be split by lightening, such as occurred at the Scottish megalith site of Brogar in 1980. Splits can also be made by using fire and water to create cleavage, such as was done at the site of Avebury in England in the 17th and 18th centuries to destroy their "pagan" resonance. It is unknown whether the Caldera boulder was intentionally split. No matter how it was created, however, the split stone is intimately and associatively linked with the rock art and forms a hallway or passage way for the viewer standing inside of it between the stream and the petroglyphs (Figure 8.1, inset).

Roughly six meters in length and three meters high, the split "passage" rock focuses the viewers' gaze at the eastern face of the petroglyph boulder. This face is more heavily eroded than the western face, and is comprised of mainly geometric designs, while the western side is predominantly marked with anthropomorphic designs. The viewer standing within the split boulder can also see the crater of the Volcán Barú, 25 kilometers distant. In the current era, the sun sets in a range from 246°–294°. The setting sun passes exactly through the midline of the split rock, angled at 288°, and over the top of the petroglyph boulder twice during the year. This would occur roughly May 14 and July 31. Since the crack in the boulder is wide, the sun of the summer solstice would presumably also shine through it, since it sets at 294° around June 21 (only 6° away from the midline of the split rock). These time periods all fall within the midway point of the wet season, when the seasonal stream behind the passage rock and petroglyphs will be full of water and fish, creating what likely felt like a very auspicious series of conjunctions or possibly marked agricultural or ritual events.

References to front/behind and top/bottom in reference to the Caldera stone are the most convenient ways to describe the site. These dyads are an obvious link between the body and its experience of the material world (Tilley 2004a:4). It is the excavation of the "lifeworld" of such embodied experiences, as Merleau-Ponty (1962) termed it, which forms the crux of phenomenological efforts in archaeology. Perception is central to this effort, and yet what we as archaeologists deem to be "material" links in very directly to what we ourselves perceive or exclude from perception or academic visibility.

Unexpected Materialization and Materiality: The Huacal Petroglyphs

Other than the Caldera petroglyph boulder, which is marked on tourist maps and hence frequently referenced by visitors needing local guides, petroglyphs in the Boquete area are not commonly known or perceived to be of interest. The presence of rock art in the area has largely been ignored by formal academic study and unnoticed by local residents in the overall region (though see Kunne 2003). The notable exception to this is the work of Septimo and Joly (1998) and Miranda de Cabal

Unthinkable Materiality in the Volcanic Context

(1974), who record ethnographic stories regarding rock art in the Ngöbe and Doraz languages, respectively, as well as in Spanish.

One commonly known petroglyph is found near the Boquete municipal water source, and it has been caged in with metal fencing so is not accessible or readily visible. If one has a local friend who is friendly with the family concerned, another petroglyph boulder can be found in a back yard, where it is used for washing dishes and clothes and is surrounded by chickens. A third petroglyph, close to a path that serves a residential and agricultural area known as Huacal, is known by many who live in its close vicinity, though at the inception of this project it was covered completely by mud and overgrowth and so the exact location of it was only roughly remembered. None of these petroglyphs, comprised primarily of spirals, abstract lines, and cupules, were deemed important by prior archaeological studies due to the inability to date or "interpret" their designs. Neither did the local residents deem them important, as unlike the Caldera boulder they generated neither local nor tourist interest. In essence, they were immaterial.

Once I began archaeological survey in a coffee field near the Huacal petroglyph, however, my survey team and I rapidly identified another rock art boulder. Still more followed in rapid succession. In the course of a two-week period, at least two dozen petroglyphs "materialized" in a field where none had perceptually existed prior, despite over 40 continuous years of farming the property by the same family. As coffee trees are planted by hand roughly two meters apart from one another and then need to be maintained by cutting the overgrowth with a machete on a regular basis, the design-covered rocks had not exactly been in locations that were infrequently visited. They were not identified, however, as "cultural" items. Instead they were categorized as part of the general natural environment and were not of particular interest.

This division between natural and cultural elements seems to be separated by an inconstant and mutable line of categorization. One of the most striking stones in the Huacal petroglyph field is actually unmarked. The eight meter long, three meter wide boulder is flat, and provides what appears to be a natural stage or platform. A small stream surfaces from under one of its corners. It is a unique form, and is made even more unique by its presence in the midst of roughly two dozen smaller stones marked with petroglyphs. The fusion of the larger stone's physical form and placement in the midst of a swarm of rock art make it a likely repository for associated past ideas, memories, histories, and mythologies, and yet it is itself not marked in the same sense as the surrounding rock art boulders. As in the Inka landscape, where both marked and unmarked stones could be designated as *wakas* and part of the ritual geography, the boundaries of nature/culture and visible/invisible seem to be slippery demarcations in the overall Huacal context. Kathleen Morrison discusses this aspect saliently in the case of South India, where the marked landscape and unmarked landscape merge into mutable, meaningful combinations over long periods of time (Morrison 2004).

The definition of what is considered data with which to create purportedly objective knowledge about natural and social processes is very much one which is intertwined with culturally-held mindsets and conceptions (Hacking 1990). The prior invisibility of the Huacal petroglyph site represents a problem in the perception of their materiality, the sense that they somehow lacked materiality altogether. The two significant systematic surveys in highland Chiriquí in the last 30 years, Linares and Ranere (1980) and Shelton (1984), each mentions in passing the discovery of rock art during survey but excludes it from all analysis and discussion. Rock art is seen as non-data, in a sense, due to the inability to date it or definitively decipher its original purpose.

Lacking both carbon-based pigments and stylistic methods for chronological placement of the petroglyphs of the Boquete area, there is a strong possibility that the creation of the designs will never be dated. Despite what can or cannot be achieved with the dating of rock art, however, there are distinct aspects of intention that should not be ignored. As they are a direct result of human action and durable elements of the permanent landscape, the failure to examine the petroglyphs as material culture grossly overlooks their significance. Landscape marking needs to be seen in the context of its larger physical surrounding, with which it is intertwined (Tilley 2004a). Marking does not necessarily need to be seen as inherently symbolic, but does provide an index of the marker and distinguishes a place from any other (Davis 1989). Alpine rock art showing maps of agricultural landscapes are thought to designate identification with territory, for example, though they are also extended to be a mixture of thought, mind, and dream of Neolithic-Copper Age shepherds who created them in the sense of modern graffiti as markers of place and passage (Arca 2004).

A common observation in rock art studies is that the designs are associatively placed in relation to prominent geographical features and permanent water. Like at the site of Caldera, the Huacal petroglyphs are located within direct line-of-sight to the volcano (not a given in Boquete due to the presence of many deep valleys and obstructive ridges) to the west, and are in close association with a stream. The Huacal petroglyphs are additionally situated in a valley that provides direct view to two geodesic rocky outcroppings, including the Artilleria geodesic point seen from the Caldera boulder. These distinctive features of the local landscape provide unobstructed 360° views of the surrounding landscape, and from them the only more prominent landscape feature is the volcano itself. A local myth, as related to me by a local resident, states that caves in each of the geodesic points "speak" to the volcano, which speaks back (personal communication, March 22, 2004). This brings up interesting multi-sensory elements, as the rocks are perceived to have both visuality and sounds. Like the petroglyph rocks, however, the volcano itself resists easy classification within Cartesian divisions of nature versus culture.

The Volcán Barú in its Social Context

The Volcán Barú is the highest point of the isthmus of Panamá, and is frequently cited in the context of national pride as a point from where one can see two oceans, the Caribbean and the Pacific. The volcano has not erupted within recent or even generational memory, as the most recent eruption of Barú occurred anywhere from 450 and 700 years ago. Despite the fact that the current residents have no experience with eruption, however, the volcano is still a very active part of daily life for those around it.

The names of towns and villages in the area give a strong indication of identification with the volcanic landscape, with names like *Caldera*, *Volcán*, and *Volcancito*. The Chiriquí portion of the InterAmerican Highway has recently been dotted with fresh new road signs. Each of these has a schematic drawing of the Volcán Barú as background for whatever road information is listed. A heart is placed within the volcano, while a cow on the left of the volcano represents the farming basis of the region and the provincial flag of Chiriquí is placed on the right. The volcano is, in essence, the heart of the region.

In the small agricultural and resort town of Boquete, directly under the shadow of the volcano, a number of small local businesses draw on Barú as a symbol of local identity. A pizzeria, *La Volcanica*, is marked by a sign with a handle-bar mustached Italian kissing his fingers and winking in front of an image of Barú's crater. The ice machines found at any gas station proclaim themselves to contain *Hielo Barú* (Barú Ice), and like the pizzeria also picture a cloud-topped image of the volcano. The local supermarket incorporates the volcano into its stylized neon logo and into its name, the *Super Barú*. The t-shirts which the employees wear at the *Super Barú* grocery store proclaim from under a stylized image of the volcano, the store is "Chiricano like you;" it is a part of the community. At the checkout counter, it is possible to buy a small, self-published paperback book by a local resident titled *El Volcán Barú* (Landau 2000). The book mixes poetry about the volcano, citations and quotes from various scientific studies, and photos along with the author's suggestion of names for interesting rock formations ("the frog," "the elephant trunk"). It is obvious that there is something highly connotative and imaginative about the volcano.

Thinking the Volcano

A tangle of associations exists in the layers of our inherited modern perceptions of volcanoes and eruption. The commonly known myths of Pele in Hawaii are layered in the western mind with the inherited mythology of the Greek god Hephaestus (later the Roman god, Vulcan). In both, creative power of fire and the procreative power of sex are strongly linked (Frierson 1991:88). Elizabeth Barrett Browning and Emily Dickenson each used volcanic imagery as metaphor for an energy that is creative, erotic, and specifically female (Frierson 1991:91). Correlations between eruption and the lunar cycle provide further links to a more feminine association to volcanic eruption (Handwerk 2002). Bataille, in turn, wrote of volcanoes being the solar anus (Bataille 1985). According to Stephens' widely read publication, *Incidents of Travel in Central America*, young women were thrown into the crater of Masaya volcano in Nicaragua to appease its eruptions (Stephens 1969[1841]). People on the island of Java throw live chickens into the Bromo volcano once a year in order to placate it (Sigurdsson 1999:13).

Volcanic imagery and symbolism of the 18th- and 19th-century French, British, and American painting traditions was symbolically linked to political or societal struggle and revolution. This compared incipient scientific understanding of eruption to the political events of the period, paralleling massive, underground strength and the potential ability to

UNTHINKABLE MATERIALITY IN THE VOLCANIC CONTEXT

tear a country or society apart (Sivard n.d.). A recent bestseller, *Pompeii*, uses the 79 A.D. eruption of Vesuvius and its destruction as satirical parable for modern American culture post September 11, 2001 (Harris 2003). Eleanor Antin, acclaimed as a driving force in feminist, postmodern art, uses the same eruption in the photographic series *The Last Days of Pompeii*. She describes her work as excavation, elaborately staging sensual recreations of an imagined past. Antin's work also implicitly parallels the United States to Rome on the brink of disaster, but more explicitly intends to infuse life and texture into the envisionment of pre-eruptive Vesuvian daily life. Though variable and historically based, in each of these contexts exists a transmittable essence of Benjaminian aura that links back to the volcano itself (Benjamin 1968).

It is this multi-dimensionality and lack of universality so readily visible in the accrued modern context which is most often neglected in archaeological assessments of volcanic regions. Large-scale cultural change versus stasis following eruptions and natural hazard considerations provide the focus in a number of archaeological analyses of prehistoric volcanic regions (e.g. Linares and Ranere 1980; Sheets and McKee 1994; Torrence and Grattan 2002). While unquestionably important, these accounts neglect more socialized elements of the non-eruptive volcanic landscape. The lack of focus upon more socialized elements of volcanic regions provides an impoverished understanding of past life within them.

It is hardly revolutionary to say that volcanoes were symbolically or culturally important in the past or in archaeological conception. Fetishized illustrations and imaginations of Laetoli, Santorini, Etna, and Pompeii during or post-eruption are common in popular literature. Mountain top worship (*apu*), which included both volcanoes and normal mountains, was widely practiced throughout the Andes (Reinhard 1985). Myths and stories exist from nearly every culture that experienced volcanism. Archaeologists, however, have been hesitant to excavate the stratigraphic layers of meaning attached to the physical presence of the volcano. Landscape garden designers in the 16th through 18th centuries sought to push the boundaries of that period's search for the sublime, until in the end they began to create miniature versions of volcanoes that could mimic eruption for clients. As Thacker (1984:74) states, the designers and clients "embraced the ultimate and hitherto unthinkable wildness, the volcano." This quote is apt to the archaeological context; in essence the volcano's experiential role within the social context has been archaeologically unthinkable.

How does one think the volcano, then? The volcano is certainly not a product, good or artifact in the sense discussed by Appadurai (1986). It could, however, potentially be attributed a biography in the sense of authors such as Hoskins (1998). The volcano is already anthropomorphized to the point of being considered active, sleeping, or dead, and hence already is easily viewed as having a lifespan and life history. Perhaps the volcano is best seen as a material "thing" that is enmeshed within the social world (Attfield 2000:15). As a thing, the volcano can be seen easily to have the agency Gell (1998) attributes to material objects. Agency is particularly blatant in the event of eruption, but operates in more nuanced but just as powerful a way during non-eruptive periods. It is this overly strong display of eruptive agency, however, that overshadows the archaeological assessment of the lived experience within volcanic regions during non-eruptive time periods. People and cultures are placed as passive recipients of this over-weighted agency and seen as capable of responding only as systemic pawns or monolithic cultural units, when in fact a much richer and more textured social relationship exists in volcanic regions over the long term.

Nature/culture and the concept of the hybrid

A volcano is a site of complexly intertwined natural and cultural interactions that combine to create a unique socialized landscape. A Cartesian attempt to separate the natural and cultural elements in such a context neglects the fact that it is a medley of real, remembered, and imagined elements that confuse the lines of definition. This socialized landscape is both physically durable and culturally mutable; the physical landmark of the volcano is draped with multiple layers of meanings and significances over time. Landscape marking may be created in one time period, but then exist and change over every time period that follows (Morrison 2004). Per Latour (1991), divisions between binaries can be seen as contingent and uncertain rather than fixed and secure, and the concept of the hybrid is more accurate a conception of categorization. Both rock art and the volcano in the Chiriquí study area are hybrid meldings of the natural and cultural elements. Rock art is comprised of stones visibly marked with meanings or intention, and the volcano is interlinked in the volcanic landscape as identical stone invisibly marked and remarked with meanings.

Archaeological assessments and hazards studies of volcanic regions tend to divide nature and culture in an artificially divisive way. Any interaction is one-directional from the volcano, which either acts to wreak danger and destruction or provide a boon in fertile soils for the human populations that create the intersection between natural and cultural worlds by living in the volcano's midst. This leads to a sterile view that is steeped in environmental determinism and neglects the very mutual and recursive relationship that people have with their environments. It also leads to the invisibility represented by the petroglyphs discussed at Huacal; once categorized as natural, they remained categorized that way until suddenly being shifted into visibility and the category of cultural. Both the petroglyphs and the volcano are simultaneously forms created without human agency and forms given intelligibility through human inscription.

This merging and interlinking of nature and culture into the hybrid form is apparent in a sample of examples that traverse the span of human occupation in the Boquete area. Distinctive dacite columns from a lava flow were transported to construct prehistoric tombs six kilometers away from the source. This evokes a direct referencing or appropriation of nature into culture and merging of the two. The dacite columnar jointing that provided the tomb columns is located beside the fenced-in petroglyph beside the main water source for the Boquete area. This natural spring emerges from the ground beside the petroglyph boulder, which is immediately adjacent to the wall of columnar joints. The Caldera petroglyph boulder is located in close proximity to a volcanic hot spring that is widely storied amongst the indigenous community to have curative powers. It is especially linked to fertility, and couples who desire a child are instructed to sit in its waters at midnight during the full moon. As of a week before this chapter was written the bottom of the volcanic crater, visible only from the rim that requires an arduous seven hour hike to reach, had been marked with stones that spelled out in large letters that "Christ is coming" in Spanish.

Particularly in times of eruption, the volcano is a site of *synaesthesia*, or an overlapping and blending of many senses (per Tilley 2004a:28). Sharp sounds, harsh colors, bitter smells all combine to provide a strong sensory experience of eruption. Sulphur gases smell like rotten eggs and hence like decay, but are also associated with the volcanic springs which are used in the Boquete area by indigenous peoples to cure skin maladies and provide overall health benefits. In a sense, then, one can imagine eruption bringing about perceptions of death–decay–healing in a cycle that is linked to the volcano. The non-eruptive volcano, however, also exerts a strong sensory presence.

Karen Holmberg

Gestalt, Figure/Ground, and Rock-Art in Context

The petroglyphs of Chiriquí are interpreted in a variety of ways. Many local residents when asked will surmise that the petroglyph designs are landscape maps that trace the contours of the ridges and mountains in order to guide prehistoric travelers up and down the isthmus. In this conjecture, spirals are interpreted as portraying the volcano and lines are rivers (Joly 1997). This sort of a theory has precedence in a number of locations worldwide. Bradley (1997) describes a somewhat similar scenario in the European context, in that rock art is suggested to portray landscape shapes. In this sense, rock art is iconic of the visual setting. Stirling (1950:234) suggested a slightly modified version of the map theory for the Chiriquí petroglyphs, claiming that the rock art lines represented trails that led to tombs rich in gold, represented by cupules.

Harte (1959) surmised that Panamanian petroglyphs were intended to convey a plethora of information: warnings of danger, maps of clan movement, bravery in battle and skill in hunting, and records of disasters and times of prosperity. The local Ba'hai community holds that petroglyph symbols are Semitic writing shared by the Kuna, Ngöbe, Maya, Navajo, Quechua, and Iroquois, amongst others. In these accounts, the interpretation of the symbols will lead to world peace and indigenous empowerment (Dragna 2004). Metaphysical groups in the area believe the rock art sites provide gateways to other worlds (personal communication, November 23, 2004).

Each of these interpretations of the Chiriquí rock art focuses upon the interpretation of the designs. Rock art, however, is "landscape art" (Whitley 2001:1). Meaning is not simply encoded in the rock art image but derived in relation to the stones themselves and the way that both the stones and the designs were related to an experience of the overall landscape. The marking needs to be seen in its larger context and setting, with the realization that it was created by and creative of human experience.

The concept of *gestalt* is usefully invoked in terms of landscapes and their contexts. As Tilley (2004a:25) points out, there are no non-contextual ways to look at landscape or place, in the sense that it is simply a matter of scale and level of analysis. Certain places may contain other places within them. The search for shape, form, or pattern through gestalt conceptions draws the Boquete area petroglyphs and the volcano into a unit of analysis where they can be seen as parts of the whole in the local sense of place. It again highlights the primacy of perception, in that form is taken as a pre-conceptual unit of perception. The famous Rubin example of figure/ground perception, in which one can either see the profile of two faces or the outline of a vase depending on whether one foregrounds the black or the white forms, is metaphoric for the changeability of human figure/ground perceptive abilities. We only perceive parts of the "figure" (i.e. "reality") as a momentary object of subjective attention. In respect to volcanic landscapes, we need to query the figures we choose and include the ground. Through gestalt, landscape features can be "thought" together and apart-but-interlocked; neither the whole nor the parts can be thought of alone. In this perspective, both the rock art and the volcano are complementary elements of the overall Chiriquí landscape.

There is no mental template or instinct to prompt people to reference the volcano or the placement of rock art. One holistic view of any landscape is generally not feasible, due to the "undisciplined material aspects of place" and the ways that time and landscape merge in ways that the stratigraphic record does not (Morrison 2004). Past life experiences were neither static nor unchanging, nor is there any reason to believe that meanings of material culture remained static either. Hence, a number of possible interpretations of the Boquete area petroglyphs are offered below in addition to the theories already cited. These likely overlapped and combined with one another fluidly, with weight given to different elements in different temporal contexts. Perhaps none of them were applicable at given periods of time. Meaning likely shifted in importance and relevance throughout the still-continuing lifespan of the petroglyphs of the Boquete area and their relation to the volcano.

Multiple Vantages and Mutable Interpretations

The Boquete area petroglyph designs can be potentially viewed as an aide mémoire with links to oral tradition that is now lost. This interpretation is applied to the Dreamtime "Songlines," or routes taken by Ancestral Beings, which marked sacred, living, and mythological sites for Australian Aboriginals (Flood 2004:183). These rendered tracks linked Dreaming sites, which were not necessarily marked in a materially discernible way. Their importance was derived and passed on through the oral tradition.

The rock art served in the Aboriginal context as memory anchors for the locations of ochre, food supplies, and permanent water. The Caldera, Huacal, and the municipal water source petroglyphs in the Boquete area are strongly associated with nearby water sources, which could indicate their linkage to memory marking for essential resources.

The petroglyphs can also be potentially conceived of as manifestations of myths that are physically anchored to the landscape. In a local Doraz ethnohistoric story, the Caldera petroglyph boulder will one day rise into the sky and explode due to earthquake and fire below it (Miranda de Cabal 1974). This can be interpreted as a reference to volcanic eruption and the Volcán Barú. The fact that the Caldera boulder is situated in a volcanic rock field and associatively aligned with the sun and the volcano binds the elements of myth, landscape, and marking into a plausible amalgam. A local Ngöbe myth narrates the original creation of all petroglyphs worldwide as the product of one Ngöbe woman waiting for her sons, who are the sun and the moon (Septimo and Joly 1986). The sons come from fire and ash, and the mother is the earth. While this could potentially be seen as a reference to the creation and fertility linked to volcanic areas, it at bare minimum highlights an interesting emphasis on the artistic contribution of women and their link to rock art in the isthmian context.

Petroglyphs can also be seen as marks of ownership or territoriality, and as such would serve as permanent statements of place and identity. The menhirs, or standing megalithic stones, erected in Neolithic through Bronze Age Brittany, are seen in this context as a response to post-Mesolithic transformation and the transition to farming (Tilley 2004b:33). The transition to maize-based agriculture is commonly thought to have allowed the first significant occupation of the Chiriquí highlands (Linares et al. 1975), which were prior to that transition (ca. 2,000–3,000 B.P.) uninhabitable. If that is the case, agricultural territory would have certainly been of key importance particularly in areas with richer soils or access to water. The marking of ownership of territory, or identification with that territory, could be seen as a viable purpose for marking the landscape.

The ways in which each of the above suggestions of meaning can work in tandem is apparent in the Andean context. The association of mytho-history and ritual practice in the Inka perception of landscape was deeply intertwined (Zuidema 1964; 1990). The 41 *ceque* lines that connected the 328 *wakas* of the Cuzco region combined both marked and unmarked elements of the landscape into a cohesive whole. Unmarked *wakas* were no less potent than those that were marked, and strongly exemplify the element of hybridity of natural and cultural elements. *Ceque* lines often crossed canal intakes, springs, or important points along canal systems, and as such divided social spaces (Farrington 1992:372; Sherbondy 1986:85–92). Social groups' access to land and water was confirmed by rituals performed at the wakes belonging to them.

Roberto Perez-Franco, an MIT-trained Panamanian engineer, has developed a series of evocative and convincing hypotheses of the designs on the western face of the Caldera petroglyph boulder. In these conceptions, the designs and where they are located on the stone relates to solar and lunar phases and could be linked to agricultural and/or ritual practices (Perez-Franco 2004). Designs indicate a sequence of attempts to demarcate the locations of the solstice and equinox sun and 12 moon cycles of the year, finally culminating in one "correct" calendar. This functional interpretation of the designs as a means of marking the passage of time does not apply to the more abstract and scattered designs of the Huacal petroglyphs. The interpretation highlights, however, the idea that the choices of which rocks are marked are strategic in order to link cultural and natural elements into a cohesive whole in the landscape.

In the Armenian context, researchers interpret a rock art site to portray a volcanic eruption (Karakhanian et al. 2002), and see cupules near the volcano image as indicative of oil-burning rituals to prevent eruption (Karakhanian, personal communication 2004). The intention of the Boquete rock art as an apotropaic element in relation to the potentially threatening volcanic environment is additionally conceivable. The most recent study of the Volcán Barú's eruptive history places eruptions at 250 A.D., 1030 A.D., and 1380 A.D. (Behling 2000). Prior studies found evidence for an eruption in 600 A.D. (IHRE 1987; Linares et al. 1975). If, per the belief of Linares and Ranere (1980), the highlands have been occupied by sedentary agricultural populations for 2–3,000 years, this provides a number of prehistoric intersections between violent andesitic eruptions and social groups. Particularly given the power of even a small volcanic eruption to poison the water source and prevent crops from growing, the location of petroglyphs in close association with water sources could have been intended as a talisman.

Mesolithic peoples in western Europe watched as their old landmarks, resources, and favorite places for settlement were erased by 16 meters of post-glacial sea level rise. Fresh water was polluted, fields became rivers, and social relationships and memories that were linked to the places were lost along with them. The menhirs erected after this period, then, could have served as new landmarks that were intended to act as guardians of fresh water and the overall sense of place (Tilley 2004b:84). The location of petroglyphs in the Volcán Barú area almost exclusively in locations from which the volcano crater can be seen and in close association with water makes this explanation a possible factor in their creation and use. The location of the municipal water source petroglyph boulder between the largest natural spring and the end of a massive, columnar jointed lava flow could add plausibility to this theory. Like volcano effigies found at the Terminal site of Tetimpa, Mexico, in line-of-sight to Popocatépetl volcano (Plunket and Urunuela 1998), the petroglyphs may have been part of an active effort to ward off the potential harm of eruption.

The petroglyphs could variously be seen in the light of respectful obeisance to the volcano. This concreted past thought and action is similar to the context of the ancient Egyptian settlement of Deir el-Medina, where rock graffiti left by people traveling to the Valley of the Kings represents a *proskynemata,* or obeisance to the local deities (Meskell 2004). This is a reflection of awe and piety in the presence of the potent symbolic landscape. Particularly in the volcanic landscape of Boquete, where the frequent earthquakes remind one regularly of the human scale's frailty and mortality in contrast to the power and permanence of the earth, awe and reflection upon the potency of the landscape can be easily imagined.

Over the lifespan of the Boquete area petroglyphs, the merging of their interpretations and meanings likely shifted in the ebb and flow of the lives of those who lived around them. The rock art cannot be seen as having ever had one primary or static purpose, function, or interpretation. Petroglyphs represent human thought, action, intention, and communication and as such are an important element of interpreting and peopling the prehistory of western Panamá.

The Thinkable Volcanic Landscape of Western Panamá

One of the challenges of archaeological work in highland western Panamá is the ephemeral nature of the prehistoric artifactual record. Neither bodies nor buildings tend to evidence the ca. 12,000 years of habitation and visitation in the isthmus due to acidic soils and high rainfall. In addition, the richness of the portable artifacts – particularly gold work – aided in the transportation of a significant amount of the artifact record to private collections or smelting ovens in Seville over the past 500 years. By broadening the boundaries and definitions of what are considered data, however, the field of materials available for study expands greatly. In Panamá, any artifact or tomb is known as a *huaca*, a term derived from the Quechua word used in the Inka context. In essence, in looking to rock art within its landscape and as a part of that landscape is a return to the original derivation of the word now used to signify material culture in Panamá.

Highland Panamá's perceived dearth of data is in fact only a reflection of the need for research methods and vantages that address materials that were previously delegated to the realm of the invisible. Research using phytoliths (Piperno 1999) and DNA (Kolman et al. 1995), for example, is seeking information from microscopic or previously overlooked forms of data to help interpret the lacunae in the larger isthmian past. These sources of data were both literally and metaphorically immaterial prior to very recent scientific advances. Other sources of information, however, have been invisible simply due to their relegation to the category of immaterial. Petroglyphs, the Volcán Barú, and the web of associations and interpretations that bind them into a socialized web of meaning fall in to this category. While rock art is concentrated in the Pacific side of western Panamá, it is found throughout the isthmus in contexts that obviously do not directly reference a volcano. It is the contention of this chapter that each rock art context is different, but each in its own way relates to the larger natural and social environment that surrounded it at the time of its creation.

I would suggest rock art can be seen as shared emblems of past social memory (per Küchler 1999; 2002). From this perspective the petroglyphs in the Boquete context are more correctly defined as forgotten memory in the seeming distance and inaccessibility of the emic meanings of their designs. If material remembering does in fact require spatio-temporal anchoring, as Meskell (2004) discusses in the case of New Kingdom Egypt, then the permanence and materiality of the Boquete petroglyphs could have provided that function in the past. Without the associated oral tradition, however, the petroglyphs are shoved into a lifeworld in which they are disembodied and fragmental. As products and initiators of human cognition and action, however, their presence is still powerful and important and is tightly interconnected with the larger landscape.

The Volcán Barú, and the petroglyphs that surround it in Boquete, suffer from an academic invisibility or "unthinkability" due to the unexamined elements of their materiality. The concepts of *gestalt* and the realization that our own figure/ground perspectives of data and non-data are not fixed in archaeological conception highlight the inherent inconstancy of binaries like nature/culture, mind/body, and literal/metaphorical. The amalgam of landscape is not encoded meaning or encrypted signs; it is agentic, auratic, and lived. Devoid of the original contextual knowledge of their creation and use, the petroglyphs that surround the Volcán Barú are a source of both information and enigma. No one interpretation of them is either possible or desirable, but what is irreducible is that they provide an anchor of the past within the present and evidence past thought, intent, and communication, hence the irresponsibility of ignoring them as non-data. Both the rock art and the volcano itself challenge easy or static Cartesian definition; they are best given voices as hybrid forms. The critical examination of what we consider visible, material, and thinkable in the recursive and ongoing lived human experience forms the crux of the archaeological challenge.

Acknowledgments

Many grateful thanks to the Wenner-Gren Foundation and Fulbright Program for funding the field work project from which this chapter developed. Lynn Meskell and the School of American Research seminar that she organized receive the largest credit due for this volume; without her mentorship and unflagging encouragement none of these thoughts would have been put down on paper. Many thanks also go to Rosemary Joyce, who did her best to untangle and clarify my thoughts once they were down on paper, though I am fully culpable for those that are still tangled. Mark A. Smith was an integral part of the field project and analysis and I am grateful for his boundless capabilities. I am also indebted to the kind support of the Smithsonian Tropical Research Institute in Panamá, particularly Richard Cooke, and to Luz Graciela Joly of the Universidad Autónoma de Chiriquí. Luz Graciela, in particular, has been integral in the protection and investigation of Chiriquí rock art sites and is a constant source of energy and inspiration.

References

Appadurai, Arjun 1986 The Social Life of Things: Commodities in Cultural Perspective. Cambridge: Cambridge University Press.

Arca, Andrea 2004 The Topographic Engravings of Alpine Rock-Art: Fields, Settlements and Agricultural Landscapes. *In* The Figured Landscapes of Rock-Art. C. Chippindale and G. Nash, eds. Pp. 318–349. Cambridge: Cambridge University Press.

Attfield, J. 2000 Wild Things: Material Culture of Everyday Life. New York: Berg.

Bataille, Georges 1985 Visions of Excess: Selected Writings 1927–1939. Minneapolis: University of Minnesota Press.

Behling, Hermann 2000 A 2860-Year High-Resolution Pollen and Charcoal Record from the Cordillera de Talamanca in Panama: A History of Human and Volcanic Forest Disturbance. The Holocene 10(3):387–393.

Benjamin, Walter 1968 Illuminations. New York: Schocken Books.

Bradley, Richard 1997 Rock Art and the Prehistory of Atlantic Europe. London: Routledge.

Davis, Whitney 1989 Finding Symbols in History. *In* Animals Into Art. H. Morphy, ed. Pp. 170–189. London: Unwin Hyman.

Dragna, Gary 2004 Routes Millenarian Indigenous. Electronic document. http://www.uraba.8k.com.

Drooker, Penelope, ed. 2001 Fleeting Identities: Perishable Material Culture in Archaeological Research. Carbondale: Southern Illinois University.

Farrington, I. 1992 Ritual Geography, Settlement Patterns and the Characterization of the Provinces of the Inka Heartland. World Archaeology 23(3):368–385.

Flood, Josephine 2004 Linkage Between Rock-Art and Landscape in Aboriginal Australia. *In* The Figured Landscapes of Rock-Art. C. Chippindale and G. Nash, eds. Pp. 182–200. Cambridge: Cambridge University Press.

Frierson, Pamela 1991 The Volcano as Western Metaphor. *In* The Burning Island: A Journey Through Myth and History in Volcano Country, Hawai'i. B. Dean, ed. Pp. 85–104. Nature and Natural Philosophy Library. San Francisco: Sierra Club Books.

Gell, Alfred 1998 Art and Agency: An Anthropological Theory. Oxford: Oxford University Press.

Hacking, Ian 1990 The Taming of Chance. Cambridge: Cambridge University Press.

Handwerk, Brian 2002 Are Volcanic Eruptions Tied to Lunar Cycle?, Vol. accessed February 13, 2004: National Geographic News.

Harris, Robert 2003 Pompeii. New York: Random House.

Harte, Eva 1959 Petroglyphs in Panama. Panama Archaeologist 2:58–69.

Hoskins, J. 1998 Biographical Objects. London: Routledge.

IHRE 1987 Final Report on the Reconnaissance Study of Geothermal Resources in the Republic of Panama. P. 72. Panama City: Instituto de Recursos Hidraulicos y Electrificacion (IRHE – IDB – OLADE).

Joly, Luz Graciela 1997 Mapas Mayas en pierdra? Los petroglifos de Palo Santo, Chiriqui. *In* El Panama America. P. 3A. Panama.

Karakhanian, A., R. Djrbashian, V. Trifonov, H. Philip, S. Arakelian, and A. Avagian 2002 Holocene-Historical Volcanism and Active Faults as Natural Risk Factors for Armenia and Adjacent Countries. Journal of Volcanology and Geothermal Research 113(1):319–344.

Kolman, Connie, Eldredge Bermingham, Richard Cooke, R. H. Ward, Tomas Arias, and Francoise Guionneau-Sinclair 1995 Reduced mtDNA Diversity in the Ngobe Amerinds of Panama. Genetics 140(May):275–283.

Küchler, S. 1999 The Place of Memory. *In* The Art of Forgetting. A. Forty and S. Küchler, eds. Pp. 53–72. Oxford: Berg.

—— 2002, Malanggan: Art, Memory and Sacrifice. Oxford: Berg.

Kunne, Martin 2003 Arte rupestre de Panama. *In* Arte rupestre de Mexico oriental y centro america. M. Kunne and M. Strecker, eds. Pp. 223–239. Indiana, vol. 16. Berlin: Gebr. Mann Verlag.

Landau, Carlos 2000 El Volcan Baru. Boquete, Panama: published by author.

Latour, Bruno 1991 We Have Never Been Modern. C. Porter, trans. Cambridge, MA: Harvard University Press.

Linares, Olga, and Anthony Ranere, eds. 1980 Adaptive Radiations in Prehistoric Panama. Vol. 5. Cambridge, MA: Harvard University.

Linares, Olga, Payson Sheets, and Jane Rosenthal 1975 Prehistoric Agriculture in Tropical Highlands. Science 187:137–145.

MacCurdy, George 1911 A Study of Chiriquian Antiquities. Vol. 3. New Haven.

Merleau-Ponty, Maurice 1962 Phenomenology of Perception. London and New York: Routledge.

Meskell, Lynn 2004 Material Biographies: Object Lessons from Ancient Egypt and Beyond. Oxford: Berg.

Miranda de Cabal, Beatriz 1974 Un pueblo visto a traves de su lenguaje. David, Panama: private press.

Morrison, Kathleen 2004 On Putting Time in its Place: Landscape History in South India: paper presented at the University of Pennsylvania ethnohistory workshop, November 11.

Perez-Franco, Roberto 2004 The Solar-Lunar Calendar of Caldera. Seminar-workshop: Archaeological Visions of Boquete for Tourism, Boquete, Panamá, December 5.

Piperno, Dolores 1999 The Origins and Development of Food Production in Pacific Panama. *In* Pacific Latin America in Prehistory. M. Blake, ed. Pp. 123–134. Pullman, Washington: Washington State University Press.

Plunket, Patricia, and Gabriela Urunuela 1998 Preclassic Household Patterns Preserved under Volcanic Ash at Tetimpa, Puebla, Mexico. Latin American Antiquity 9(4):287–309.

Reinhard, Johan 1985 Sacred Mountains: An Ethno-Archaeological Study of High Andean Ruins. Mountain Research and Development 5(4):299–317.

Septimo, Roger, and Luz Graciela Joly 1986 Kugue kira nie ngabere (sucesos antiguos dichos en Guaymi). P. 110: Asociación Panameña de Antropologia.

——— 1998 Ñaglon bata sö (El sol y la luna). *In* Pueblos Indigenos de Panama. C. Picon, J. Alemancia, and I. Solcher, eds. Pp. 21–26. Panama: UNESCO.

Sheets, Payson, and Brian McKee, eds. 1994, Archaeology, Volcanism, and Remote Sensing in the Arenal Region, Costa Rica. Austin: University of Texas Press.

Shelton, Catherine 1984 Formative Settlement in Western Chiriqui, Panama: Ceramic Chronology and Phase Relationships. Ph.D. thesis, Temple University.

Sherbondy, J. 1986 The Canal Systems of Hanan Cuzco. Ph.D. thesis, University of Illinois at Urbana-Champaign.

Sigurdsson, Haraldur 1999 Melting the Earth: The History of Ideas on Volcanic Eruptions. New York: Oxford.

Sivard, Susan n.d. The Volcano in European and American Art, 1770–1865. Ph.D. thesis, Columbia University.

Stephens, John Lloyd 1969[1841] Incidents of Travel in Central America, Chiapas, and Yucutan. Vol. 2. New York: Dover.

Stirling, Matthew 1950 Exploring Ancient Panama by Helicopter. National Geographic Magazine 97:227–246.

Thacker, Christopher 1984, The Volcano: Culmination of the Landscape Garden. *In* British and American Gardens in the Eighteenth Century. R. Maccubbin and P. Martin, eds. Pp. 75–83. Williamsburg, Virginia: The Colonial Williamsburg Foundation.

Tilley, Christopher 2004a, The Materiality of Stone. Oxford: Berg.

——— 2004b Sprouting Rhizomes and Giant Axes: Experiencing Breton Menhirs. *In* The Materiality of Stone. Pp. 33–86. Oxford: Berg.

Torrence, Robin, and John Grattan 2002 The Archaeology of Disasters: Past and Future Trends. *In* Natural Disasters and Cultural Change. R. Torrence and J. Grattan, eds. Pp. 1–18. One World Archaeology, vol. 45. London and New York: Routledge.

Whitley, David, ed. 2001 Handbook of Rock-Art Research. Walnut Creek: Altamira.

Zuidema, R. 1964 The Ceque System of Cuzco: The Social Organization of the Capital of the Incas. Leiden: E. J. Brill.

——— 1990 Inca Civilization in Cuzco. Austin: University of Texas Press.

9
Afterword

Daniel Miller

Materiality as a term always speaks to a paradox, which is the assumed greater reality of that which we do not apprehend over that which is merely evident (Miller In press). In all religions for example, the assumption is that what we see in front of us is largely vestigial and superficial. The real lies in the cosmological world of which things are mere tokens and signs. Since almost every society that is the subject of archaeological exploration and excavation would have understood itself in cosmological terms, this places the very practice of archaeology in an analogous relationship to its own subject of enquiry. A contemporary archaeologist is by and large considered profound or at least good at their work largely to the extent to which they are able to transcend the merely manifest in the objects which they uncover and see through these fragments to the reality of the social and cultural lives of which they are mere remnants. So today an archaeologist looks down upon their forebears who labeled the peoples they discovered with terms such as the "bell-beaker" folk or the "Acheuliean hand-ax" people, precisely because there is a sense that this phase of archaeology lacked anthropology. It lacked the sensitivity to see beyond the mere artifact to appreciate that those artifacts were no more the totality of the peoples who used them, than we are condensed into the furniture or clothes we use today.

As such the sensibility of the archaeologist to the paradox of materiality, in which reality lies behind, not in front of, artifacts, is directly analogous to the ways in which the peoples whose remains are being excavated themselves may well have understood that the merely mundane artifactual presence in the world, belies the true grandeur and profundity of the divine and spiritual world compared to which they are themselves poor vessels, mere broken fragments and shards. So the importance of an engagement with the concept of materiality for the archaeologist is that it helps us to grant to those we study a perspicacity equivalent to that which we seek for ourselves. An understanding that the artifacts excavated speak not merely to a social system but inevitably to the cosmological system, to the reality that for most peoples in the past only truly existed in the immaterial, not merely the material world.

But there is another more fortuitous aspect to the word materiality which helps guide us to the ways in which this same process operates. Consider the way we colloquially use the word "materialized." For example when someone returns from an event and we say "Ok so what materialized?" The word here refers metaphorically to the concrete sense of the material, by virtue of asking what consequences accrued from some action or event. What materialized is to ask which out of several possibilities actual came to be. To my mind what this collection accomplishes is a rapprochement between the first sense of materiality as an acknowledgment of the cosmological origins of the material worlds we encounter, and this sense that artifacts also for us, and for the people who lived before us, often answer the question "what materialized?" meaning what were the particular consequences of past events out of the various possible consequences that might have accrued from their presence in the world.

The theme that emerges again and again in these chapters is that of the direct analogy between what the academics seek to achieve and the aims of those same people who are the subject and object of academic enquiry. Perhaps the clearest example here of the fundamental paradox of materiality comes from Nakamura's work on the figurines of neo-Assyria. In effect this becomes an essay on the magical foundations of archaeology as a means for materializing not simply the everyday activities of the people of ancient Assyria but rather a conjuring up of the universe to which they in turn paid obeisance. In all such cases we need a sense of the Kantian resistance of the art work to its immediate apprehension. The source of our reverence for things is in their opacity, their reluctance to make material the "real" world which lies behind their mere appearance as things. In the same way, in Gaitán's chapter we encounter the image of schoolchildren crowded around a toothbrush as an archaeological object entranced, by the sense of the archaeologists as shamans who reveal through mundane things a reality that is entrancing to the extent that it was previously hidden, or in Hasinoff's we see how an exhibition is constructed of "Indian" artifacts precisely as a work of Protestant revelation in which reality lies not in how Indians made the artifacts but in how god made the Indians.

This is how Nakamura understands the role of the figurines themselves. Mere miniatures of clay provide a sense of the limitation of both humanity and of the merely material in apprehending reality. Indeed the neo-Assyrian may be informed by the not too distant Biblical texts, in which we have not just abundant metaphors of humanity with the gods as skilful potters, forming humanity from real clay, but also the sense that objects are such poor vessels of mimesis that in Judaism (and later on Islam) all representation was banned as a sign of the hopelessness of this very task of mimesis. For Nakamura there are many layers of concealment which become revelations of the power of mimesis, as the fragile, miniaturized form of the figurine established both the grandeur of its creator and the evocation of our need for protection by the still grander forces of the divine. As such the neo-Assyrians can be understood as themselves archaeologists, attempting to apprehend, through little pieces of clay, a totality that they could never directly encounter, but through creative imagination and reconstruction could at least hope to learn about their own place in this world and by extension a glimpse of their place in the real world of cosmology.

One of the primary ways in which archaeology rendered itself a part of a larger anthropology was by recasting artifacts as the material revelation of relationships. This, as evident in the contribution by Lazzari, has again the desired effect of equalizing the task of the archaeologist and the anthropologist. Since for the social anthropologist relationships are no more materially present than they are for archaeologists. For both they have to be imagined out of revelatory artifacts that speak to relationships Indeed in the recent influential work of Strathern persons are themselves understood in Melanesia as objects that materialize the relationships that are presumed to have been responsible for their coming into being. An idea very close to our colloquial question "what then materialized?" As Lazzari notes these relationships are often in themselves hybrids of social and material form. Indeed there is a neat alignment with Munn's notion of an expansion of space-time as the experience of cultural connectedness and the way this is made more potent by a mountainous landscape in which the connectivity of people is often that of both the valleys they pass through and the objects they are thereby

AFTERWORD

able to barter. No doubt there were also kinship connections that once also made manifest this connectivity.

This space-time becomes ordered as people delineate worlds that are thereby envisaged as intrinsically separate but potential connected. So that in one place a genre of objects is restricted to the domestic area, and in another to the world of ritual. As Lazzari notes, this creation of universes is in turn analogous to the creation of style, the configurations and dimensions around which the conceptual and visual world is organized. Style is not just form here, it is also the references of place and thus relationships between places. This seems very reasonable, inasmuch as it actually helps us to think of the Kula ring as a kind of Melanesian style, a way of re-configuring the relationships between people into an imagined circle that then becomes the circuits of both people and more particularly valuables. The Kula ring, amongst other things, is clearly a design which could in turn be called a style.

The effect of this revelatory potential of archaeology is that it transforms our sense of who we are in relation to our pasts. The discovery recently of Homo Floriensis forces us to confront the idea of parallel hominid branches that fascinates us because it implies that we do not actually control the action of self-discovery, but find out who we are in dynamic relation to potentially unprecedented discoveries about our own histories. Again the archaeologist appears a shaman finding objects that reveal our true condition in unexpected ways. This dynamic quality is central to the findings of Weiss, who uses it to turn around our assumptions about the process of objectification. For the bushmen living in the Northern Cape of South Africa it is the solid rock face and its attendant rock-art that gives fluidity to identity and the means for appropriating their self-construction, which becomes a means of resistance to the pathologizing objectification suffered during the colonial encounter.

Whether or not the people who actually engraved the rock painting site of Wildebeestkuil were ancestral is unimportant. There are many ways in which a sense of appropriation may be achieved. On the one hand the very firmness and solidity of the landscape speaks to the firmness of the inhabitants and the courage in the face of colonial persecution, on the other their ritual practice and beliefs can be read into the representations depicted in the paintings as though they had produced them. The powers of shamans are invoked as our pilots that fly us between apparently incommensurable worlds and bring forth as objects the signs of universes we do not otherwise encounter, including those of the ancient past. The main constraint upon such appropriation would have been the power of colonial authority, but today there is a new alignment, such that the ability of the bush people to reaffirm their specificity through re-attachment to the landscape as heritage is understood as a bulwark against the alienating effects of modernism. In much the same way the tourists see the authenticity of the inhabitants as a sign of support against what they see as a preponderance of artificiality and superficiality of the modern world. Today the indigenous finds a new rhythm as the "autochthonous bearers of the rainbow nation or an African renaissance."

The distance traveled to reach the ideal of a rainbow nation from the past oppression of colonialism is evident by comparing this case with two matched chapters, those of Hasinoff and Gaitán. Prior to this emancipation most peoples of the world were rather more likely to be seen themselves as the material sign of another greater reality – that of god's civilizing purpose for the world. As part of the Protestant Mission's "object lessons" to the faithful, the "Indian" artifacts became the objects, and the lesson became the truth of a certain version of social evolution. The primitive represent the stunted lines of only partially evolved humanity that will only come to full fruit under the benign light of god's rays, which thanks to the work of the mission can now penetrate the dense fog of primitive ignorance and superstition. Just as Jesus once made mundane artifacts the means of miraculous revelation, so now the materiality of Indian life can show the miracle of how people can be saved and resurrected through mission work. As such the greater the realism of representation the better and the more fully the lesson would be learnt.

During this same period there were, as Hasinoff makes clear, alternative forms of revelation that seemed manifest in these artifacts. When seen as "arts and crafts" then they could reveal both a connection with nature lost in the modern world or a fine utilitarianism depending upon the value the viewer sought to resurrect. But for mission it was much more the central paradox of materiality that was the route to salvation. Both the savagery of pre-Christian form and the enlightenment of the converted could as material signs help conjure the evidence that gave credence to the ultimate purpose "the assimilatory success of of American Christianity, itself impelled by Manifest Destiny."

The mirror image of this example is found in Gaitán. In Hasinoff the outsiders are testimony to the place of god's civilization as embodied in the presence of the viewer. For the 19th-century bourgeoisie of Bogotá regarding themselves as the periphery, the center of civilization was somewhere far removed – in this case distant Paris. If hand made artifacts revealed the lack of civilization of the Indians, artifacts could make Colombians feel they were themselves mere Indians in comparison to the refinements of civility found in Paris. The power of Gaitán's chapter lies in the evocative potential of the toothbrush as archaeology and reveals not the mass industrial plastic item we automatically associate this activity with today, but a handcrafted bone and bristle object that once became the very signature of imported refinement.

Indeed if the imported toothbrush is regarded as the refined form which signified the *habitus* of the civilized, it seems almost churlish not to try and imagine behind the excavated toothbrush, the ephemeral but perhaps at the time devastating smile that was, one imagines, the most effective manifestation of their use. Again it is our ability to imagine bone and pig hair formed into the means by which one person could literally dazzle another with the brightness and whiteness of that hitherto unreachable perfection that may correspond to an excavation of civilization.

If Hasinoff and Gaitán form an obvious pair, so finally do Palus and Holmberg. This issue of our imagination as to what materialized, i.e. what were the consequences of the very existence of some material form, finds its clearest expression in these two chapters. In the case of Holmberg the issue is one of acknowledgment of a materiality that is so given and massive that we can end up not "seeing it" as the context for the more parochial material we do look at. With Palus we are concerned with the emergence of a new phenomenon that challenges the very sense of what is material and immaterial. Though curiously once something like electricity becomes ubiquitous it suffers from the same problem as a volcano, we quickly take it for granted and thus struggle to manage what Palus achieves, which is a reconstruction of what might be called our original naïveté.

Holmberg employs recent writing by Tilley and others on the paradox of materiality that pertains to landscape. In general as I have argued elsewhere material culture possesses a humility in that the more important it is as the context in which we live the more inclined we are to relegate it to unseen context and backdrop so that it becomes in effect immaterial. Landscape seems a particularly clear example of this paradox. In the case of Holmberg the problem is that we see the boulder that was spawned by the volcano because of its petroglyphs, but we don't see the volcano itself. It is a typical result of the fact that human perception depends upon focus, so that to concentrate on the foreground often masks the background to our vision. Metaphorically she suggests this is just as true of the academic as of the oracular sight. This is particularly unfortunate since the materiality of a volcano is also expressed in its longevity. Although we struggle to know how it was seen in the past, it would be a pity to refuse that commonality represented by acknowledging that clearly it was present in the past as it is today, and that the first response to the prehistoric materials is to recognize that they were themselves a response to the questions of materiality that literally issued forth from the volcano itself.

To gain a sense of how the presence of a phenomenon gives rise to an engagement with materiality that hinges on the metaphorical, the imaginative, and the technological issues of consequence from its very existence, we can turn to the penultimate chapter by Palus which also helps us come full circle to the first chapters. Palus makes clear that when electricity came to Annapolis it was not at all certain what exactly would be revealed by its light. It did not attract industry to the town in quite the way expected, it produced industry more vicariously to the degree to which workers could work longer hours. But just as in the very first chapter on the neo-Assyrians, we can see how a new material presence is first and foremost an implement of cosmological imagination. Materialization is always also an act of imagination, to think what kind of thing this could be, a process only made more obvious because of the very ambiguity of electricity as materiality. So the discoveries of the internal connections that make up the human nervous system made more sense when they were seen as analogous to the invisible movement of electricity outside the body. It is hardly surprising that one of the main early expectations was of direct medical use. Something that the book and film *One Flew Over the Cuckoo's Nest* reveals was later put into practice with often devastating effects.

As such Palus's work on electricity helps clarify some of the themes that pertain to the volume as a whole. For archaeologists it seems both natural and appropriate to think of materiality in the sense of a discovery of the capacity of humanity made manifest in that which humanity produces. But it is a truth of objectification that it is only ever through this dialectical process that we discover who as humanity we are. So when electricity arrives it is as though we suddenly have a new prosthetic arm which with one twist can turn on lights, and with another can bring

Afterword

forth sound broadcast in another country. Many things now lie at the tips of our fingers that did not previously exist and thereby our sense of what we can do in the world is changed. But the best way of understanding this dynamic is certainly not through the image of "Terminators," the science fiction imagination of barely tamed prosthetic forms. Rather it lies much closer to the mundane and everyday ways of creating and appropriating worlds that are found throughout these chapters, the discovery of what one can do with a toothbrush or how to appropriate a rock engraving as one's landscape.

In all such acts of materialization we are fascinated with the idea that the manifest is merely vulgar and the reality lies in a more profound world that remains entrancing precisely because it is opaque. It is the very charm of archaeology that at most it will never find more than a hint of what it seeks. It is the very attraction of theory as used in many of these chapters that the opacity of language can hint of a still more profound apprehension than that which can be conveyed in an academic work. It is the sensitivity to religious paraphernalia, either figurines or protestant intimations of savagery, that implicate god or gods as the true origin of what merely appears to be. Indeed it is the paradox that we all suffer from in the study of material culture. We see this finally in the way in which we are often denigrated for choosing to study material culture. We are assumed to have failed to appreciate the superficiality of the material, when by rights we should be studying society, culture, ideology, and the deconstructed, all of which are much more real than the merely apparent which we choose to focus on. We poor materialists are seen as a vulgar and simplistic lot. But as these chapters expertly reveal, it was ever thus.

Reference

Miller, D. ed. In press Materiality. Chapel Hill: Duke University Press.

Index

Note: page numbers in italics refer to illustrations or figures

Aconquija mountains *139*; caravan trails 137–8, 140; ceramics 138, 143–6; lithics 138, 143–6; roads/herding posts 138, 140; social connections 148; spatial practices 148–9; *see also* obsidian
Adorno, T. 49, 164
Afrikaners 11, 62
after-life beliefs 62
AIDS epidemic 10–11
Akkadian language 27, 37
Allotment Act 108
American Arts and Crafts Movement 111
American Indian League 106, 109–12; *see also* Native Americans
American Museum of Natural History: burden basket 112–14; ethnological artifacts 97, 117–18; World in Boston 114–18
ANC government 13
Anderson, B. 184
Andes region 130, 199
Andrefsky, W. 145
Annapolis: and Baltimore 170; electric lights 164–5, 172–3, 218; electricity consumption 184; US Naval Academy 171, 174
Annapolis Electric Light Company 165, 171, 172–3, 177
Annapolis Gas Light Company 171, 177
anthropology 14, 116–17, 212, 214
Antigal de Tesoro 138, *146*
Antin, E. 199
apotropaic function: figurines 20–2, 31–3, *35*, 40n1; Neo-Assyrian magic 28–9; performances 136; petroglyphs 205, 206; ritual 20–1, 28–9; texts 19, 28–9
Appadurai, A. 50, 51–2, 76, 200
Arbousset, J. T. 58
arc lights 173–4
archaeology: anthropology 212, 214; ethnography 76–7; evolutionary approach 133; functionalism 133; materiality 1–2, 4, 7, 212–13; post-structural 133
Arendt, Hannah 181
Argentina, northwest *139* (*map*); ceramics 132; communities 137; cultural areas 141; Formative period 129, 137–8, 142, 151n2; hunter-gatherers 136–7; obsidian 131–2, 143–4; *see also* Aconquija mountains

INDEX

Armenia 205
art 52, 108–9, 129
artifacts 32; culture 1; ethnological 97, 117–18; fetishization 83, 86, 88–9; lifeworld 141; material culture 2; regionality 130; resistance 10; tourism 46
artisan economies 8; *see also* crafts
Asendorf, C. 168, 170
Asher, A. L. 27
Asher-Grève, J. M. 27
āšipu: *see* priest-exorcist
assimilation 97, 106, 118–19
Assur 18, 19
Atherstone, Dr 57
Australian Aboriginals 203–4
authenticity 14–15, 56
automatism 23, 38
Avebury 193

Ba'hai community 202
Bakhtin, M. 25, 32, 38, 40n5, 129, 148
Balfour, H. 58
Balibar, E. 55–6
Baltimore 170
Bamiyan Buddhas 56
barter 130, 145
baskets: burden 112–14, 120n7; Pomo 112–14, 115, 117; utilitarian/decorative 113–14; wire 9–10, 12–13
Bataille, G. 63, 198
Beard, G. 162, 167–9
being-in-the-world (Heidegger) 181, 182
Benjamin, W. 28, 164, 199
Berossos' *Babyloniaka* 37
betel bag 76–7
Black, J. 35
blankets 107, 114
Bleek, W. 57, 59–60, 62
Board of Home Missions 97, 101–2
Boas, F. 120–1n10

body 40n9; experience 194; inscription 128; Marx 126–7; materiality 128; neurasthenia 162, 168–9, 170; skin color 169
Boers 11, 56, 57, 59
Bogotá 71, 72–4, 85, *86*, 216–17
Bolivar, S. 74–5, 91
Boquete area 208; apotropaic rock art 205; dacite columns 201; earthquakes 206; petroglyphs 194–7, 203–6, 207; *see also* Volcán Barú
Borges, J. L. 83
Bottéro, J. 27
Bourdieu, P.: *doxa* 80–1, 147; elective asceticism 86; *habitus* 2–3, 80–1, 151n4
bourgeoisie 71, 82–3, 85–6, 216–17; *see also* elites
Boussingault, J.-B. 71, 88
Bradley, R. 202
British Association for the Advancement of Science: *Notes and Queries on Anthropology* 117
British Museum 58
Brittany 204
Bromo volcano 198
Browning, E. B. 198
Brush 166
Brush Arc Lighting Company 164–5
Brush Electric Light Company 173
bundling 4, 32
burial 36–7
Bushman myth 51, 56, 57
Bushmen 12, 59, 215

Caillois, R. 34
Caldera petroglyph 191–4; as calendar 194, 205; setting *193*; split boulder *192*; Volcán Barú 204
caravan trade 130–1, 137, 149
ceque lines 204–5

INDEX

ceramics 1, 13; Aconquija mountains 138, 143–6; Antigal de Tesoro *146*; Argentina, northwest 132, 142; decorated 141–2, 145–7; and lithics 129, 136, 140–3, 148; and obsidian 148, 149–50; sedentary lifestyle 136–7; social life 141, 147
de Certeau, M. 184
Chiriquí 190, 191, 197–8, 202, 204
Christianity: expansion 102; Native Americans 97, 101, 103, 104, 118–19; *see also* Protestantism; Roman Catholicism
civility 71–2, 82, 83
civilization, scale of 11
class/identity 80
clay 40–1n14, 142
clothes 104
Cody, Buffalo Bill 99
Coetzee, J. M. 9
Colloredo-Mansfeld, R. 14, 149
Colombia 74–5, 79–80; *see also* Bogotá
colonialism 12, 47–8, 56–63, 64
commodities: automatism 23; circulation 128–9; consciousness 133; exchange value 84; fetishism 74, 87, 90–1, 127, 164, 186; gift exchange 48; hybrid 109; standardized 75
communities 46, 52, 137
consciousness 133
consumption: electricity 166, 177–8, 180–1, 184; elites 86; heritage 49–51, 53; imports 79; luxuries 72; materiality 47, 48–9; objectification 49
control 179
Coombes, A. E. 50, 53, 58
cosmologies 59, 61, 212, 214
courtesy 82, 83

Craft South Africa 13
crafts: and development 8–9; modern materials 12–13; Native Americans 97, 110; technique/aesthetics 107, 114, 118–19
creation myths 40–1n14
culture: Afrikaners 11; appropriation 52, 53–4, 215; artifacts 1; materiality 6–7, 190; morality 83; nation 13; Native Americans 115–16; nature 7, 130, 200, 205; preservation 109, 191; spiritual/material needs 9; tooth-brushing 81–3
cuneiform script 27
Cuzco region 204–5

dacite columns 201
dance of blood 58
Dantzer, D. 56
Daumas, F. 58
Dawes Act 108
Deacon, H. J. 61
death 24, 62, 63
Deir el-Medina 206
Deleuze, G. 29, 36, 40n6
Derrida, J. 23, 33–4, 36, 38, 39, 55
Descartes, R. 127, 200
development 8–9, 12
Dickenson, E. 198
discourse/social analysis 132
Dixon, R. 113, 120n8
Doraz ethnohistoric story 204
Dowson, T. 60, 65–6n5
doxa 80, 147
Dreaming sites 203–4

earthquakes 206
Edison, T. 165, 166, 174
education 107–8, 110
Egypt 5–6, 206, 207
eland 62, 63

INDEX

electricity: advertisement 165; archaeology 163, 185–6; blackouts 178, 179–80; consumption 166, 177–8, 180–1, 184; experiments 163; extension of working hours 178; heat 165, 166; lighting 164–5, 172–3, 218; materiality 162–3, 164, 168–9, 217; medical practices 163, 166, 167–70, 218; nervousness 163–4, 179–80; objectification 218–19; safety 165, 166
electrocommunications 186
electrotherapy 167–8
Elias, N. 82
elites 82, 86
enchantment 30–1, 144
Enki 34, 37
Enlightenment thinking 5
enlivening 29–30, 40n13
ethnicity 9–10, 85
ethnography 76–7
evangelism: object lessons 112–13; progressivism 105, 115; World in Boston 99, 103, 114
Evening Capital 165, 170–1, 172
evolutionary approach 133
exchange value 84
existentialism 182
experience 26, 194

Fanon, F. 12
fashion 13, 111
Faubion, J. D. 58
Ferguson, James 8
fetishes 3; blurring taxonomies 5–6; Boussingault 71; domesticated 87; Marx 49; toothbrush 72, 74, 91
fetishism 3; artifacts 83, 86, 88–9; commodities 74, 87, 90–1, 127, 164, 186; methodological 76–7; technique 164

figurines: apotropaic 20–2, 31–3, 35, 40n1; magic 28; miniatures 214; Neo-Assyrian 18, 19, 32–3, 36–7, 213
flake scarring 54, 55
Formative period, Argentina 129, 137–8, 142, 151n2
Foucault, M. 58, 179
France 84, 204, 206
Frankfurt School 49, 65n3, 164, 181, 183
Freud, S. 168
functionalism 133

Gaitán Ammann, F. 7, 74, 213, 216–17
galvanism 163
Gaonkar, D. P. 55
Garland, E. 51
Geertz, C. 2
Gell, A. 133–4, 200
gestalt concept 202–3, 208
gift exchange 48, 145
gods 5–6, 39
Gordon, R. J. 51
governmentality 58
Green, A. 35
Guenther, M. 61

Habermas, J. 135
habitus 2–3, 80–1, 151n4, 184, 217
Halbwachs, M. 126
hallucinogenic drugs 146
Handbook and Guide to the World in Boston 96, *100*, 103
handwork: *see* crafts
Harte, E. 202
Hasinoff, E. 7, 214, 216
Hawaii 198
heat/light 165, 166
Hegel, G. W. F. 4, 46–7, 49, 65n2, 127
Heidegger, M. 4, 179, 181–2

INDEX

Hephaestus 198
heritage: consumption 49–51, 53; destroyed 56; identity 50; objectification 52, 54; production/consumption 53; tourism 50–1
heritage politics 50
Holmberg, K. 4, 7, 217–18
Homo floriensis 215
Horkheimer, M. 164
Hoskins, J. 76, 200
House Museum Quinta de Bolivar 91
huaca (artifact/tomb) 207
Huacal area 194–7, 201
Huffman, T. 13
human/animal blending 34, 36
Humboldt, A. von 85
Humphrey, M. E. I. 109
Humphrey, W. B. 105, 106, 109–12, 117
hunter-gatherers 136–7
hybridity 34–6, 85, 109

identity: appropriation 51; authenticity 14–15; class 80; community 46; ethnicity 9–10, 85; heritage 50; materiality 8; object biography 78; recast 13, 14, 53
imaginary 150
immateriality 98, 99, 179
incandescent lights 174, *181*
India, South 196
Indian Christian Chapel 101
Ingenio Arenal 138, 144
Ingold, T. 146
Inka landscape 195–6, 204–5, 207
interpretation 6, 40n8
Investing in Culture, Chief Director 13–14
invisibility/materiality 195, 201, 208

Islam 214
Ivison, D. 14

Jay, M. 181
Jesus Christ 98–9, 216
Joly, L. G. 194
Judaism 214

Keane, W. 2, 4
Khoesan 10, 57
Khwe San: SADF 52–3, 55; spiritual practices 54; Wildebeestkuil 46
King, T. 104–5
Kopytoff, I. 76, 78
Kula ring 215
KwaZulu Natal 10–11

landscape: as chronotope 130; cultural/natural 7, 130; *gestalt* concept 202–3; lifeworld 136; materiality 217–18; petroglyph markers 196; regionality 147–8; rock art 61–2, 202; sea level rises 205–6
landscape garden volcanoes 199
landscape studies 128
language 133
Latour, B. 4–5, 6, 200
Lazzari, M. 4, 7, 214–15
Lefebvre, H. 134
Levi-Strauss, C. 23
Lewis-Williams, D. 61
lifeworld: artifacts 141; *habitus* 3, 151n4; landscape 136; materiality 135; Merleau-Ponty 194; mundane 135–6, 142; petroglyphs 207–8; presence 149; representation 149
lighting 162–3, 165, 173–4, *181*; *see also* electricity
lightning strikes 57
Linares, O. 196, 205

INDEX

lithics: Aconquija mountains 138, 143–6; and ceramics 129, 136, 140–3, 148; decorated 141–2; domestic use 143; knapping quality 144; social life 141; tools 142
Luckmann, T. 135, 142
Lukács, G. 49, 134
luxuries 72

machine truths 164, 170
magic: death 24; figurines 28; Marx 22–3; materiality 21–2; mimesis 27–8, 31; objects 36; presentation 23–4; secrecy 32; senses 25–6, 29–30; thinking mode 39; Wittgenstein 24–5
Mallowan, M. 18
Mandela, N. 13
Manifest Destiny doctrine 97, 106, 118, 216
Marcuse, H. 164, 170, 181–2, 183, 185
Marx, K.: body 126–7; *Capital* 126; commodity fetishism 127; fetish 49; and Hegel 65n2; magic 22–3; Marcuse 182; objectification 65n3; social fact 150; social/material 134
Maryland Public Service Commission 177
Masaya volcano 198
material culture 2, 115–16, 133
material culture studies 1, 48
materiality: archaeology 1–2, 4, 7, 212–13; body 128; bundling 4, 32; civility 71–2; consumption 47, 48–9; cultural context 6–7, 190; electricity 162–3, 164, 168–9, 217; embodiment 128; identity 8; invisibility 195, 201, 208; landscape 217–18; lifeworld 135; magic 21–2; meaning 4, 78–9, 219; metaphorical usage of term 213; mimesis 32; modernity 49, 85–6; object biography 77–8; obsidian 149; protection 31–3; religion 212; social life 126–7, 134; technology 179; toothbrush 89–90
Matthews, C. 170
Mattick, B. 89–90
Mauss, M. 4, 21, 126, 131, 142
Mbeki, T. 9, 15
meaning: interpretation 40n8; materiality 4, 78–9, 219; obsidian 147; rock art 200
medicine: electricity 163, 166, 167–70, 218; somatic theory 169
Melanesian studies 76–7
menhirs 204, 206
Menke, C. 30
Merleau-Ponty, M. 26, 40n2, 127–8, 134, 135, 194
Meskell, L. 2, 39, 77, 206, 207
Mesopotamia 26–7, 30–1
methodological fetishism 76–7
Miller, D. 1–2, 3, 46–7, 65n2, 65n3, 75–6
mimesis: magic 27–8, 31; materiality 32; priest-exorcist 30, 33–4, 36; religion 214
mind/matter dichotomy 127, 134
miniatures 33–4, 199, 214
Miranda de Cabal, B. 194–5
mission schools 107–8
missionaries: exhibitions 96–7, 114–15; Native American crafts 110; *Notes and Queries on Anthropology* 117; *see also* World in Boston
modernity 5, 49, 79, 85–6
Moffat (missionary) 63
morality/culture 83
Morgan, L. H. 1
Morrison, K. 196
Morus, I. R. 163

INDEX

mundane 135–6, 142
Munn, N. D. 4, 214
mythologies: Bushman 51, 56, 57; creation 40–1n14; Inka landscape 204–5; Neo-Assyrian Empire 38–9; Ngöbe 204; Pele 198

Nakamura, C. 4, 213, 214
nation/culture 13
National Heritage Day 9–10
nationalism 55–6
Native American Folk-lore 105–6
Native Americans 97; art 108–9, 110; assimilation 106, 118–19; baskets 111–12, 120n7; blankets 107, 114; Christianity 97, 101, 103, 104, 118–19; classifications 99–101; culture 106, 115–16; dwellings 100–1, 120n3; education 107–8; fashion 111; missionaries 110; performances 104–6; preserving culture 109; Protestantism 214; self-representations 103–4; stereotypes 99; technique/aesthetic 118–19; World in Boston 107–9; *see also* American Indians; Native Americans; World in Boston
natural/supernatural 27
nature/culture 200, 205
Navajo weaving 107, 114
Ndebele dress designs 13
Neo-Assyrian Empire: apotropaic magic 28–9; cosmology 214; figurine deposits 18, 19, 32–3, 36–7, 213; mythologies 38–9; ritual 31
Neolithic-Copper Age markers 196
nervousness 163–4, 169, 179–80
Netherworld 37, 38
neurasthenia 162, 167–70
New Granada 79, 85, 87; *see also* Colombia

New York City 164–5
Ngöbe myth 204
Nimrud site 18, *20*
Nye, D. 166

object biography 4, 75–6, 77–9
object lessons 96; evangelism 112–13; narrative 102–3; Protestantism 98–9, 216; stewards 115
objectification: consumption 49; electricity 218–19; god 5–6; heritage 52, 54; Marx 65n3; Miller 46–7
objects: magic 36; presence 142, 164; representational 141; social mediators 133–4; Word 98–9; *see also* artifacts; object biography
obsidian: Argentina, northwest 131–2, *139 (map)*, 143–4; ceramics 148, 149–50; knapping quality 144; materiality 149; meaning 147; Ona source 141, 143; power 145
O'Hanlon, M. 116
One Flew Over the Cuckoo's Nest 218
O'Neill, J. 135
oracles 5–6
oral tradition 203–4
original unity worldview 26–7
ostrich egg shell jewelry 10
other/self 36, 51
Ouzman, S. 55
ox 63

Palus, M. M. 7, 217, 218
Panamá: archaeology 207; *huaca* 207; prehistoric artifactual record 206–7; rock art 190, 207–8; *see also* Volcán Barú
panopticon image 59
past/future concepts 37
Pasteur, L. 84

INDEX

Pele mythology 198
Perez-Franco, R. 205
Péringuey, L. 56, 57
petroglyphs: apotropaic function 205, 206; Boquete area 194–7, 203–6, 207; Caldera 191–4, 204, 205; Chiriquí 190, 202; designs 194, 202; Huacal area 194–7, 201; human thought 206; lifeworld 207–8; markers 196, 204; social significance 192; splitting 193–4; unmarked stones 195–6; Volcán Barú 204, 205, 206; water sources 201, 204, 206; *see also* rock art
phenomenology 135, 181, 182
philanthropists 109, 120n6
Philip, J. 59
Platfontein 52, 55
Pomo basket 112–14, 115, 117
Pompeii 199
Popocatépetl volcano 206
post-Apartheid society 54–5
postcolonialism 14
postmodernism 14
post-structural archaeology 133
pottery: *see* ceramics
poverty 8–9
Povinelli, E. A. 55
praxis 135, 181, 182
Presbyterian Church of America 97, 101–2
preserving culture 109, 191
priest-exorcist 29–30, 33–6
primitivisms 9, 12
progressivism 103–4, 105, 107, 115, 118
Protestantism: anthropology 116–17; education 107–8; immateriality 98, 99; Native Americans 214; object lessons 98–9, 216
psychotherapy 168
Purdy, C. *112*, 113
purification (Latour) 6

railways 164
rain-making 52, 54, 60
Ranere, A. 196, 205
rationality 25–6
regionality 130, 147–8
reification 164
religion 212, 214; *see also* Christianity
representation 149
revisionism 50
Riley, E. S. 171
ritual 28–9, 31, 198
rock art: Alpine 196; Armenia 205; Bushmen 215; Caldera 192–4; cosmology 61; dating 196; designs 191–2, 196–7; landscape 61–2, 202; meaning 200; memory anchors 204; multi-sensory 197; Panamá 190, 207–8; potency 54, 55, 64; settlers 62–3; shamanism 48, 61; signifier 60; sorcery 54; as title-deeds 57; Volcán Barú 190–1; Wildebeestkuil 46–7, 51–6; women's contribution 204; *see also* petroglyphs
rock graffiti 206
Rockwell, A. D. 167–8
Roman Catholicism 98–9

Sack, S. 14
St Louis World's Fair 105
salvage anthropology 108
salvage ethnography 105
San: belief systems 48; cosmology 59; culture refashioned 56; ethno-commodification 51; naming of newborns 62; shamans 60
San José 140
Santa María 140
Scattolin, M. C. 147
Scheelkoos 56, 57
Schivelbusch, W. 164
Schutz, A. 135, 142

INDEX

sea level rises 205–6
sedentary lifestyle 136–7, 149
Seemann, B. 192
self/other 36, 51
senses: body 40n9; eye/ear 103; magic 25–6, 29–30; Merleau-Ponty 127–8; rationality 25–6; synaesthesia 201
Septimo, R. 194
settlers 62–3
Shalmaneser, Fort 20
Shalmaneser III 18
shamanism 65n1; dance of blood 58; death 63; depicted 61–2; rain-making 60; rock art 48, 61; Wildebeestkuil 47, 215–16
Shelton, C. 196
Simmel, G. 134
Simon, L. 166, 167, 174
Sin-shar-ishkun 18
skin bags 10, 12
Smith, A. 59
social analysis/discourse 132
social anthropology 116
social boundaries 141
social evolutionism 116–17
social fact 150
social life: Aconquija 148; ceramics 141, 147; materiality 126–7, 134; sedentary lifestyle 136–7, 149; technology 149; temporality 130
somatic theory of illness 169
sorcery 54
South Africa: artisan economies 8; Department of Arts and Culture 8; genocide 59; indigenous peoples 7–8; National Heritage Day 9–10; post-Apartheid society 7–8, 14, 50, 54–5; SADF 52–3; *see also* Wildebeestkuil
Southern Africa 47–8
space/time 129–30, 131, 133, 148–9, 214–15

Stephens, J. L.: *Incidents of Travel in Central America* 198
Stewart, S. 36
Stirling, M. 202
stone circles 60
stones, marked/unmarked 195–6
Stow, G. W. 56–7, 60, 62
Sumerian language 27
supernatural/natural 27
synaesthesia 201

Taussig, M. 30, 36, 61, 180
taxonomy 2, 4–6
technique, fetishization 164
technocracy 184
technology: critical theory 164; as epistemology 181–2; hierarchy of 11–12; Marcuse 183; materiality 179; nervousness 169; social life 149
telecommunications 162, 168
Terminators 219
texts, apotropaic images 19, 28–9
Thacker, C. 199
Thompson, R. C. 30
Tilley, C. 2, 202–3
time/space: *see* space/time
tooth-brushing 81–3, 85–6
toothbrush: archaeological object 213; bone 75, 80, 88; bone bag 75, 79; designs 83–4, 87; fetishized 74, 91; French 73, 84, 87; *habitus* 217; manufacture 84; materiality 89–90; as signifier of taste 81, 217; theft of 88
tourism 8, 46–7, 50–1
translation, Latour 6
Trigger, B. 106
trophy art 58
Truth and Reconciliation Commission 13
Turing, A. 5
Tylor, E. B. 3, 9–10, 11, 100–1, 116

INDEX

under-development 12
underworld 34, 37–8, 41n19
Ur 18, 19
Uribe, Don Diego 90
US Naval Academy 171, 174
utility companies: private 166–7, 171–2; public *175–6*

Vélez, Paula Arango de 72–4, 81
Venda ceramics 13
Vico, G. 25, 134
vitalism 167–8
Volcán Barú: Caldera petroglyph 191–4, 204; eruptions 205; need for research 208; petroglyph location 206; rock art 190–1; sight-lines 197; social context 197–8; stone writing in crater 201
volcanoes 198–9, 201, 206, 218
Vulcan 198

wakas, Cuzco region 204–5
water sources 201, 204, 205, 206
Watts, W. 172
weapons, miniature 19
weaving 107, 114
Weiss, L. M. 7
Westinghouse incandescent light *181*

Wiggermann, F. A. M. 29
Wild West Shows 99
Wildebeestkuil 51–6; /Xam San 56–7; authenticity 56; colonialism 56–63, 64; cultural appropriation 215; lightning strikes 57; potency of rocks 54; removal of engravings 57–8; shamanic rituals 47, 215–16; stone circles 60; tourism 46–7
wish-manifestation 24–5, 28
Wissler, C. 112
Wittgenstein, L. 24–5
Woolston, C. H. 98–9
working hours, extended 178
World in Boston 96–7; evangelism 99, 103, 114; floor plan *100*; *Handbook* 96, *100*, 103; Indian Christian Chapel 101; Native Americans 99–103, 107–9; as object lesson 119; stewards 101–3, 115

/Xam San 47, 51, 56–7
!Xun 46, 52–5

Young People's Missionary Movement 97, 102

Zulu wire baskets 9–10, 12–13

Made in the USA